Microsoft®
Visual Basic®
2005 Express Edition
Programming
for the Absolute
Beginner

JERRY LEE FORD, JR.

THOMSON

COURSE TECHNOLOGY

Professional ■ Technical ■ Reference

ISBN: 1-59200-814-3

Library of Congress Catalog Card Number: 2005923914

Printed in the United States of America

06 07 08 09 10 PH 10 9 8 7 6 5 4 3 2

Publisher and General Manager, Thomson Course Technology PTR:
Stacy L. Hiquet

Associate Director of Marketing:
Sarah O'Donnell

Manager of Editorial Services:
Heather Talbot

Marketing Manager:
Heather Hurley

Acquisitions Editor:
Mitzi Koontz

Marketing Coordinator:
Jordan Casey

Project Editor:
Argosy Publishing

Technical Reviewer:
Jonathan Harbour

PTR Editorial Services Coordinator:
Elizabeth Furbish

Copyeditor:
Ginny Kaczmarek

Interior Layout Tech:
Jill Flores

Cover Designer:
Mike Tanamachi

Indexer:
Katherine Stimson

Proofreader:
Sara Gullion

THOMSON

COURSE TECHNOLOGY

Professional ■ Technical ■ Reference

Thomson Course Technology PTR,
a division of Thomson Course Technology
25 Thomson Place
Boston, MA 02210
http://www.courseptr.com

Dedication

To Alexander, William, Molly, and Mary.

About the Author

Jerry Lee Ford, Jr. is an author, educator, and an IT professional with more than 16 years of experience in information technology, including roles as an automation analyst, technical manager, technical support analyst, automation engineer, and security analyst. Jerry has a master's degree in business administration from Virginia Commonwealth University in Richmond, Virginia. He also is the author of 14 other books, including *VBScript Professional Projects*, *Microsoft Windows Shell Scripting and WSH Administrator's Guide*, *Learn VBScript in a Weekend*, *Microsoft Windows Shell Scripting for the Absolute Beginner*, *Learn JavaScript in a Weekend*, and *Microsoft Windows XP Professional Administrator's Guide*. He has more than five years of experience as an adjunct instructor teaching networking courses in information technology. Jerry lives in Richmond, Virginia, with his wife, Mary, and their children, William, Alexander, and Molly.

Acknowledgments

This book represents the culmination of efforts provided by a number of individuals. I would like to thank Mitzi Koontz, who served as the book's acquisitions editor. Special thanks also go to Kevin Haley and Jonathan Harbour for serving as the book's development and technical editors. I would also like to acknowledge Ginny Kaczmarek for lending her copy editing services. Finally, I'd like to thank everyone else at Thomson Course Technology PTR for all their hard work.

CONTENTS

Chapter 7 PROCESSING LOTS OF DATA WITH LOOPS 227

Chapter 8 ENHANCING CODE STRUCTURE AND ORGANIZATION 271

INTRODUCTION

Welcome to *Microsoft Visual Basic 2005 Express Edition Programming for the Absolute Beginner*. Visual Basic 2005 Express Edition is the newest incarnation of Visual Basic. This particular version of Visual Basic has been developed for first-time programmers and computer hobbyists. It is designed to enable the development of applications that execute on computers running a Windows operating system.

Unlike other current versions of Visual Basic, Visual Basic 2005 Express Edition is limited in scope. It provides a subset of Visual Basic functionality found in other versions of Visual Basic. For example, it cannot be used to develop software for smart device applications or to develop Web-based applications.

Microsoft created Visual Basic 2005 Express Edition with the individual user in mind, intending it to provide a lightweight programming experience. Microsoft's intention is to introduce Visual Basic programming to as many people as possible. This new version of Visual Basic costs significantly less than previous versions, making it affordable to just about anyone. (In fact, just prior to the publishing of this book, Microsoft announced that it would make Visual Basic 2005 Express Edition available as a free download until November 6, 2006.) Yet Visual Basic 2005 Express Edition still packs plenty of punch, providing a powerful, yet easy to learn, programming language from which first-time programmers can quickly learn how to develop their own fully featured Windows applications.

WHY VISUAL BASIC 2005 EXPRESS EDITION?

Visual Basic 2005 Express Edition makes for an excellent first programming language. It is one of a number of programming languages supported by the Microsoft .NET Framework. The .NET Framework provides an environment that supports application development by providing everything that programmers need to test, debug, and run Windows applications. Other .NET-supported programming languages include Visual C++ .NET, Visual C# .NET, and Visual J# .NET. Of these languages, Visual Basic is the easiest to learn and use. It is certainly the most popular.

If you want to develop Windows applications, Visual Basic 2005 Express Edition will suit your needs well. Once you have mastered the basics of programming using Visual Basic 2005 Express Edition, you'll find yourself well prepared to upgrade to the full version of Visual Basic 2005, where you can then apply your programming skills to the development of Windows and Web-based applications. In addition, you'll be able to apply what this book has taught you to the development of applications that support smart devices such as the Pocket PC or PDAs (*personal digital assistants*).

WHO SHOULD READ THIS BOOK?

This book is designed to teach you how to develop Windows applications using Microsoft Visual Basic 2005 Express Edition. Although a previous programming background is helpful, this book does not assume that you have any previous experience with Visual Basic or any other programming language. However, a good understanding of computers and Microsoft Windows operating systems is expected.

Whether you are an experienced programmer looking for a jump start on learning Visual Basic 2005 Express Edition, or a first-timer looking for a friendly programming language and a book that will help you to begin your programming career, you will be happy with what this book has in store for you. You will find that this book's unique games-based teaching approach makes learning easier and a lot more fun.

WHAT YOU NEED TO BEGIN

This book was written using Microsoft Visual Basic 2005 Express Edition for its examples. All of the figures and examples that you see as you read along will show Microsoft Visual Basic 2005 Express Edition running on Windows XP. Therefore, if you are using a different Windows operating system, or if you are using a different version of Visual Basic, such as the version of Visual Basic supplied with Visual Studio 2003, you may notice small differences in the way some things look. However, you should still be able to follow along with the examples shown in this book with little, if any, trouble.

If you don't already have Microsoft Visual Basic 2005 Express Edition, you should be able to download a copy from msdn.microsoft.com/vstudio/express/vb/ through November 6, 2006. After this date, Microsoft may begin selling Visual Basic 2005 Express Edition for profit on-line and at your local computer or office supply store. Before you purchase Visual Basic 2005 Express Edition, you'll want to make sure that your computer has enough horsepower to run it. First off, your computer must run one of the following operating systems:

- Windows 2003 Server
- Windows XP Home Edition
- Windows XP Professional
- Windows 2000 Professional

In addition, you'll want to make sure that your computer meets the minimum hardware requirements specified in the following table. However, minimum requirements are just that. In order to really take advantage of Visual Basic 2005 Express Edition, you'll be a lot better off if your computer meets the table's recommended requirements.

TABLE A: MINIMUM REQUIREMENTS FOR RUNNING VISUAL BASIC 2005 EXPRESS EDITION		
Requirement	**Minimum**	**Recommended**
Processor	600 MHz Pentium	1 GHz Pentium
Memory	192 MB	256 MB
Hard Disk	1.3 MB	2 GB

That's it. All you'll need is a copy of Visual Basic 2005 Express Edition running on your computer and this book. You'll find that everything you need to write, test, and compile Visual Basic programs is provided as part of the Visual Basic 2005 Express Edition package.

WHAT'S ON THE COMPANION WEB SITE?

- **Appendix A, "What's on the Companion Web Site?"** This appendix outlines the materials that you will find on the book's companion Web site, which will include all the sample programs you see in this book as well as links to a collection of useful Visual Basic Web sites.

- **Appendix B, "What Next?"** In this appendix, I'll provide you with parting thoughts and give you some final advice on how to continue to further your Visual Basic programming education.

- All source code for programs and projects featured in this book.

An Introduction to Visual Basic 2005 Express Edition

Microsoft developed Visual Basic 2005 Express in hopes of attracting a new generation of programmers to Windows. Microsoft has put a great deal of time and effort into creating the best possible development environment for Windows applications. In this chapter, you will begin your Visual Basic programming journey by learning some necessary background information. You will then get the chance to jump right in and get your feet wet by developing your first Visual Basic application. Through the development of this application, you will learn the basic steps involved in creating a Windows application as well as get a preview of just what makes Visual Basic the most popular programming language ever developed.

Specifically, you will learn:

- What Visual Basic 2005 Express is and what it can do
- What .NET is and how it works with Visual Basic 2005 Express
- What Visual Studio is and how Visual Basic fits into it
- The five basic steps involved in developing a Visual Basic application

Project Preview: The Joke Machine

In this chapter, as in all the chapters to follow, you will learn how to create a computer game using Visual Basic. Simple game projects provide a fun and engaging learning experience while you learn about Visual Basic .NET 2005.

In this first chapter, you will learn how to create the Joke Machine game. The Joke Machine game begins like most other Windows applications, displaying a window that controls the game's execution. Compared to most Windows applications, the Joke Machine game is relatively simple, consisting of just two buttons, a label, and a text box. However, the development of this game will demonstrate powerful programming techniques that make up the foundation of any Windows application.

When first started, the Joke Machine will appear on your desktop as shown in Figure 1.1.

FIGURE 1.1

The initial window of the Joke Machine game.

The game is very simple, containing just two buttons, each of which displays a joke and its punch line when clicked. Figure 1.2 shows the first joke displayed by the game.

FIGURE 1.2

Viewing the first joke told by the Joke Machine game.

Figure 1.3 shows the joke that appears when the Joke Machine's second button is clicked.

FIGURE 1.3

Viewing the
second joke told
by the Joke
Machine game.

By the time you have created and run this game, you'll have learned the five basic steps involved in writing and executing a Visual Basic application.

A FEW OPENING WORDS

Learning a new computer programming language is a challenging experience. But it can also be very enjoyable and fulfilling. In this chapter, we'll start your Visual Basic programming journey by going over background information that you'll need in order to advance to later chapters. This will include a brief overview of what Visual Basic 2005 Express is and what it can do. It will also include a high level explanation of what .NET is and how it interacts with Visual Basic 2005 Express.

In this chapter, you will also learn how to create your first Visual Basic application. You may find it a little intimidating to begin putting together a Visual Basic application before you have had a chance to learn a little more about the language. This is to be expected. But don't worry about it. Just follow along and perform the steps that I'll lay out exactly as shown and you'll be able to get the application working. You'll find that as a result of writing your first program and stepping through the application development process, you'll develop a better understanding of just what Visual Basic and .NET are and will be better prepared to understand the chapters that lay ahead of you. The most important thing for you to do as you go through this chapter is to try and focus on the big picture and not to get too caught up in the details.

A QUICK OVERVIEW OF VISUAL BASIC

Visual Basic is *visual* because of the process that programmers go through to create the part of the application that users see, also known as the GUI (*graphical user interface*). Visual Basic is *Basic* because it was created based on the BASIC (*Beginners All-Purpose Symbolic Instruction Code*) programming language.

Visual Basic is a programming language that is used to develop Windows applications. This means that once you have written a Visual Basic application and compiled it into executable code, the application can run on its own. It doesn't require anything else to execute except for the Windows operating system.

Right from its initial release by Microsoft, Visual Basic earned a reputation for being very easy to learn while simultaneously delivering development capabilities previously only made available by more complex programming languages. As a result, it quickly became the most popular programming language in the world. Today, you'll find that Visual Basic is taught in colleges all over the world. It is also used by companies internationally to create Windows applications that drive mission-critical business processes.

DEFINITION

Compiling is the process of translating the code statements that make up a computer application into a format that can be executed by the computer operating system.

There are a number of reasons why Visual Basic is so popular. Three of the most important reasons include its support of the following:

- Drag-and-drop GUI design
- Rapid application development
- Object-oriented programming

GUI Development

One of the first things that you will come to appreciate about Visual Basic as you work your way through this book is the ease with which it enables you to create a really slick looking GUI.

DEFINITION

A GUI (graphical user interface) is the part of the application that the user sees and can interact with using the mouse.

When you first begin working on a Windows application, Visual Basic automatically creates a new blank window for you. It also provides you with a collection of Windows components, such as buttons, check boxes, and text boxes, that you can then add to the window by clicking on and dragging them over to the window and placing them where you want them.

Rapid Application Development

Visual Basic is a RAD (*rapid application development*) Windows application tool. RAD allows you to quickly create a mockup of your application so that you can show users what the application will look like even thought it lacks the underlying code that actually makes work. This allows users to provide early feedback and helps programmers to deliver a final product that meets user expectations.

DEFINITION

RAD (rapid application development) is a process whereby programmers quickly create a mockup of an application's GUI for initial review by the users for whom the application is intended in order to demonstrate how the application will ultimately look and operate.

Object-Oriented Programming

Visual Basic is also an *object-oriented programming* (OOP) language. OOP refers to the coding part of creating a Visual Basic application as opposed to the development of its GUI. From an OOP perspective, everything in a Visual Basic application is treated like an object. Objects store infor-

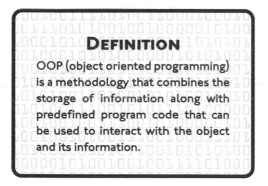

DEFINITION

OOP (object oriented programming) is a methodology that combines the storage of information along with predefined program code that can be used to interact with the object and its information.

mation about themselves and provide access to this information. Objects also provide the ability to perform tasks and react to events. For example, in Visual Basic, a button is an object. Any information about a button is stored alongside the button, such as its size, color, and what actions the button initiates if it gets clicked. As you will learn in Chapter 9, "Getting Comfortable with Object-Oriented Programming," OOP supports code sharing and reuse and can greatly simplify program development.

A Little Visual Basic History Lesson

Microsoft introduced Visual Basic version 1.0 in 1991. Up until this time, the only programming language available to programmers for Windows application development was Microsoft C. Microsoft C was powerful for sure, but it took a lot of time to master. In addition, it was not easy to use. In fact, it used to take many hundreds of lines of complex code statements to accomplish things that you can do with Visual Basic today with just a few lines of code.

Like all initial releases of new programming languages, the first version of Visual Basic had plenty of bugs. Things began to get a lot better when Microsoft released Visual Basic version 3.0. Version 3.0 also introduced built-in support for database access.

Visual Basic 4.0 appeared in 1995, creating a major impact on the programming world and solidifying Visual Basic's place as a major application development tool. Visual Basic 5.0 came next, adding support for OOP. Visual Basic 6.0 then came along, adding support for ActiveX data objects, expanding Visual Basic's database capabilities and making Internet database access possible.

Although it was a little slow in anticipating the way the Internet was changing the world, Microsoft decided that the Internet was a critical part of Visual Basic's future. At the same time, Microsoft wanted to create an application development environment that would support multiple programming languages (which it accomplished through the development of the .NET Framework). So Microsoft went back to the drawing board and completely redesigned the way Visual Basic worked from the bottom up. The end result was something totally new, Visual Basic .NET 2002. With the release of Visual Basic .NET 2002, Web development became as integral a part of Visual Basic as Windows development.

Visual Basic .NET 2002 was really a totally new version of Visual Basic. Microsoft literally started over when it built this version. As a result, there was no intention of providing for backward compatibility with Visual Basic 6.0 or any previous version of Visual Basic. Therefore, Visual Basic programmers could not automatically upgrade their applications from Visual Basic 6.0. This confused a large portion of the Visual Basic community, which had invested years and effort and a lot of money in projects based on Visual Basic 6.0.

IN THE REAL WORLD

Because of its popularity, Visual Basic 6.0 will still be with us for a long time. So many large projects were developed using it, and the cost of rewriting these projects is steep. If you visit http://msdn.microsoft.com/vbasic, Microsoft's Visual Basic Developer Center Web site, you'll see that Microsoft still supports and provides regular updates for Visual Basic 6.0.

TRAP Microsoft did include a code migration tool with Visual Basic .NET 2002, which automatically launched any time a Visual Basic 6.0 program was loaded. Unfortunately, the migration tool was only capable of upgrading relatively simple programs.

In 2003, Microsoft updated Visual Basic .NET, releasing the next version as Visual Basic .NET 2003. This version added support for program development on mobile Web appliances such as PDAs and smart devices such as the Pocket PC. Improvements were also made to Web services and to the code migration process.

Finally, in 2005, Microsoft released Visual Basic .NET 2005. In addition to fixing a few bugs left in the previous version of Visual Basic .NET, Visual Basic .NET 2005 made significant enhancements to the language's Web development capabilities. Microsoft also introduced Visual Basic 2005 Express in 2005 in an effort to attract a new generation of programmers.

TRAP In order to run an application created using Visual Basic .NET, a computer must have the .NET Framework installed on it. Microsoft has upgraded the .NET Framework several times since its introduction. Visual Basic .NET 2002 was designed to work with Microsoft .NET Framework 1.0. Visual Basic .NET 2003 was designed to work with Microsoft .NET Framework 1.1, and Visual Basic .NET 2005 works with Microsoft .NET 2.0. Although an application created using Visual Basic .NET 2002 will run on any computer that has any version of .NET installed on it, an application written using Visual Basic .NET 2003 requires that .NET 1.1 or 2.0 be installed. In similar fashion, an application written using Visual Basic .NET 2005 requires that .NET 2.0 is installed.

Visual Basic's Cousins

Visual Basic is just one of three computer programming languages developed by Microsoft based on the Basic programming language. The other two languages include:

- VBA (*Visual Basic for Applications*)
- VBScript

Microsoft created Visual Basic first and then created these other two languages in large part by extracting functionality from Visual Basic. As a result, once you have mastered the ability to create Visual Basic applications, you shouldn't have any trouble leveraging what you have learned when learning how to program with these other languages. A brief overview of VBA and VBScript is provided in the next two sections to give you an idea of the differences between Visual Basic and these two close cousins.

VBA

Microsoft introduced VBA in 1993. The current version of VBA is version 6.3, which Microsoft released in 2001. VBA is designed to provide applications with a Visual Basic-like programming language. Microsoft has embedded support for VBA into numerous Microsoft products, including:

- Microsoft Word
- Microsoft Excel
- Microsoft Access

- Microsoft PowerPoint
- Microsoft FrontPage
- Microsoft Outlook

For example, using VBA for Microsoft Access, Access programmers can create entire applications to automate application features provided by Microsoft Access. Unlike Visual Basic applications, which can be compiled into standalone programs that can be run directly from the Windows desktop, VBA applications require a host application such as Microsoft Access in order to run.

 To find out more about VBA and Microsoft Access, read Microsoft Access VBA Programming for the Absolute Beginner by Michael Vine, ISBN 1592000398.

 To find out more about VBA and Microsoft Excel, read Microsoft Excel VBA Programming for the Absolute Beginner by Duane Birnbaum, ISBN 1931841047.

VBScript

VBScript is a scripting language. In order to execute, VBScripts need to be executed by an execution host. Examples of execution hosts that support VBScript execution include Internet Explorer and the WSH (*Windows Script Host*). Execution hosts provide scripts with an environment in which they can execute as well as access to resources that exist within that environment. For example, VBScripts can be embedded within HTML pages and executed within the Internet Explorer Web browser. In addition to running embedded VBScripts, the browser provides the scripts with access to browser and Web page resources such as frames, buttons, and browser controls. By embedding VBScripts inside HTML pages, Web programmers can make their Web pages more dynamic by writing scripts that can create rollover effects, create cookies, generate pop-up dialogs, and so on.

Similarly, VBScripts that execute under the control of the WSH allow script developers to automate a host of Windows desktop tasks, including the creation of user accounts, desktop shortcuts, printer management, and so on. WSH-run VBScripts can even modify the Windows registry and control network resources such as network drives and printers.

INTRODUCING VISUAL BASIC 2005 EXPRESS EDITION

Visual Basic 2005 Express is a special version of Visual Basic that Microsoft created especially to attract first-time programmers. Its primary purpose is to provide a simplified and streamlined introduction to Windows application development. It provides complete support for

Microsoft's .NET Framework and can be used to create Windows applications. Like every other version of Visual Basic, it is relatively easy to get started with and can be used to create world-class desktop applications.

If you have not done so yet, now would be a good time to pause and install Visual Basic 2005 Express. The first time that you start it up, you'll see the screen shown in Figure 1.4.

FIGURE 1.4

Visual Basic 2005 Express starts by displaying information about available Visual Basic resources.

DEFINITION

An IDE (integrated development environment) is a workspace (the collection of menus, toolbars, and Windows) provided by Visual Basic with which you create new Visual Basic applications.

As you can see, Visual Basic 2005 Express has a standard Windows menu and a default toolbar at the top of its *IDE* (*Integrated Development Environment*). Prominently displayed in the middle of the IDE is the Start Page window. This window is divided into a number of sections. The Recent project section lists projects that you have recently worked on and provides open and create project commands that you can click on to edit or start a new Visual Basic project. The Getting Started section has links that provide you with instruction to assist you in getting ready to start writing programs. The Visual Basic Express Headlines section provides access to recent articles and other technical resources. The MSDN: Visual Basic 2005 Express edition section consists of links that make it easy for you to reach out to various resources available to you on the Internet.

What Can Visual Basic 2005 Express Edition Do?

Visual Basic 2005 Express was created by Microsoft to support the development of Windows applications. It is awfully good at creating Windows applications that run on the Windows desktop. For example, using Visual Basic 2005 Express, you can create applications that:

- Create Windows games
- Create Windows desktop applications
- Generate reports and text files
- Work with graphics
- Interact with the Windows file system
- Access local databases

To help make application development as easy as possible, Microsoft has included templates, also known as Start Kits, with Visual Basic 2005 Express. Templates are used to create a particular type of Windows application. For example, Visual Basic 2005 Express provides a template designed to speed up the development of Windows desktop applications. Templates are also available for creating specific types of applications. For example, Visual Basic 2005 Express ships with a My Movie Collection Starter Kit template that steps you through the creation of an application that helps to organize and keep track of DVDs. It even downloads cover art and other basic information from Amazon.com.

DEFINITION

A template is a collection of base files, program code, property settings, and tasks that Microsoft has predefined to assist you in creating a particular type of Windows application.

What Can't Visual Basic 2005 Express Edition Do?

Unlike other versions of Visual Basic, Visual Basic 2005 Express is limited to the development of Windows applications. Therefore, it cannot be used to create any of the following types of applications, whose development is supported by other versions of Visual Basic:

- Web applications
- Web services
- Windows services

- Windows Dynamic Link Libraries (DLLs)
- PDA applications
- Mobile device applications (cell phones, pagers, and so on)

It is important to remember that Microsoft's reason for creating Visual Basic 2005 Express was to provide first-time programmers and computer hobbyists with the opportunity to purchase an inexpensive programming language that would introduce them to Windows programming. Microsoft's intention is to provide you with everything that you need to learn how to create Windows programs using Visual Basic. Once you have mastered this, you'll be ready to move on to these other programming platforms and to justify the purchase of more expensive versions of Visual Basic.

IN THE REAL WORLD

Microsoft packages Visual Basic as a standalone product that it calls a Standard Edition. This version of Visual Basic generally sells for around $100 and will support the development of different types of Visual Basic applications other than just Windows applications. The Standard Edition of Visual Basic is intended for the individual user. Companies that develop Visual Basic applications generally purchase Visual Basic as part of a package deal that Microsoft calls Visual Studio. When purchased this way, you get access not only to Visual Basic but also to the other languages and tools that make up Visual Studio. There are several different versions of Visual Studio, and they are not cheap. At the low end is Visual Studio .NET Professional Edition, for which you can expect to pay around $500. As you would expect, it supports Windows, Web, and mobile device development using any of its supported programming languages. Next comes Visual Studio .NET Enterprise Developer, running more than $1,000, for which you'll also get an assortment of team-oriented development tools. Finally, there is Visual Studio .NET Enterprise Architect, which runs somewhere around $2,500.

HINT Because the focus of this book is on Visual Basic 2005 Express, from this point on in the book I use the terms Visual Basic and Visual Basic 2005 Express to refer to Visual Basic 2005 Express, unless otherwise specifically stated.

OTHER VISUAL STUDIO 2005 EXPRESS PROGRAMMING LANGUAGES

Visual Basic 2005 Express is just one member of a family of Visual Studio Express programming languages. A listing of other Visual Studio Express programming languages include:

- **Visual C# 2005 Express.** A Windows program development language that grew out of C, C++, and Java, which is also aimed at first time and casual programmers, hobbyists, and students.

- **Visual C++ 2005 Express.** A Windows program development language aimed at more experienced programmers with a need for greater control.

- **Visual J# Express.** A Windows program development language based on the Java programming language, which is designed for individuals with a Java programming background.

Visual C# 2005 Express

Visual C# is a relatively new programming language that Microsoft created based on a combination of C, C++, and Java. Microsoft first introduced Visual C# with the initial release of Visual Studio. Though a little more difficult to learn that Visual Basic, C# provides former C, C++, and Java developers with a program development platform that is easy to learn and leverages their existing program development skills.

Visual C++ 2005 Express

Visual C++ is an updated version of Visual C++ that now allows the development of C++ applications to leverage the power of the .NET Framework. In addition, Visual C++ 2005 Express can be used to create applications that run independently of the .NET Framework. Visual C++ is the most difficult of the Express family of languages to learn and master. It provides greater program control and more horsepower than other express languages. As a result, it is the preferred language of power-programmers.

Visual J# 2005 Express

Visual J# is an enhanced version of Microsoft Visual J++ 6.0, which has been updated to work with the .NET Framework. Though strongly tied to the Java programming language, Microsoft has added numerous extensions to the language. As a result, Visual J# 2005 Express is not compatible with Java, so you won't be able to run programs developed with Visual J# using Sun's Java Virtual Machine. However, Visual J# provides individuals with previous Java programming experience with a great language for Windows application development using .NET.

THE MICROSOFT .NET FRAMEWORK

All of the various Visual Studio programming languages, whether Express or full-featured versions, are designed to work with the Microsoft .NET Framework. Microsoft created the .NET Framework to provide a multilanguage application development environment capable of supporting the creation of applications and services for Windows, the Web, and mobile devices.

IN THE REAL WORLD

Thanks to the multilanguage development environment provided by the .NET Framework, applications created using Visual Studio .NET can involve multiple languages. For example, an application might include code written in both Visual Basic and another Visual Studio programming language such as C#. This allows companies to break application development projects into parts and to assign the various parts to programmers who are using different programming languages based on their particular areas of expertise or upon the strengths and weaknesses of a particular programming language.

The .NET Framework is at the core of the Windows application development environment. Therefore, a basic understanding of .NET is a critical part of any Visual Basic programmer's foundation.

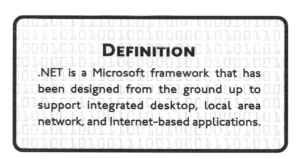

DEFINITION

.NET is a Microsoft framework that has been designed from the ground up to support integrated desktop, local area network, and Internet-based applications.

Before .NET

Before the introduction of .NET, Microsoft created and encouraged the use of the COM (*Component Object Model*). Using COM, Windows programmers were able to gain access to numerous system resources. COM also represented Microsoft's first attempt at creating an OOP standard. COM provided programmers with the ability to create component libraries made up of code that could be reused by different languages, such as Visual Basic and C++.

Before the arrival of .NET, early versions of Visual Basic depended on Windows DLL (*dynamic link library*) files for much of their core functionality. Visual Basic automatically loaded DLL files onto your computer when you installed Visual Basic. Things would get complicated when programmers finished developing their applications and were ready to deploy them. In order for their applications to work, the programmers had to make sure that all the DLLs that their applications needed to run were also installed on each user's computer. To help make this task easier to manage, Microsoft provided Visual Basic with the ability to create a deployment package that automatically collected all the DLLs required by a given application. Although this made things easier on the programmer, it also made for some very large deployment packages. In most cases, even the smallest Visual Basic deployment package would easily grow to be 30 to 40 MB in size.

Unfortunately, package deployment size was not the only DLL problem that programmers had to contend with. Problems sometimes occurred because deployment packages would replace DLL files already installed on a user's computer with older versions of DLL files. This often caused other applications on users' computers to break. This situation was so common and difficult to deal with that programmers ultimately began to refer to it as DLL Hell.

Microsoft's solution to DLL Hell is the .NET Framework. The .NET Framework is now responsible for providing Visual Studio programming languages with the functionality that they used to get from DLL files. Because DLL files are not needed to develop Windows applications, deployment packages are now a lot smaller. Now instead of worrying about what version of DLL files users have installed on their computers, programmers need only to make sure that users have the .NET Framework installed.

.NET Components

The .NET Framework is a collection of programming services that supports application development and execution on Windows operating systems, the Internet, and mobile devices such as PDAs. The .NET Framework acts as an interface between the operating system and your applications.

Figure 1.5 depicts the .NET Framework's role in the application development process. As you can see, it enables applications to be developed using any combination of .NET supported programming languages. It is responsible for translating the code created using these programming languages into a format that can be executed on the intended execution platform, whether it is a PC, Web server, or a Pocket PC device.

As Figure 1.5 shows, the .NET Framework is made up of two primary components. These are:

- .NET Framework class library
- CLR (*common language runtime*)

FIGURE 1.5

Microsoft .NET
Framework
enables the
development of
multilanguage
applications on
different
execution
environments.

The .NET Framework Class Library

The .NET class library is made up of an enormous amount of prewritten code that is available to any Visual Studio programming language. The class libraries are used to define objects within applications.

The .NET class library contains the code required to create forms, buttons, and other Visual Basic controls. For example, to create a new form within a Visual Basic application, you would call upon a predefined class that already had everything defined within it to create the new form. This saves you from having to write all the underlying low-level code yourself. If you then dragged and dropped a Button control onto the form, the .NET class library would automatically supply your application with all the underlying code, defining how the button looks and how your application can interact with it.

DEFINITION

A class is a collection of code representing a programming object, such as a form, a button, or a text box. When you create a new form or add a control to a form when building an application interface, you are instantiating new objects based on predefined classes stored in the .NET class library.

The CLR

The CLR provides the .NET Framework with a collection of services that facilitate application execution. These services include:

- Debugging
- Memory management
- Compiling
- Security
- Exception handling

In order for your Visual Basic applications to run, they must be compiled. When your Visual Basic applications are complied, the Visual Basic statements that make up your applications are translated into MSIL (*Microsoft Intermediate Language*). One of the jobs of the CRL is to convert MSIL code into binary code that the computer understands.

DEFINITION

Compiling is the process of converting the programming statements that make up a given application into a format that can be executed by the operating system.

Once converted to MSIL, it does not matter whether the original source code for the application was written in Visual Basic, C++, or any other programming language supported by Visual Studio. Because of this, you can mix and match multiple programming languages together to create a single application.

Although all this may sound rather complicated, the good news is that it all occurs under the covers. Visual Basic 2005 Express automatically takes care of all this for you as you create and save your applications. So if you find this material a little intimidating right now, don't worry. Keep pressing on, and as you get more experience, it will start to make more sense.

If you want to learn more about .NET, visit http://www.microsoft.com/net.

BACK TO THE JOKE MACHINE

OK, let's turn the focus of this chapter back to the development of its main project, the Joke Machine game. Through the development of this game, you will learn the basic steps involved in developing a Windows application. As you go through the steps involved in creating your first Visual Basic application, try and focus on the overall process that is involved and don't get caught up in the details too much, which will be explained in later chapters.

Designing the Game

The Joke Machine game's design is very straightforward, involving basic, yet fundamental Windows programming techniques. The game begins by displaying its GUI. It then waits for the user to click on a button before displaying a joke. The game continues to run, allowing the user to click either of its buttons as many times as desired. Like other Windows applications, the game can be minimized or maximized and continues to run until the user clicks on the close button in the upper right-hand corner of the window.

As you will see as you build the Joke Machine game, Visual Basic applications are typically created in five steps, as outlined below.

1. Create a new Visual Basic project.
2. Create the GUI.
3. Modify form and control properties.
4. Add program code.
5. Test the application's execution.

Each of these steps will be demonstrated in detail in the sections that follow.

Step 1: Creating a New Visual Basic Project

So let's get started. If you have not already done so, start up Visual Basic 2005 Express now. Next, create a new Visual Basic project by clicking on File and then selecting New Project. The New Project dialog appears as shown in Figure 1.6.

FIGURE 1.6

Select the Windows Application template to create a new Windows application.

The New Project dialog displays a collection of templates for you to choose from. Templates assist you in developing new applications by providing an initial starting point from which you can begin creating a particular type of application. Because the Joke Machine will run as a graphical Windows desktop application, select Windows Application. If you click on the

OK button at this point, a new application named WindowsApplication1 will be created. Instead of this name, type "Joke Machine" as the name of your new application in the Name field located at the bottom of the New Project window and click on OK.

DEFINITION

A Visual Basic project is a container that is used to store and manage the items that make up your Visual Basic application.

TRICK By default, Visual Basic stores your new applications in their own folder located in C:\Documents and Settings\Username\ My Documents\Visual Studio\Projects. However, if you wish, you can configure Visual Basic to automatically store them elsewhere by clicking on the Tools menu and selecting the Options submenu. This will open the Options window. From here you can click on Projects and Solutions and set default location where you'd like all your Visual Basic applications to be stored.

IN THE REAL WORLD

Visual Basic 2005 Express allows you to create the following three types of applications:

- **Windows Application.** A graphical Windows application that runs on the Windows desktop. Examples of this type of application include Microsoft Word, WinZip, and any Windows application that you interact with using a mouse.

- **Windows Control Library.** A custom-built control that can be added to or referenced from within a Windows application. This type of application is one in which you define your own customized Windows controls for the purposes of adding them to other Windows applications that you'll develop.

- **Console Application.** A text-based application typically run from the Windows Command Prompt. A console application is one in which the user interacts with the application by running it from the Windows Command Prompt and then typing in commands as directed by the application.

The full version of Visual Basic is capable of creating many additional types of applications. Examples include Web applications, applications for smart devices, and Windows services.

Visual Basic creates a new project for you. In the middle of the IDE, you will see a blank window as shown in Figure 1.7. Within Visual Basic, this window is referred to as a *form*. You will create the GUI for the Joke Machine by adding controls to this form. Note that by default, Visual Basic names the form Form1. As you'll see in the next chapter, you can change the name of forms to anything you wish.

FIGURE 1.7

By default, Visual Basic automatically creates a new blank form for new Windows applications.

At this point, you now have a fully functional, though not very interesting, Windows application. You can run your application by clicking on the Debug menu and selecting the Start Debugging option. You could also press the F5 key or click on the Start Debugging icon on the Standard Visual Basic toolbar. Once started, the application will begin running. The name of the application's form, Form1, is displayed in the title bar, and Minimize, Maximize, and Close buttons will appear in the upper right-hand corner of the application's window. Click on the Close button to stop your application and return to the Visual Basic IDE.

Step 2: Creating the User Interface

In order to create the interface for the Joke Machine game, you need to add controls, such as buttons and text boxes, to the form. Visual Basic makes controls available to you via the Toolbox window, which by default is displayed on the left-hand side of the IDE.

You can add controls to your form using a number of different techniques. For example, you can drag and drop a control from the Toolbox onto the form, or you can double-click on a control located in the Toolbox and Visual Basic will automatically place a copy of the control onto the form for you, which you can then move and resize.

The first control that you will add is the TextBox control. To do this, double-click on the TextBox control in the Visual Basic Toolbox. Visual Basic adds the Textbox control to the form assigning it a default name of TextBox1. Next, locate the Multiline property in the first column of the Properties Windows (located by default in the lower left-hand side of the IDE) and change its value to True. This will enable the display of multiple lines of text within the control. Using the mouse, move and resize the TextBox control by clicking and holding on to the small white squares that define its parameter, as shown in Figure 1.8.

FIGURE 1.8

Adding and resizing a TextBox control on a Visual Basic form.

Now, let's add a descriptive label to the form just above the TextBox1. Start by double-clicking on the Label control located in the Toolbox. Using the mouse, move the control just above the upper left-hand corner of the TextBox1 control. Note that Visual Basic automatically assigned the label a default text string of Label1.

Now let's add the first Button control to the form by double-clicking on the Button control located in the Toolbox. Visual Basic adds the control to the form assigning it a default text string of Button1. Using the mouse, reposition the button beneath the TextBox1 control. Add a second button to the form and reposition it just to the right of the first button. Note that Visual Basic automatically assigned this control a default text display string of Button2. At this point, your game's interface should like the one shown in Figure 1.9.

FIGURE 1.9

Visual Basic automatically adds descriptive text labels to controls as you add them to a form.

Now, let's pause for a moment and do a test run of your application by clicking on the Debug menu and then selecting Start Debugging. Within a moment, your new application will start. As you can see, it doesn't do much yet. If you click on its buttons, nothing happens. Once you are done looking at it, click on the Close button located in the upper right-hand corner of the game's dialog to close the application and return to Visual Basic's design view.

Step 3: Customizing Control Properties

Now that all of the controls that are needed to build the application interface have been placed on the form, it is time to customize each of the controls to make them look and act like they should. This will be achieved by selecting each control in turn and editing selected properties associated with each individual control.

Let's begin with the Label1 control. This control needs to be modified so that it displays a text string of "Joke Machine". To do this, click on the Label1 control. Once you have done this, you will notice that the Properties window in the lower right-hand side of the IDE has changed and now displays properties associated with the Label1 control. The name of each property is displayed in the left-hand column and the value assigned to the property is shown in the right-hand column.

Scroll down and select the Text property, which is grouped with other properties under the category of Appearance. As you will see, a text string of Label1 is currently assigned to the Text property of the Label1 control. To replace this string, highlight the currently assigned value and type in the string "Joke Machine" in its place. Now, click back somewhere on Form1 and you'll see that Visual Basic has already updated the text displayed by the Label1 control.

Next, click on the first button control (Button1) that you added to the Form1. It should be located just below the lower-left hand corner of the Textbox1 control. Change the text string stored in its Text property field to "Joke 1". Then click on the second button control (Button2) and change its Text property to "Joke 2".

Step 4: Adding a Little Programming Logic

As I mentioned earlier in the chapter, Visual Basic in an OOP language. Controls like the Button control provide a good example of how OOP works. In order to make these buttons do something when the Joke Machine is run, you'll need to associate or attach some Visual Basic programming statements to them. As you will see, every control that you attach to a Visual Basic form is capable of storing program code alongside the control. You enter this code using the Visual Basic code editor. To enter code for a given object, such as a Button control, you simply double-click on the Button. The IDE will automatically switch from the form designer, where you have just visually assembled the application's interface, to code view, where programming statements associated with selected controls are stored.

To make the Joke Machine work, all that is required is to add two programming statements. The first statement will be assigned to the Button1 control. To prepare to enter this statement, double-click on the Button1 control. The IDE will open the code designer window as shown in Figure 1.10.

TRICK   Because the IDE has so many bells and whistles, it is impossible to display every available toolbar and window at the same time. Therefore, Microsoft makes some windows share the same space. If you take a look at the code editor window in Figure I.I0, you see that it is currently sharing space with the Form designer window and the Start Page window. You can switch between these windows by clicking on their associated tabs.

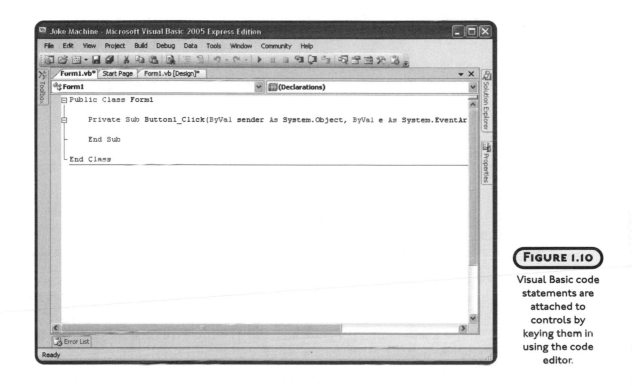

FIGURE 1.10

Visual Basic code
statements are
attached to
controls by
keying them in
using the code
editor.

TRICK

You may have noticed that the code editor window shown in Figure 1.10 takes up almost the entire display area of the IDE. I expanded it to make it easier to view and edit programming statements. One way to make more room for the code editor window is to close other windows in the IDE, such as the Toolbox, Solution Explorer, and Properties windows. The problem with this option is that you use these other windows so often that it is just too inconvenient to have to keep opening and closing them all the time. Instead, what I did was to temporarily thumbtack the Toolbox, Solution Explorer, and Properties windows to the side of the IDE. Take a look at the upper right-hand corners of the title bars for each of these three windows and you will see a thumbtack button. Clicking on the thumbtack button tells the IDE to shrink the display of the window down to a tab docked on the side of the IDE where the window is docked. As you can see in Figure 1.10, there is a tab on the far left-hand side of the IDE representing the Toolbox and two tabs on the far right-hand side of the IDE representing the Solution Explorer and Properties windows. When you are ready to view these windows again, just click on their tabs. When you do, the IDE will temporarily display them again. To make these windows remain open, click on the thumbtack button for each window again.

As you can see, Visual Basic has already generated some code for you. I'll explain what this code is in later chapters. For now, just enter the following statement, exactly as shown below. To make the statement that you are supposed to enter stand out, I have highlighted it in bold.

```
Private Sub Button1_Click(ByVal sender As System.Object, ByVal e As System.EventArgs)
Handles Button1.Click
    TextBox1.Text = "What is black and white and red all over?     " & _
    "A sunburned penguin!"
End Sub
```

Without getting into the technical details at this point of the book, the statement that you just entered assigns a string of text as the Text property value of the TextBox1 control. The text that you are assigning will display in the TextBox1 control when the Button1 control is clicked.

Next, return to the form designer view for Form1 by clicking on the tab labeled Form1.vb [Design]. Then double-click on the Button2 control. As you can see, you are now back in the code editor window, and a pair of new program statements has been added for you. Add the line of code shown below, in bold, inside the two new statements.

```
Private Sub Button2_Click(ByVal sender As System.Object, ByVal e As System.EventArgs)
Handles Button2.Click
    TextBox1.Text = "What ceases to exist when you say its name?" & _
    "Silence!"
End Sub
```

Just like with the previous statement, the code that you just added will execute when the Joke Machine is run and the Button2 control is clicked.

Step 5: Testing the Execution of the Joke Machine Application

That's it. The Joke Machine game is complete and ready to run. Press F5 to run it. As long as you didn't make any typos when modifying control properties or entering program code, it should run exactly as shown at the beginning of this chapter. Otherwise, go back and correct your typos and try running your application again.

SUMMARY

This chapter has covered a lot of ground for an introductory chapter. You learned about what Visual Basic 2005 Express is and what it is not. You learned about the history behind Visual Basic and how Visual Basic fits into Microsoft Visual Studio. On top of all this, you also learned the five basic steps involved in developing a Visual Basic application. You then put this information together and developed your first Visual Basic application, the Joke Machine.

Before you move on to the next chapter, take a few more minutes and see if you can improve on the Joke Machine game by implementing the following list of challenges.

CHALLENGES

1. Improve the Joke Machine by adding additional buttons along with additional jokes.

2. Currently, the Joke Machine game displays the text string of Form1 in the Windows title bar. Replace this text string with the phrase "Visual Basic Joke Machine". (Hint: Click on the form and modify the form's Text property.)

3. As it is currently written, the TextBox field on the Joke Machine window allows the user to enter text into it, when it should really just display the text of jokes. Prevent this behavior from occurring. (Hint: Click on the TextBox1 control and set the ReadOnly property to True.)

Navigating the Visual Basic 2005 Express Edition Development Environment

Now that you know what Visual Basic 2005 Express is and what it can and cannot be used for, it is time to get better acquainted with its IDE (*integrated development environment*) and to learn how to better work with all its pieces and parts. Mastery of the IDE is very important and will help you to work more efficiently and effectively. This chapter will review the most commonly used IDE windows and provide instruction on how to use them.

Specifically, you will learn:

- How to work with the IDE menu and standard toolbar
- The basics of working with the form designer and code editor
- About IntelliSense and how to use it to your advantage
- How to work with the Toolbox, Solution Explorer, and Properties windows

PROJECT PREVIEW: THE CLICK RACE GAME

In this chapter's game project, you will learn how to develop the Click Race game. The object of this game is for the player to use the mouse to click on a pair of buttons as many times as possible in a 30-second period. To make things more challenging, the game forces the player to alternate the clicking of each button. To play well, the player must be not only a fast clicker but also good at quickly and accurately moving the mouse.

The Click Race game starts up as shown in Figure 2.1. The game buttons that the user must click to score points are located at the bottom of the game window and are disabled (grayed out).

FIGURE 2.1

Starting up the Click Race game.

To begin playing, the player must click on the Start Game button. When this happens, the game button located at the lower left-hand corner of the window is enabled as demonstrated in Figure 2.2.

FIGURE 2.2

Players score points by clicking on the currently active game button.

The player scores a point by clicking on the button. Once clicked, the game button is disabled and the other game button is visible throughout the game. The final score remains visible after game play has ended, as demonstrated in Figure 2.3.

The Click Race game gives the player 30 seconds to accumulate as many points as possible. Game play stops at 30 seconds when both game buttons are disabled. The total number of points scored by the player is displayed as demonstrated in Figure 2.4.

By the time you have created and run this game, you'll have learned how to exercise dynamic control over Windows controls by responding to events generated by the player. You will also have learned how to work with the Visual Basic Timer control.

FIGURE 2.3

To score another point, the player must click on the second game button.

FIGURE 2.4

Game plays ends at 30 seconds when both game buttons are disabled.

GETTING COMFORTABLE MOVING AROUND THE VISUAL BASIC 2005 EXPRESS EDITION IDE

Visual Basic applications are created using Visual Basic's built-in IDE. The Visual Basic IDE provides tools such as a compiler, which translates application code into a finished executable program; a debugger, which assists in tracking down and fixing programs; and tools for managing projects.

The Visual Basic 2005 Express IDE features a standard menu, numerous toolbars, and a number of different windows. Because Microsoft has crammed so much into the IDE, there is no way that all of the available toolbars and windows can be displayed at the same time. Instead, Microsoft has come up with a number of clever ways of allowing these resources to share the same space.

Figure 2.5 shows how Visual Basic 2005 Express IDE looks the first time you use it to open up a new project.

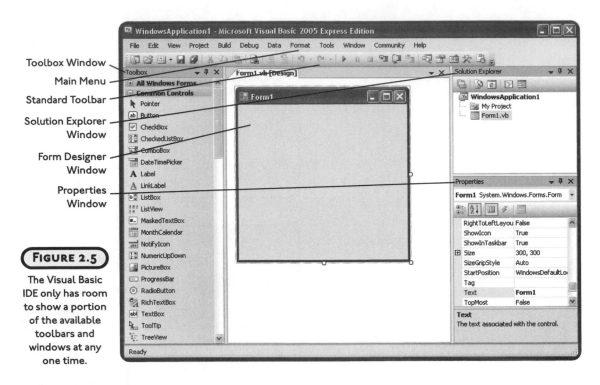

Toolbox Window

Main Menu

Standard Toolbar

Solution Explorer
Window

Form Designer
Window

Properties
Window

FIGURE 2.5

The Visual Basic
IDE only has room
to show a portion
of the available
toolbars and
windows at any
one time.

As Figure 2.5 shows, the default layout of the Visual Basic IDE features a number of different elements. Each of the key elements shown in Figure 2.5 will be covered in detail later in this chapter.

One nice feature of the IDE is AutoDock. AutoDock allows you to move windows around in the IDE by using your mouse to reposition them. As you move them near the edge of the IDE, an outline appears, showing where the IDE will automatically redock the window if you let it go. This makes it easy for you to reorganize the placement of windows within the IDE to suit your own personal preferences.

Be careful when repositioning windows within the IDE. There are so many windows available that it is all too easy to misplace them or even accidentally rearrange them.

From time to time, you will either accidentally or deliberately close a window within the IDE. Don't panic if you later discover you need it back. Instead, click on the View menu and select the appropriate window to display it again. The IDE provides so many different windows that it cannot show them all directly under the View menu. If you don't see the window that you are looking for listed there, select the Other Windows option and look for it in the submenu that appears.

Because the IDE is so packed full of features, Microsoft has had to employ a few organizational tricks in order to make everything fit. In some cases, two or more windows may share the same space in the IDE. Each tab identifies its associated windows. You can jump between windows by selecting the appropriate tab.

Another useful feature that you'll see a lot in the IDE is the presence of a thumbtack at the top of windows such as the Solution Explorer and Properties windows. The thumbtack represents an autohide feature that allows you to shrink down a window to a tab that is connected to the edge of the IDE where the window is docked. This way you free up space in the IDE for other windows without having to close any windows, and you can later restore a docked window by clicking on its tab. For example, take a look at Figure 2.6. Here you will see that the Solution Explorer window has been docked as a tab on the right side of the IDE in order to provide additional room for the Properties window.

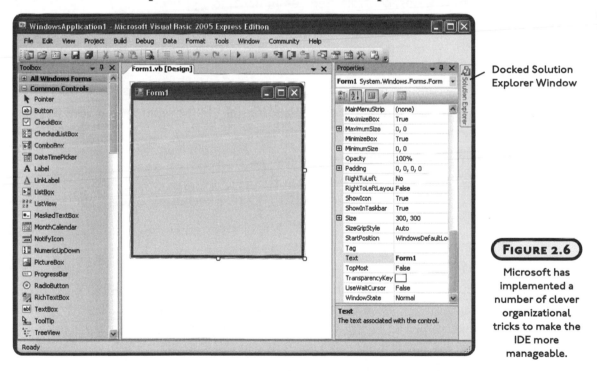

Docked Solution Explorer Window

FIGURE 2.6

Microsoft has implemented a number of clever organizational tricks to make the IDE more manageable.

The IDE is highly customizable. Click on the Tools menu and then select the Customize option to configure which of the IDE's many toolbars are displayed. In addition, you can customize any number of IDE features, such as how the form designer looks and how the code editor behaves, by clicking on the Tools menu and selecting Options.

Navigating the IDE Menu

The Visual Basic 2005 Express IDE includes a comprehensive menu, which lists and organizes the various commands and options available to you as you work. Visual Basic's IDE is a dynamic tool. It automatically changes based on the particular task that is before it.

The following list identifies the IDE menus and summarizes the functionality that they provide:

- **File.** Menu options for opening and saving projects and solutions
- **Edit.** Text-editing options such as Undo, Copy, Cut, and Paste
- **View.** Switch between the form designer and code editor and access other windows such as the Toolbox, Solution Explorer, and Properties windows
- **Project.** Add new forms, controls, and components to a project
- **Build.** Build or compile a standalone version of your application
- **Debug.** Test the execution of an application or step through a program that has been stopped with an error or a breakpoint
- **Data.** Configure connections to data sources such as a local database
- **Tools.** Collection of different options, including the Options submenu where you can customize the IDE and various project settings
- **Windows.** Select and arrange open windows
- **Community.** Access to on-line Visual Basic resources
- **Help.** Access to Visual Basic's integrated help system, including access to both local and online help topics

Working with Toolbars

As is the case with any Windows-based application, Visual Basic 2005 Express makes it easy to access certain commands using toolbars. By default, Visual Basic automatically displays its Standard toolbar, shown in Figure 2.7. The items displayed by toolbars may also change dynamically based on what you happen to be doing at the time.

The Visual Basic 2005 Express IDE includes more than a dozen toolbars, each of which provides single-click access to various commands. For some of the toolbars, you can configure whether or not they are displayed by clicking on the View menu and then selecting the Toolbars option. Optionally, you can configure the display of all the available toolbars by clicking on the Tools menu and selecting Customize.

Error List Window

Object Browser Window

Solution Explorer Window

Properties Window

Toolbox Window

FIGURE 2.7

The Standard toolbar provides access to commonly used IDE commands and windows.

TRICK You can also configure the display of toolbars by right-clicking on any visible toolbar and selecting the desired toolbar from the list that will appear.

Each icon on a toolbar performs a specific command or task. Visual Basic 2005 Express has too many toolbars to go over each of their icons in this book. You can find out about the specific function for each toolbar icon by placing your cursor over it, which results in its name being displayed as a ToolTip. However, you can get a pretty good feel for the purpose behind each toolbar based on its name.

Form Designer Basics

The form designer, shown in Figure 2.8, provides you with the ability to visually create GUIs (*graphical user interfaces*) using drag and drop. The form designer makes Visual Basic visual. The form designer shares space within the IDE with the Getting Started window and the code editor window, which is what you'll use to enter your Visual Basic programming statements.

Close Button

Maximize Button

Minimize Button

Title Bar

FIGURE 2.8

Visual Basic automatically creates a new form containing basic Windows elements each time you open up a new Visual Basic project.

> **TRICK**
> Sometimes when you are working with the form designer you may notice that there is an asterisk in the tab for the window just to the right of the form name. This asterisk indicates that you have made changes to the form that you have not saved yet. It is always a good idea to frequently save changes any time you modify your Visual Basic applications.

As you have already learned, you create an application window using a form. An application can have more than one form. As you saw when you created the Joke Machine application in Chapter 1, "An Introduction to Visual Basic 2005 Express," an application window is created by adding controls to it. These controls are copied over from the Toolbox. Once added to your form, you can customize controls by changing their size or editing their associated properties. Once you have a prototype of your form set up to look like you want it to, you'll need to add code to the controls to make them behave and work like you want them to.

The form designer makes relocating and aligning controls easy. It provides visual indicators that show the location of each control relative to the location of other controls on the form, as demonstrated in Figure 2.9.

Alignment
Indicators

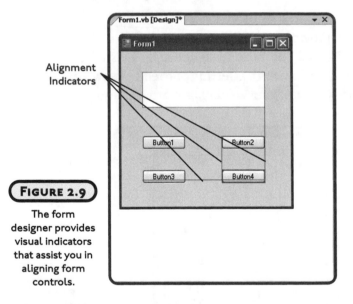

FIGURE 2.9

The form designer provides visual indicators that assist you in aligning form controls.

> **TRICK**
> You can also use commands located on the Format menu to automatically align controls on a form. For example, if you had three buttons of varying sizes on a form and wanted them all to be the same size, you could select them all by holding down the Ctrl key as you click on each button, and then click on Format, Make Same Size, and the Height and Width commands.

TRICK If you find that you are continually accidentally moving controls while working on a Windows interface, you can lock controls into place so that they cannot be moved by mistake. To do this, click on the Format menu and click on the Lock Controls command. If later you want to move a control, click on Lock Controls command again.

Understanding the Code Editor

The code editor facilitates the storage and viewing of the programming code that drives your Visual Basic applications. The easiest way to access it is to double-click on a form or one of the controls on the form. This automatically switches you from the form designer view to the code editor view as shown in Figure 2.10. Best of all, it also automatically places your cursor at the right location to begin entering code for the resource that you double-clicked on.

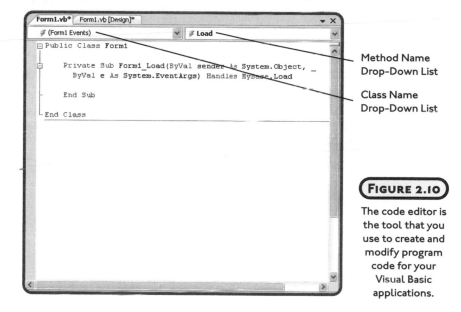

Method Name
Drop-Down List

Class Name
Drop-Down List

FIGURE 2.10

The code editor is the tool that you use to create and modify program code for your Visual Basic applications.

TRICK You can configure a number of features that affect the way the code editor looks and acts by clicking on the Tools menu and selecting Options. When the Options window appears, select the Text Editor option located on the left-hand side of the Options window and change any of the configuration settings that will be displayed on the right-hand side of the dialog.

Program code associated with a form and any of the controls placed on that form is stored alongside the form. Therefore, if a Visual Basic application contains more than one form, the code associated with each form is stored and displayed separately.

TRICK In addition to storing program code alongside a form, you can store the code in a separate module, which you can then use to refer back to a form and its controls.

At the top of the code editor are two drop-down lists. The first drop-down list is the Class Name list, from which you can select any of the controls located on the form. The second drop-down list is the Method Name list, which provides access to any event associated with the currently selected object. By using these two drop-down lists together, you can locate any code procedure. If you use these controls to look for a procedure that has not been created yet, the code editor will define a new procedure for that control and event on your behalf.

Visual Basic Assisted Code Development

One of the really nice things about Visual Basic is that it does so much work for you under the covers. For example, you don't have to figure out how to create a button or a text box. Visual Basic already makes them available to you as controls located in the Toolbox. Just as Visual Basic greatly simplifies form design, it helps streamline the code development process. For example, as you saw in Chapter 1 when you created the Joke Machine, Visual Basic automatically generates a lot of code for you. For example, create a new project and place a Label, a Textbox, and a Button on the form. Then double-click on the form and you'll see that Visual Basic automatically generates the following code for you.

```
Public Class Form1

    Private Sub Form1_Load(ByVal sender As System.Object, _
       ByVal e As System.EventArgs) Handles MyBase.Load

    End Sub

End Class
```

TRICK Actually, the format of the code statements that you will see when performing the above steps will vary slightly from the statements presented here. In order to make things fit onto the pages of this book, I will have to split some programming statements up into multiple pieces, using the continuation character (_).

As you can see, Visual Basic has already framed out the overall organization of the program statements that will make up the application. Now, using the Class Name and Method Name drop-down lists, select Button1 control and the Click event. As soon as you do this, the code editor defines a new procedure for you, as shown below.

```
Public Class Form1

    Private Sub Form1_Load(ByVal sender As System.Object, _
        ByVal e As System.EventArgs) Handles MyBase.Load

    End Sub

    Private Sub Button1_Click(ByVal sender As Object, _
        ByVal e As System.EventArgs) Handles Button1.Click

    End Sub

End Class
```

Now all that you have to do is type in the Visual Basic code statements that you want to be executed as part of these procedures, as was demonstrated in the Joke Machine project. I'll talk more about the benefits and use of procedures later in Chapter 8, "Enhancing Code Structure and Organization."

Color Coding, Automatic Indentation, and Spacing

You may have noticed back in Chapter 1 when you were creating the Joke Machine that the Visual Basic code editor did a number of things that made it easier for you to key in your Visual Basic code statements. For example, certain Visual Basic keywords were color coded in order to make them stand out. You will really learn to appreciate this feature as your applications grow in complexity and you end up writing more and more code. Color coding helps to make your code easier to read and work with by providing visual indicators that make your program code intuitively easier to follow along.

Another nice feature that you may not even have noticed is the automatic indentation of code statements, as demonstrated in Figure 2.11. By indenting groups of related code statements, your code is visually organized into logical chunks and becomes easier to read and understand.

Another really handy feature of the code editor is automatic spacing. For example, you might try to enter the following code statement, exactly as shown below.

```
TextBox1.Text="Hello"
```

As soon as you press the Enter key, the code editor changes the statement to look like the line of code shown below.

```
TextBox1.Text = "Hello"
```

FIGURE 2.11

The Visual Basic code editor automatically color codes statements and indents them to make them easier to read.

The changes to the line of code are subtle, but very important. If you look closely, you'll notice that a blank space has been added just before and after the equals sign to make the code easier to read. This is just another way that the Visual Basic code editor works to help make your coding experience as easy as possible, allowing you to focus on the task at hand without having to worry about little organizational details.

IntelliSense

A really nice feature that is directly integrated into the code editor is IntelliSense. IntelliSense was first introduced with Visual Basic 5.0. IntelliSense can be so helpful that many times you'll be able to get what you need from it without having to turn to other resources for help.

IntelliSense is responsible for displaying the pop-up boxes that you may have noticed when you were creating the Joke Machine back in Chapter 1. With IntelliSense, the Visual Basic IDE keeps an eye on your program statements as you type them and displays windows showing all the possible options available to you as you enter your code.

To better understand IntelliSense, let's look at a couple of examples. In the first example, shown in Figure 2.12, I created a form that contained a button and a text box. I then double-clicked on the button to open the code designer. I entered the word TextBox1 followed immediately by a period. In response, IntelliSense kicked in and displayed a pop-up window showing all the possible coding options available to me. In this example, I clicked on Text, which represents the TextBox control's Text property, and IntelliSense automatically appended the word to my code. All that remained for me to do was to finish writing the rest of the code statement as shown below.

```
TextBox1.Text = "Click on Me!"
```

FIGURE 2.12

IntelliSense provides dynamic assistance as you enter your code statements.

IntelliSense can help in the formation of more complex programming statements as well. For example, with the next code statement, my intention was to gray out and prevent the user from being able to click on the Button1 button. I started the statement by keying in the name of the Button1 control followed by a period. IntelliSense then kicked in, as shown in Figure 2.13, and displayed a pop-up window showing me all of my available options. I clicked on Enable and IntelliSense then appended that word to the code.

FIGURE 2.13

IntelliSense can assist you in the creation of complex code statements and in reducing typo mistakes.

Next I typed a space and pressed on the equals (=) key. Once again, IntelliSense jumped into action, displaying a pop-up window showing the two options that were available to me. (Also, just to the right of the pop-up dialog, a ToolTip was displayed, explaining what the Enabled method does.) I selected False and IntelliSense completed the code statement by appending the word False to the end of it.

TRICK   Another nice IntelliSense feature is the ability to use the Ctrl and Space keys together to tell the code editor to start it up. For example, suppose you created a form with a large number of controls and were having trouble remembering the name of a particular control for which you wanted to write some code. In this scenario, you could type the first letter or two of what you thought the control might be named and then could press and hold down the Ctrl key while also pressing the Space key. When you do this, IntelliSense starts and displays the names of all available resources that begin with those letters, as demonstrated in Figure 2.14.

FIGURE 2.14

Using the Ctrl and Space keys to manually start up IntelliSense.

What's in the Toolbox?

The Toolbox window, shown in Figure 2.15, contains all of the controls that are available to your Visual Basic applications. By dragging and dropping an icon from the Toolbox onto a Visual Basic form, you automatically add its functionality to your application. For example, in this book you will learn how to work with controls such as Label, Button, and TextBox.

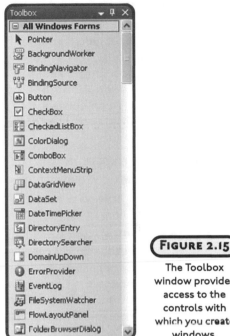

FIGURE 2.15

The Toolbox window provides access to the controls with which you create windows.

The Label control allows you to place a string of text anywhere on a form. The Button control allows you to add as many buttons to your form as you need. You can then customize the appearance of each button and add code to it in order to make your application perform a specific task whenever the user clicks on it. The TextBox field provides the ability to collect text input directly from users. These are just a few of the dozens of controls that are available to you.

By default, the Toolbox window displays a list of controls with their names just to the right of each control. Toolbox controls are organized into the following groups:

- **All Windows Forms.** A list of all available controls.
- **Common Controls.** Commonly used interface controls.
- **Containers.** Controls that can be used to organize other controls.
- **Menus & Toolbars.** Controls that facilitate the creation of menus and toolbars.
- **Data.** Controls that facilitate the establishment of a connection to a local database.
- **Components.** Controls that facilitate the collection of information regarding how the computer is operating.
- **Printing.** Controls that provide access to print features.
- **Dialogs.** Controls that provide access to various dialog windows.
- **General.** Contains controls that do not fit in the above categories.

TRICK

Because there are so many available controls in the Toolbox, you have to scroll down to view them all. Once you learn to identify each control by its graphic icon, you can modify the Toolbox window so that it only displays a list of icons. This enables you to view the available controls at one time with no scrolling. To set this up, right-click on the Toolbox window and select the List View option from the drop-down menu that appears. Also, if you forget what a given control icon represents, just place you cursor over it and its name is displayed as a ToolTip.

There isn't enough space in this book to cover every Visual Basic 2005 Express feature, such as all of the Toolbox controls. However, rest assured that as you work your way through this book, you'll learn how to work with a lot of other controls.

TRICK

Visual Basic provides access to more controls than are displayed by default in the Toolbox. You can view these additional controls and add them to the Toolbox as necessary by right-clicking on the Toolbox and selecting Choose Items. This opens the Choose Toolbox Items dialog where you will find additional controls listed on either of two tabs. The first tab is .NET Framework Components. It stores controls that are designed to work with the .NET Framework. The second tab is listed as COM Components. The controls listed here are legacy controls for which .NET equivalent controls have yet to be developed. To add a control, select it and click on OK.

Working with Solution Explorer

Solution Explorer displays the projects and files that make up your Visual Basic applications. Solution Explorer organizes its contents in a hierarchical format, starting with the solution, followed by its member's projects, and then all the files that make up those projects, as demonstrated in Figure 2.16.

You can also use the Solution Explorer to locate and open a file by double-clicking on it. If you select a file that is associated with both the form designer and code editor, you can select which tool you wish to work with by clicking on the appropriate icon as shown in Figure 2.16.

View Designer

View Code

Refresh

Show All Files

Properties

FIGURE 2.16

Using Solution Explorer, you can manage the projects and files that make up your Visual Basic applications.

Understanding How to Use the Properties Window

Properties are a key component in the development of any Visual Basic application. By specifying the values assigned to a form using the Properties window, you are able to specify its initial appearance and behavior. Later, in your program code, you can modify the value of many properties and dynamically change them as your application executes.

Every control that you can place on a form when creating your application's graphical interface also has its own collection of properties. By setting property values associated with a control, you can specify control text, size, color, location, and behavior.

You have already seen how to work with control properties back in Chapter 1 when you created the Joke Machine. All you have to do is select a control and its associated properties are automatically displayed in the Properties window, as demonstrated in Figure 2.17.

As you can see, the name of each property is shown in the left-hand column of the window, and any values assigned to those properties are shown in the right-hand column.

By default, the Visual Basic IDE organizes the display of properties by category. This assists you in finding the right properties to modify when you are not sure what the name of the property you are looking for is but you have a good guess as to what category it belongs to. However, as you become more comfortable with Visual Basic programming, you may find

FIGURE 2.17

Examining the properties associated with a Button control.

that you prefer to have control properties listed alphabetically, so that you can quickly scroll down and locate the one that you know you are looking for. You can switch between category and sort view by clicking on either the Categorized or Alphabetical icons located at the top of the Properties window, as shown in Figure 2.17.

For most controls, all that you have to do to modify one of their associated properties is to type a new value for it in the Properties window. However, some properties have a finite number of available values. When this is the case, an iconic arrow is displayed when you select the properties. For example, as demonstrated in Figure 2.18, only two possible values are available for the Button control's Enabled property (True or False).

For some properties, such as the Font property, you'll notice that when you select them, three ellipses are displayed in the value field. When you click on the ellipses, a dialog appears, from which you can select the appropriate value. For example, Figure 2.19 shows the dialog that appears when you want to modify the values associated with the Font property.

Properties

Button2 System.Windows.Forms.Button

DialogResult	None
Dock	None
Enabled	True
⊞ FlatAppearance	True
FlatStyle	False
⊞ Font	Microsoft Sans Serif, 8.25pt
ForeColor	■ ControlText
GenerateMember	True
Image	☐ (none)
ImageAlign	MiddleCenter
ImageIndex	☐ (none)
ImageKey	☐ (none)
ImageList	(none)
⊞ Location	**182, 165**
Locked	False
⊞ Margin	3, 3, 3, 3
⊞ MaximumSize	0, 0
⊞ MinimumSize	0, 0

Enabled
Indicates whether the control is enabled.

Select True
or False

FIGURE 2.18

When only a finite number of values are available for a property, the Properties window displays them in a drop-down list for your selection.

Font

Font:	Font style:	Size:	
Microsoft Sans Serif	Regular	8	OK
Microsoft Sans Serif	Regular	8	Cancel
T MT Extra	Italic	9	
O MV Boli	Bold	10	
T OCRATTRegular	Bold Italic	11	
T OzHandicraft BT		12	
O Palatino Linotype		14	
T PosterBodoni BT		16	

Effects
☐ Strikeout
☐ Underline

Sample

AaBbYyZz

Script:
Western

FIGURE 2.19

Sometimes you will be presented with an additional dialog from which you can select the values that you want to assign to a given property.

You can edit most, but not all, of the properties belonging to a given object at design time, which is when you are developing your application using the IDE. However, some properties are only available at run-time, which is not until your application has been finished, saved, and then executed. For example, the font type and size associated with a control is always available at design time, whereas the text entry for a control that holds user input, such as a TextBox control, won't be available until your application is running. You cannot, therefore, set properties only available at run-time from within the Properties window at design time.

The Component Tray

Most of the controls on the Toolbox work by copying an instance of the control onto a Visual Basic form. Once added to a form, you can modify the control and access its properties. However, some controls don't actually appear on your forms when you add them because they don't take a visual form that users can see and interact with. Perhaps the best example of this type of control is the Timer control.

A Timer control provides the ability to trigger activity at certain time intervals. For example, the Click Race game that you will learn how to create later in this chapter uses a Timer control to limit the amount of time that the player has to play the game. So if the Timer control does not appear on a form, how can you see that you have successfully added it to your application, and how do you access its properties at development time? The answer is by using a component tray located at the bottom of the form designer.

Any time that you add a control that cannot appear on a form, Visual Basic automatically displays it in a component tray, as demonstrated in Figure 2.20.

As you can see in Figure 2.20, the Timer control has been added to the form. You can now select it and set its Properties just like any other control that you can add to a Visual Basic form.

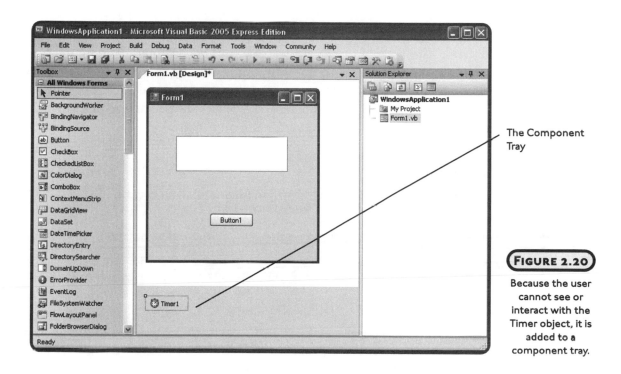

The Component Tray

FIGURE 2.20

Because the user cannot see or interact with the Timer object, it is added to a component tray.

Other Windows

There are a number of other IDE windows available to you as you develop your Visual Basic applications. Some are very specialized, and you will only need to work with them at certain times. For example, the Error List window automatically appears if you attempt to run a program with an error in it within the IDE. Table 2.1 lists these other windows, which are discussed, where relevant, in later chapters.

TABLE 2.1: ADDITIONAL IDE WINDOWS

Windows	Description
Object Browser	Provides the ability to view objects and their members
Error List	Displays information about errors that occur when testing your applications
Immediate	Provides the ability to issue commands and test expressions while testing your applications
Task List	Displays tasks that Visual Basic identifies as needing to be done

Back to the Click Race Game

In the Click Race game, the player is required to click on two buttons as many times as possible in order to score points in a 30-second period. However, in order to rack up points, the player must click on one button and then the other button before returning to click on the first button. Therefore, the game requires that the player be not only quick with the mouse button, but also quick and precise in moving the mouse around.

Designing the Game

The Click Race game is played on a single window. It is made up of a form and six controls shown in Table 2.2.

TABLE 2.2: FORM CONTROLS FOR THE CLICK RACE GAME

Control	Description
TextBox1	Displays the number of valid mouse clicks
Label1	Descriptive label for the text box
Button1	One of two game buttons
Button2	One of two game buttons
Button3	Button used to start game play
Button4	Button used to close the game
Timer1	Timer control used to control the length of a game

Step 1: Creating a New Visual Basic Project

The first step in creating the Click Race game is to start Visual Basic and open a new project.

1. If you have not already done so, start up Visual Basic 2005 Express and then click on File and select New Project. The New Project dialog will appear.
2. The Click Race game runs as a graphical Windows desktop application, so select Windows Application.
3. Next, type Click Race as the name of your new application in the Name field located at the bottom of the New Project window.
4. Click on OK to close the New Project dialog.

Visual Basic will now create a new project, including an initial form, in its IDE.

Step 2: Creating the User Interface

Now it is time to add the controls required to assemble the game's interface. The overall layout of the game's interface is shown in Figure 2.21.

FIGURE 2.21

Completing the interface design for the Click Race game.

1. Let's begin by adding a TextBox to the form. By default, Visual Basic assigns the name Textbox1 to the control.

2. Then let's add a Label, which Visual Basic automatically names Label1, to the form.

3. Move and resize TextBox1 and Label1 to the approximate location shown in Figure 2.21.

4. Add the first button to the form and place it in the lower left-hand corner. Visual Basic assigns it the name Button1.

5. Add the second button to the lower right-hand corner. Visual Basic assigns it the name Button2.

TRAP It is important that you not get the buttons mixed up. You will need to know which button is which when it is time to begin adding code to the application.

6. Then add the third button to the upper right-hand corner of the form. Visual Basic assigns it the name Button3.

7. Next, add a fourth button just beneath it. Visual Basic assigns it the name Button4.

8. Finally, add a Timer control to your form, which Visual Basic names Timer1. The Timer1 control will actually be displayed on a Component Tray.

The layout and design of your Visual Basic form is now complete and should look like the example shown in Figure 2.21, except that the Timer1 control is displayed in a Component Tray just below the form.

Step 3: Customizing Form and Control Properties

Before you start customizing the properties associated with the controls that you just added to the form, let's change one of the properties belonging to the form itself. Specifically, let's modify the form so that it displays the text string of Click Race Game in its title bar. To do this, click anywhere on the form, except on top of one of its controls, and then locate the Text property in the Properties windows and replace the default value of Form1 with Click Race Game.

The first control to modify is the Textbox1 control. Table 2.3 lists all of the properties that you should modify and shows what their new values should be.

TABLE 2.3: PROPERTY CHANGES FOR THE TEXTBOX1 CONTROL	
Property	**Value**
BackColor	Info
ForeColor	HotTrack (on the System Tab)
ReadOnly	True
Font	Arial
Font	Regular
Font	Size 14
Size	132, 29

Once you have completed making the property changes for the TextBox1 control, let's work on the Label1 control by making the property changes shown in Table 2.4.

TABLE 2.4: PROPERTY CHANGES FOR THE LABEL1 CONTROL	
Property	**Value**
Font	Arial
Font	Bold
Font	Size 12
Text	Number of Clicks

Now, referring to Table 2.5, modify the properties associated with Button1, Button2, Button3, and Button4.

TABLE 2.5: PROPERTY CHANGES FOR THE BUTTON1 THROUGH BUTTON4 CONTROLS		
Button Name	**Property**	**Value**
Button1	Text	Click Me!
	Font	Arial
	Font	Regular
	Font	Size 9
Button2	Text	Click Me!
	Font	Arial
	Font	Regular
	Font	Size 9
Button3	Text	Start Game
	Font	Arial
	Font	Regular
	Font	Size 9
Button4	Text	Exit
	Font	Arial
	Font	Regular
	Font	Size 9

There are two additional property modifications that need to be made. They are to the Timer1 control located in the Component Tray. By default, the Timer1 control's Interval property is set to 100 by Visual Basic at design time. Interval represents the amount of time in milliseconds that passes during each interval measured by the timer control. It is a lot easier for people to think in terms of seconds than in terms of milliseconds. So let's change the value assigned to Interval1 to 1000 as shown in Table 2.6.

TABLE 2.6: PROPERTY CHANGES FOR THE TIMER1 CONTROL

Property	Value
Interval	1000
Enabled	True

Lastly set the Timer control's Enabled property equal to true. Otherwise it will not execute when the application is executed.

That's all the property modifications that are required for the Click Race game. Now it is time to give life to the application by adding the programming code that will make the game run.

Step 4: Adding a Little Programming Logic

OK, it is time to start coding. If you double-click on Form1, Visual Basic starts things off for you by adding a number of lines of code, as shown below. Actually, what you'll see in the code editor window is slightly different than what you see here. Take a look at the end of the second line of code shown below. Notice that it ends with the underscore character. In Visual Basic the underscore character is used as a continuation character. I added it where I did so that I could make the code statement a little easier to read by breaking it out into two lines. Other than this cosmetic change, everything else is exactly the same.

```
Public Class Form1

    Private Sub Form1_Load(ByVal sender As System.Object, _
       ByVal e As System.EventArgs) Handles MyBase.Load

    End Sub

End Class
```

Visual Basic 2005 Express is an OOP (*object-oriented programming*) language. In order to work with an object, you must define an instance of the object in your application. In the case of the above code, in the first statement, Visual Basic defines an object named Form1 on your behalf, which extracts everything its needs from the Visual Basic Class Library. All code for the Form1 object or any of the controls that you have added to the form is placed somewhere after the Public Class Form1 statement and before the closing End Class statement. These two statements define the beginning and end of the code affecting the Form1 object.

TRICK

In between the Public Class Form1 statement and the End Class statement are two more statements. These statements identify the beginning and end of the Form1 Load event procedure. Take a look at the first of these two statements and you will see that the first statement assigns the procedure the name Form1_Load. You can change the name of the procedure to anything that makes sense to you.

The Load keyword refers to the form's Load event. Events occur in Visual Basic whenever something happens. For example, when a form first appears or loads, the Load event for that form executes. Therefore, this procedure executes when the application starts (for example, when the form first loads). Don't worry if this explanation is a little difficult to grasp just yet. I shared it with you now just to try and give you a feel for what Visual Basic is doing. I'll go over procedures and events in much more detail in later chapters.

Now it is time to begin adding code to the Click Race game. Again, since you won't start learning how to formulate Visual Basic statements until Chapter 4, "Working with Menus and Toolbars," just follow along and make sure that you enter any Visual Basic statements exactly as I'll show you.

For starters, add the two statements shown below in bold exactly where shown. These statements define two variables that the application will use to keep track of how many times the player has clicked on the game's buttons and how long the game has been running.

```
Public Class Form1

    Dim intCounter As Integer = 0
    Dim intTimerCount As Integer = 0

    Private Sub Form1_Load(ByVal sender As System.Object, _
        ByVal e As System.EventArgs) Handles MyBase.Load

    End Sub

End Class
```

Next, add the two statements shown below in bold in the Form1_Load procedure. These statements execute as soon as the form loads and gray out the two buttons used to play the game.

```
Public Class Form1

    Dim intCounter As Integer = 0
    Dim intTimerCount As Integer = 0

    Private Sub Form1_Load(ByVal sender As System.Object, _
      ByVal e As System.EventArgs) Handles MyBase.Load

        Button1.Enabled = False
        Button2.Enabled = False

    End Sub

End Class
```

Now click on the Form1.vb [Design] tab to return to the designer view and then double-click on Button1. This switches you right back to the code editor, where you will see that Visual Basic has added a new procedure named Button1_Click. Add the four statements shown below in bold to this procedure exactly as shown. The first statement adds a value of 1 to the intCounter variable, which the game uses to track the total number of mouse clicks made by the player. The second statement displays the value of the value of intCounter in the Textbox1 control so that the player will know that a click has been counted. The next two statements gray out or disable Button1 and enable Button2 (because the game forces the player to alternate the clicking of these two buttons).

```
Private Sub Button1_Click(ByVal sender As System.Object, _
  ByVal e As System.EventArgs) Handles Button1.Click

    intCounter = intCounter + 1
    TextBox1.Text = intCounter
    Button1.Enabled = False
    Button2.Enabled = True

End Sub
```

Now click on the `Form1.vb [Design]` tab to return to the designer view and then double-click on `Button2`. This switches you back to the code editor. You'll notice that Visual Basic has added a new procedure named `Button2_Click`. Add the four statements shown below in bold to this procedure. As you can see, these statements look almost exactly like the four statements that you added to the previous procedure, except that the last two statements switch the enabling and disabling of the two game buttons.

```
Private Sub Button2_Click(ByVal sender As System.Object, _
  ByVal e As System.EventArgs) Handles Button2.Click

    intCounter = intCounter + 1
    TextBox1.Text = intCounter
    Button1.Enabled = True
    Button2.Enabled = False

End Sub
```

Now it is time to add some code to the game's Start button (`Button3`). Start by clicking on the `Form1.vb [Design]` tab to return to the designer view and then double-click on `Button3`. This switches you back to the code editor. You'll notice that Visual Basic has added a new procedure named `Button3_Click`. Add the six statements exactly as shown below to this procedure. This procedure is used to start or restart the game at any time. The first two statements reset the values assigned to the game's two variables back to zero. The next statement clears out `Textbox1`. Two statements that follow enable `Button1` and disable `Button2`. The last statement restarts the `Timer1` control.

```
Private Sub Button3_Click(ByVal sender As System.Object, _
  ByVal e As System.EventArgs) Handles Button3.Click

    intCounter = 0
    intTimerCount = 0
    TextBox1.Text = ""
    Button1.Enabled = True
    Button2.Enabled = False
    Timer1.Enabled = True

End Sub
```

Now let's fix up the Exit button (`Button4`) so that it will close the Click Race game when the player clicks on it. Click on the `Form1.vb [Design]` tab to return to the designer view and then double-click on `Button3`. This switches you back to the code editor, where you'll see that

Visual Basic has added a new procedure named Button4_Click. Add the following statement to it, shown in bold, exactly as shown below. This statement tells Visual Basic to exit the application.

```
Private Sub Button4_Click(ByVal sender As System.Object, _
  ByVal e As System.EventArgs) Handles Button4.Click

    Application.Exit

End Sub
```

Now all that is left to do is to add some code to the Timer1 control so that it will limit the player's turn to 30 seconds. Click on the Form1.vb [Design] tab to return to the designer view. Double-click on Timer1. Visual Basic automatically adds the Timer1_Tick procedure to your application. Add the five Visual Basic statements shown below in bold to this procedure. The first statement tells the Timer1 control to keep track of the number of seconds that it has run. Remember that you previously configured the Timer1 object's Interval property so that the Timer1 control would execute every second. The next four statements will execute as soon as the Timer1 control has run for 30 seconds, at which time the two game buttons will be disabled, thus ending the player's turn.

```
Private Sub Timer1_Tick(ByVal sender As System.Object, _
  ByVal e As System.EventArgs) Handles Timer1.Tick

    intTimerCount = intTimerCount + 1

    If intTimerCount = 30 Then
      Button1.Enabled = False
      Button2.Enabled = False
    End If

End Sub
```

Step 5: Testing the Execution of the Click Race Game

OK. That's it. The Click Race game should be ready to go. Try running it by pressing the F5 key. If any errors occur, go back and double-check the code statements that you added to make sure that you did not make any typos.

SUMMARY

This chapter provided detailed coverage of the most commonly used windows in the Visual Basic 2005 Express IDE. This included learning how to work with its menu and toolbars. You also learned how to work with the form designer and the code editor. In addition, you learned about IntelliSense and how to use it effectively. On top of all this, the chapter provided you with additional information on how to work with and take advantage of the Toolbox, Solution Explorer, and Properties windows.

Before you move on to Chapter 3, "Creating an Application Interface," take a few minutes to further improve the Click Race game by implementing the following challenges.

CHALLENGES

1. Spice up the Click Race game by redecorating it a bit. For example, play around with the background and foreground colors of the form and other controls to create a color scheme that is more to your personal liking.

2. If you place the cursor over one of the edges of the Click Race game's window, you can resize it, resulting in a less-than-attractive result. Prevent this behavior by locking the dimensions of the window into place. (Hint: Click on the form and set the FormBorderStyle property equal to one of the "Fixed" border styles in the drop-down list that will appear.)

3. As it is currently written, the Timer1 control keeps on ticking after the player's turn ends. This is OK because the Timer1 control is restarted as soon as the player clicks on Start again. However, allowing the Timer1 to keep running does waste CPU processing cycles. It would be more efficient if you had the Timer1 control disable itself at the end of the player's turn. (Hint: Add Timer1.Enabled = False as the last statement in the Timer1_Tick procedure.)

4. Make the game a little slicker by adding a Textbox that displays the amount of time that the player has left as the game progresses. (Hint: Add a Textbox to the form. Make sure it is named TextBox2 and then modify the code associated with the Timer1 control as shown below in bold.)

```
Private Sub Timer1_Tick(ByVal sender As System.Object, _
    ByVal e As System.EventArgs) Handles Timer1.Tick

        intTimerCount = intTimerCount + 1
        If intTimerCount = 30 Then
```

continued

```
                Button1.Enabled = False
                Button2.Enabled = False
            Timer1.Enabled = False
        End If

        TextBox2.Text = intTimerCount

    End Sub
```

CHAPTER

3

CREATING AN
APPLICATION INTERFACE

In this chapter, you will learn how to spice up your Visual Basic application's graphical user interface. In doing so, you will learn how to make your applications look and behave like the professional Windows applications that you work with every day. This will include learning how to create ToolTips, designing a status bar, and posting an icon representing your application in the System Tray located on the Windows taskbar. You will also learn how to save time when creating your Visual Basic applications by taking advantage of two easily accessible built-in dialogs. In addition, you'll get the chance to put to practical use some of the tricks that you'll learn in this chapter's game project, the Speed Typing game.

Specifically, you will learn how to:

- Create and write text to a status bar
- Display additional information as ToolTips
- Associate a custom icon with your Visual Basic application
- Display an application icon in the System Tray
- Use the `MessageBox.Show` method and the `InputBox` function to display messages and collect user input
- How to control the tab order in which controls are accessed
- How to specify the location where your Visual Basic application first appears on the user's desktop

- How to specify the type of border used to frame your application windows
- How to create a splash screen for your application

PROJECT PREVIEW: THE SPEED TYPING GAME

In this chapter's game project, you will learn how to develop the Speed Typing game. The object of this game is to see how good and fast a typist the player is. The game begins by displaying a text string, which the player is then supposed to retype exactly as shown.

The player must type the string exactly. If an extra space is added between words or if a typo is made, the game calls a strike on the player. The game tests the player's typing skill using five different levels. The player gets 15 seconds to type in the text string associated with each level. To advance to the next level, the player must first successfully complete the current level. The player also gets a strike if the time runs out before the current text string is typed.

Each level is a little bit harder than the level that precedes it. The game ends when the player either successfully completes all five levels or when three strikes are accumulated. At the end of game play, the game ranks the player's skill level as beginner, intermediate, advanced, or expert. Figures 3.1 through 3.5 demonstrate the overall flow of the Speed Typing game.

FIGURE 3.1

The Speed Typing game begins when the player clicks on the Go button.

Custom Icon

Status Bar

FIGURE 3.2

Players advance by typing in the required text string within the allotted amount of time.

FIGURE 3.3

Players who fail to type the required text in time receive a strike.

FIGURE 3.4

Players who make a typo when keying in the required text string receive a strike.

FIGURE 3.5

The player's typing skill level is analyzed and displayed at the end of game play.

By the time you have created and run this game, you'll have increased your understanding of Windows application interface design and will have had the opportunity to implement several of the graphical interface design techniques that are presented in this chapter.

PUTTING TOGETHER A GRAPHICAL USER INTERFACE

The first thing users typically see when they start up a Windows application is its graphical user interface. Today, most users have enough experience working with computers running Windows that they approach each new application with certain expectations. For starters, they expect application windows to be well organized and clearly presented. Users also expect other things, such as being able to tab between controls in a logical order and to see messages displayed in a status bar located at the bottom of windows.

Users also want to be able to move the pointer over a control in order to see a ToolTip explaining what the control does. Users expect to see a unique icon representing your applications' executable file, and they may also want to see that icon posted in the Windows taskbar's System Tray. In short, they expect your Visual Basic application to provide the same basic features that are found in most other Windows applications. In this chapter, you will learn how to implement each of the features described above. Depending on the type of application you are working on, users may also expect to see menus and toolbars. You'll learn how to add these types of controls to your Visual Basic application in Chapter 4, "Working with Menus and Toolbars."

Specifying a Windows Starting Position

By default, Windows opens your Visual Basic application's windows at the location of its choice. Sometimes this is in the middle of your screen, sometimes it's not. However, if you want, you can exercise control over the screen position that Windows chooses. This is accomplished by setting the form's `StartPosition` property. The `StartPosition` property can be set to any of the values shown in Table 3.1.

By specifying one of the values shown in Table 3.1 at design time, you can exercise various levels of control over where your form is initially displayed and in what size it will appear.

TABLE 3.1: VALUES SUPPORTED BY THE FORM STARTPOSITION PROPERTY

Property	Description
Manual	The form's Location property determines where the form is displayed and the form's Size property specifies its bounds.
CenterScreen	The form is centered in the middle of the screen and the form's Size property specifies its bounds.
WindowsDefaultLocation	Displays the form at a location chosen by Windows but the form's Size property specifies its bounds.
WindowsDefaultBounds	Displays the form at a location chosen by Windows using bounds (size) also chosen by Windows.
CenterParent	The form is centered within the bounds of its specified parent, which could be the Windows desktop or another form in the application.

Specifying Windows Border Style

By default, Visual Basic allows users to resize a form's window border at run time. However, this can result in some undesired consequences, as demonstrated in Figure 3.6. As you can see, once resized, the window shown in Figure 3.6 suddenly looks very unprofessional, with far too much empty space on the right-hand side of the window.

FIGURE 3.6

Unless you specify otherwise, Visual Basic will allow users to change the size of your application's window.

The easiest way to deal with this situation is to control the form's border style using the FormBorderStyle property. Table 3.2 outlines each of the available FormBorderStyle property values.

TABLE 3.2: AVAILABLE OPTIONS FOR THE FormBorderStyle PROPERTY	
Value	**Description**
None	Displays the form without a border
FixedSingle	Sets up a fixed single line form border
Fixed3D	Sets up a fixed three-dimensional form border
FixedDialog	Sets up a thick fixed form border
Sizable	Sets up a resizable border
FixedToolWindow	Sets up a tool window border that cannot be resized
SizableToolWindow	Sets up a tool window border that can be resized

DEFINITION

A tool window is one that does not appear in the Windows taskbar when the application is running.

Dynamically Altering Title Bar Messages

Unless you change a form's Text property, Visual Basic displays the name of the form in its title bar, as shown in Figure 3.7.

Title Bar String

FIGURE 3.7

By default, Visual Basic displays a form's name in its title bar.

Typically, you will set the form's Text property to display any text string you wish using the Properties window. In addition, you can set it with code at run time, as demonstrated below.

```
Private Sub Button1_Click(ByVal sender As System.Object, _
  ByVal e As System.EventArgs) Handles Button1.Click

        Me.Text = "Speed Typing Game"

End Sub
```

This code is associated with the click event belonging to the Button1 control on the form. When the button is clicked, the code executes, updating the text string displayed in the title bar, as shown in Figure 3.8.

FIGURE 3.8

Programmatically changing the text string displayed in the window's title bar.

TRICK   Note the use of the keyword Me in the previous example. Me is a Visual Basic keyword that refers back to the parent object that is currently executing, which in the case of the previous example was form1.

By programmatically changing the text string displayed in the form's title bar using code, you create the ability to dynamically change its contents. However, you should exercise this capability very carefully. Most users don't look at the title bar, and even when they do, they don't go back and view it over and over again, so they'll miss any text changes that you have posted to it.

TRICK   If you plan to post dynamic text content, you should look at setting up a status bar on your form, as discussed later in this chapter.

Setting Up Control Tab Order and Focus

Users can interact with controls that appear on your Visual Basic applications by using their mouse to click on or select them. However, users can also use the keyboard Tab key. By repeatedly pressing the Tab key, focus is transferred from control to control. You can visually tell which control has focus by examining it. Controls such as buttons are highlighted when they receive focus, whereas controls such as textboxes display a blinking cursor.

DEFINITION

Focus is a term used to identify the currently selected control (the control that will receive any keyboard input).

The tab order between controls is based, by default, on the order in which you add the controls to the form. Each time you add a control to a form, it is assigned a tab index number. The first control added to the form is assigned an index number of 0, and each control that is added after that is assigned an index number that is incremented by 1. So by carefully adding controls to a form in the exact order in which you wish them to be accessed via the Tab key, you can control the form's tab order. However, in most cases this option is too bothersome to try and implement. Instead, most programmers add controls in any order they wish and then come back and specify the tab order.

TRICK   By default, each control's TabStop property is set to True. If you set this property to False, your application will not include the control in the tab order.

One way to modify tab order, after you have added all the controls to a form, is to set each control's TabIndex property. Specify 0 for the default control (the control that initially receives focus when the form loads) and 1 for the control that will be the next control in the tab order. However, a better way to specify tab order is to click on the View menu and select the Tab Order option. This tells the IDE to display numbers in the corner of each control representing each control's order within the tab index, as demonstrated in Figure 3.9.

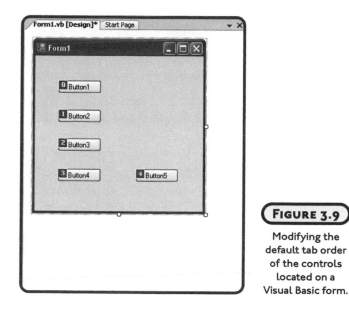

FIGURE 3.9

Modifying the
default tab order
of the controls
located on a
Visual Basic form.

To modify the tab order, just click on the control that should be first, followed by each remaining control in the order that you wish them to be ordered. When done, click on the Tab Order option located on the View menu a second time to remove the tab order indicators.

Adding a Status Bar to Your Application

One feature that you may wish to add to windows in your Visual Basic applications is a status bar. A status bar is a window control, typically located at the bottom of a window where applications display all sort of information as they run. Examples of information commonly displayed by status bars include the current date and time, help information, hints, error information, or the name of a currently open file.

TRICK   Although the IDE automatically places the status bar at the bottom of the form by default, you can move it to any edge of the form by setting the Dock property, which supports any of the following values: Right, Left, Top, Bottom, and Fill.

A status bar can display different types of data, including text and icons. Status bars can also be divided up into panels, enabling one status bar to display many different types of information, each in its own defined section of the status bar, as demonstrated in Figure 3.10.

FIGURE 3.10

A Windows status bar displaying the current date and application status information in two separate panels.

In order to add a status bar to a window in a Visual Basic application, you must add the StatusBar control from the Toolbox to the appropriate form. Once added, you can configure the StatusBar control by modifying any of the properties shown in Table 3.3.

TABLE 3.3: CONFIGURING PROPERTIES BELONGING TO THE STATUSBAR CONTROL

Property	Description
Text	A text string to be displayed in the status bar
SizingGrip	A visual indicator in the right-hand corner of the status bar indicating that it can be resized
Panels	Adds or removes panels from the status bar
ShowPanels	Determines whether the status bar displays panels

To get a better understanding of how to work with the StatusBar control, let's work on a couple of examples. In order to use the StatusBar control you must first add it to your ToolBox window, as outlined in the following procedure.

1. Right-click on the Toolbox window and select Choose Items from the context menu that appears.

2. The Choose Toolbox Items window appears. By default the .NET Framework Components tab is selected.

3. Scroll down and select the StatusBar control.

4. Click on OK.

Once you have added the StatusBar control to the Toolbox windows, you can add a status bar to your application and write some text for it, as outlined below.

 You can also implement a status bar on your application using the StatusStrip control. For information on how to use this control, refer to Visual Basic's online help.

1. Create a new Visual Basic application.

2. Add a Button control and a StatusBar control to your application's form.

3. Modify the button's Text property to Push me.

3. Select the StatusBar control and then modify its Text property to display the string Hello World!

Now, press the F5 key to run your application, and you should see that Hello World! is displayed in the left-hand side of the status bar. Stop your application in order to return to design mode. Next, let's modify the application's status bar by organizing it into two panels and displaying separate pieces of information in each panel as outlined below.

 You might want to set the StatusBar control's SizingGrip property to False if you plan on preventing users from being able to resize your application window. Otherwise, your users are going to get confused.

1. Select the StatusBar control and then set its ShowPanels property equal to True.

2. Next select the Panels property and click on the ellipsis (...) button shown in its value field to open the StatusBarPanel Collection Editor window.

3. Click on the Add button to define the first panel. A panel named StatusBarPanel1 will be displayed in the Members pane.

4. Modify the StatusBarPanel1 object's Text property for the first panel to say Ready.

6. Modify the StatusBarPanel1 object's AutoSize property to equal Spring.

7. Click on the Add button again to define a second panel. By default, the panel will be named StatusBarPanel2.

8. Modify the StatusBarPanel2 object's Text property of the second panel to say Click on the button.

9. Modify the StatusBarPanel2 object's AutoSize property to equal Spring.

FIGURE 3.11

Using the StatusBarPanel Collection Editor, you can organize a status bar into any number of panels.

10. Click on OK to close the StatusBarPanel Collection editor.

TRICK You can control the amount of space allocated to each status bar panel by specifying any of the following values for the AutoSize property.

- **None.** Does not display a border

- **Spring.** Shares space with other panels that have their AutoSize property set to Spring

- **Contents.** Sets panel width based on its current contents

Press F5 to run your application. Now your application's status bar displays two separate pieces of information, each in its own status bar panel. Or course, to make a status bar truly useful, most applications need to be able to dynamically change its contents as the application runs. For example, if you have defined a status bar named StatusBar1 that does not have any panels, you could add the following statement to the click event of the Button control. When clicked, the text Hello World! is displayed in the status bar.

```
Private Sub Button1_Click(ByVal sender As System.Object, _
        ByVal e As System.EventArgs) Handles Button1.Click

        StatusBar1.Text = "Hello World!"
End Sub
```

If, on the other hand, you organized your status bar into multiple panels, you could place a text string in each panel by adding the following statements to the click event of the Button control.

```
Private Sub Button1_Click(ByVal sender As System.Object, _
     ByVal e As System.EventArgs) Handles Button1.Click

     StatusBar1.Panels(0).Text = "Hello World!"
     StatusBar1.Panels(1).Text = "Today is " & Now()

End Sub
```

 TRICK Now **retrieves the current date and time as set on the computer running your Visual Basic application.**

As you can see in Figure 3.11, the StatusBar control organizes panels into a collection, assigning each panel in the collection an index. The first panel has an index of 0. The next panel has an index of 1, and so on. Each StatusBarPanel object in the collection is its own object and can display its own content. To write a text string to a particular panel, you must specify its index position within the collection. Figure 3.12 shows how the two-panel example from above looks after the user has clicked on the button.

FIGURE 3.12

Status bars provide an effective tool for communicating information with users.

TRICK

If you wish, you can set up your application so that it can respond when the user clicks on the status bar. This is achieved by adding whatever code you wish to the Click or PanelClick events, depending on whether you have set up a simple or panel-based status bar.

```
Private Sub StatusBar1_PanelClick(ByVal sender As System.Object, _
        ByVal e As System.Windows.Forms.StatusBarPanelClickEventArgs) _
        Handles StatusBar1.PanelClick

        MessageBox.Show("Status bar has been clicked.")

End Sub
```

Posting a NotifyIcon in the System Tray

Using a NotifyIcon control, you can add or remove an icon representing your Visual Basic application in the System Tray, as demonstrated in Figure 3.13. By placing an icon in the System Tray, you provide the user with an alternative way of communicating with your Visual Basic applications. For example, you might want to place an icon in the System Tray in the event that an error occurs in your application when it is in a minimized state. Alternatively, you might make the icon blink in order to catch the user's attention. You can even set things up so that your application reappears when the user clicks or double-clicks on the icon.

FIGURE 3.13

The Windows System Tray provides single- and double-click access to various Windows utilities, processes, and applications.

DEFINITION

The System Tray is an area located on the far right-hand side of the Windows taskbar that displays icons representing active system processes, utilities, and applications.

NotifyIcon are implemented by adding a NotifyIcon control from the Toolbox onto your form. Actually, the NotifyIcon component will appear on the component tray, just below the IDE form designer. Once added, you can edit its properties, which include:

- **Icon.** Specifies the name and location of the icon to be displayed in the System Tray
- **Text.** Specifies text to be displayed as a ToolTip when the user moves the pointer over the icon
- **Visible.** Enables or disables the display of the icon in the System Tray

By default, the Visible property is set equal to True at design time, meaning that the application's NotifyIcon will be displayed as soon as your application begins to execute. You can programmatically enable the display of the NotifyIcon by executing the following statement where appropriate in your application code:

```
NotifyIcon1.Visible = True
```

Alternatively, you can disable the display of the NotifyIcon as demonstrated below.

```
NotifyIcon1.Visible = False
```

 TRICK To grab the user's attention, you can create a look that alternates the execution of the two previous statements every second, thus causing the icon to blink repeatedly in the System Tray. You will learn how to work with loops later, in Chapter 7, "Processing Lots of Data with Loops."

You can also set up your application to react to events, such as the Click and DoubleClick events for the NotifyIcon, as demonstrated below.

```
Private Sub NotifyIcon1_MouseDown(ByVal sender As System.Object, _
    ByVal e As System.Windows.Forms.MouseEventArgs) _
    Handles NotifyIcon1.MouseDown

    MessageBox.Show("The Notify Icon has been clicked.")

End Sub
```

Adding a Splash Screen to Your Application

One thing that you might want to do to spice your application up a bit is to give it a *splash screen*. The IDE makes the creation and setup of a splash screen very straightforward. All that you have to do is create a new form and then tell the IDE to make it your application's splash screen.

DEFINITION

A splash screen is a window that appears briefly when an application first loads. Application developers use splash screens to display product information or to distract users while their application loads.

The following example demonstrates the steps involved in adding a splash screen to your Visual Basic applications.

1. Open a new Visual Basic Windows application project and expand the default form to approximately twice its normal size to make it distinguishable from its splash screen. Place whatever controls you wish on it.

2. Click on the `Project` menu and select the `Add Windows Form` option. The Add New item window appears.

3. Select the Splash Screen icon from the available list of templates, enter `Splash-Screen.vb` as the Window's name in the Name field, and click on the `Add` button.

4. The IDE will display the `SplashScreen` form. By default is will already have its `BackgroundImage` property set to display a graphic depicting three intertwined rings. You can change this property to use any bitmap image you wish.

5. Visual Basic automatically displays text on the Splash Screen window representing your application's name, version and copyright date. You do not need to modify this information. Visual Basic will automatically fill their values for you.

6. Click on the `Properties` option located at the bottom on the `Project` menu. A new window will appear in the IDE.

7. Make sure that the Application tab is displayed as shown in Figure 3.14.

FIGURE 3.14

Configuring a Visual Basic application to begin by displaying a splash screen.

8. Using the Splash screen drop-down list at the bottom of the window, select SplashScreen as your application's splash screen.

Now, close the Properties Window and press F5 to run your application. Just before the main menu starts, you should briefly see your splash screen appear. After a moment, it will close and your application's main windows will be displayed, as demonstrated in Figures 3.15 and 3.16.

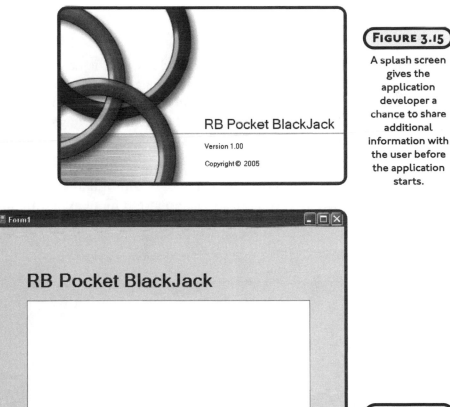

FIGURE 3.15

A splash screen gives the application developer a chance to share additional information with the user before the application starts.

FIGURE 3.16

The application's main window appears as soon as the splash screen closes.

Leveraging the Convenience of Built-in Dialogs

In some applications, you may want to interact with and collect information from the user using more than one window. One way to accomplish this is to create additional forms and to call upon each form when needed. You've just seen one way to do this using a splash screen. You'll learn how to create and display your own custom windows in later chapters. Another option available to you is to take advantage of a couple of built-in options for displaying pop-up windows.

The MessageBox.Show Method

Sometimes all your application may need to do is ask the user a simple question. You can always add controls to a form to collect this information, or even create a new form especially for this purpose. Optionally, you may be able to collect the information you want using the MessageBox.Show method, which is made available through the .NET Framework. The MessageBox.Show method is used to display a pop-up window that contains a custom text message along with an icon and buttons.

Figure 3.17 provides an example of the kind of pop-up window the MessageBox.Show method is capable of producing. As you can see, it supports a number of different features.

FIGURE 3.17

The MessageBox. Show method is perfect for displaying a small amount of text information.

The MessageBox.Show method supports 21 different formats, meaning that you can pass it different information in different ways depending on what you want it to do. As a demonstration of this, take a look at Figure 3.18. As you can see, as soon as I typed MessageBox.Show(, IntelliSense kicked in and started offering its assistance in the formulation of the rest of the statement. Take note of the up and down arrows surrounding the 1 of 21 text at the beginning of the first line of text in the IntelliSense window. By clicking on these up and down arrows, you can scroll through and view each of the different variations of the MessageBox.Show method.

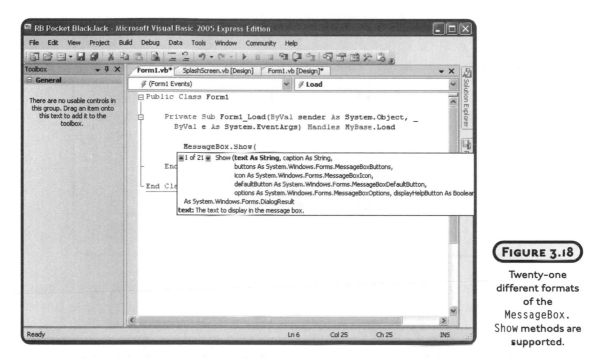

FIGURE 3.18

Twenty-one different formats of the MessageBox. Show methods are supported.

Regardless of which format of the MessageBox.Show methods you choose to use, they all require the same basic information in order to execute, as outlined in Table 3.4.

TABLE 3.4: PARAMETERS AVAILABLE TO THE MESSAGEBOX.SHOW() METHOD

Parameters	Description
Text	The text string to be displayed in the pop-up windows
Caption	The text string to be displayed in the pop-up window's title bar
Buttons	The button or group of buttons to be displayed in the pop-up window
Icon	The type of icon to be displayed in the pop-up window
DefaultButton	The button that will serve as the default button
Options	Display options that affect how the pop-up window and its text are displayed

The text and caption parameters are simply text strings. The Buttons parameter is used to specify any of six different sets of buttons, as shown in Table 3.5.

TABLE 3.5: BUTTONS AVAILABLE TO THE MESSAGEBOX.SHOW() METHOD	
Button	**Description**
AbortRetryIgnore	Displays Abort, Retry, and Ignore buttons
OK	Displays an OK button
OKCancel	Displays an OK and a Cancel button
RetryCancel	Displays a Retry and a Cancel button
Yes/No	Displays a Yes and a No button
YesNoCancel	Displays a Yes, a No, and a Cancel button

The MessageBox.Show method also allows you to display an icon to further help inform the user about the nature of the pop-up windows and the information it is trying to convey or collect. Table 3.6 identifies the various icons supported by MessageBox.Show.

TABLE 3.6: ICONS AVAILABLE TO THE MESSAGEBOX.SHOW() METHOD	
Icon	**Description**
Asterisk	Displays an Asterisk icon
Error	Displays an Error icon
Exclamation	Displays an Exclamation Mark icon
Hand	Displays a Hand icon
Information	Displays an Informational icon
None	Displays the pop-up window without displaying an icon
Question	Displays a Question Mark icon
Stop	Displays a Stop icon
Warning	Displays a Warning icon

You can also specify which button should be used as the default button. You specify which button to make the default button based on its position. Table 3.7 lists the available selections.

TABLE 3.7: DEFAULT BUTTON VALUE OPTIONS FOR THE MESSAGEBOX.SHOW() METHOD

Button	Description
Button1	Makes the first button the default
Button2	Makes the second button, if present, the default
Button3	Makes the third button , if present, the default

You can also specify any of the values listed in Table 3.8 for the Options parameter.

TABLE 3.8: OPTIONS VALUES FOR THE MESSAGEBOX.SHOW() METHOD

Button	Description
DefaultDesktopOnly	Displays the pop-up window on the active desktop
RightAlign	Displays the text in the pop-up windows as right aligned
RtlReading	Displays the text in the pop-up windows as left aligned

To help make the MessageBox.Show method easier to understand, let's look at a few examples. In this first example, I'll create a pop-up window that asks the user a question, displaying Yes and No buttons and the Stop icon. I'll also make the Yes button the default button and right-align the message text (including the caption text).

```
Private Sub Button1_Click(ByVal sender As System.Object, _
      ByVal e As System.EventArgs) Handles Button1.Click

      MessageBox.Show("Click on Yes to continue or No to Stop.", _
        "MessageBox.Show Example 1", _
        MessageBoxButtons.YesNo, MessageBoxIcon.Stop, _
```

```
            MessageBoxDefaultButton.Button1, _
            MessageBoxOptions.RightAlign)


End Sub
```

When executed, this example generated the pop-up window shown in Figure 3.19.

FIGURE 3.19

Prompting the
user for
permission to
continue.

Next, let's look at an example where I'll only supply the first two parameters. As the following statements show, I only supplied the parameters for the Text and Caption.

```
Private Sub Button1_Click(ByVal sender As System.Object, _
        ByVal e As System.EventArgs) Handles Button1.Click


        MessageBox.Show("This is an informational message.", _
            "MessageBox.Show Example 2")


End Sub
```

When executed, this example generated the pop-up window shown in Figure 3.20.

FIGURE 3.20

Displaying a
simple
informational
message.

In addition to displaying informational messages for users, you can use the MessageBox.Show method to collect and analyze the user's response, as demonstrated in the following example.

```
Private Sub Button1_Click(ByVal sender As System.Object, _
        ByVal e As System.EventArgs) Handles Button1.Click


        Dim UserResponse As String
```

```
UserResponse = MessageBox.Show("Please click on a button", _
   "MessageBox.Show example 3", _
   MessageBoxButtons.AbortRetryIgnore)

MessageBox.Show("You clicked on " & UserResponse)
```

End Sub

In this example, the user is asked to click on one of the three buttons displayed by the pop-up window. A number representing the button that the user clicked is passed back and stored in a variable name UserResponse. A second MessageBox.Show method is then used to display the user's response as shown in Figures 3.21 and 3.22.

DEFINITION
A variable is a piece of memory where data is stored by your application as it runs.

FIGURE 3.21

Prompting the user to select from three options.

FIGURE 3.22

Viewing the results of the button selection made by the user.

As you can see in Figure 3.22, a numeric value was passed back representing the button that the user clicked on. Table 3.9 defines the range of values that may be returned by the MessageBox.Show method.

TRICK Visual Basic also supplies the MsgBox function as another tool for displaying information in a pop-up dialog. However, all of the functionality provided by the MsgBox function is already provided by the MessageBox.Show method.

The InputBox Function

Another option for interacting with the user and collecting user input is the Visual Basic InputBox function. The InputBox function provides you with the ability to collect text-based information from the user, as demonstrated in Figure 3.23.

TABLE 3.9: RETURN VALUES ASSOCIATED WITH THE MESSAGEBOX.SHOW() METHOD

Button	Description
OK	1
Cancel	2
Abort	3
Retry	4
Ignore	5
Yes	6
No	7

Caption   Text Message

FIGURE 3.23

Examining the composition of a pop-up window generated by an InputBox function.

The basic syntax of the InputBox function is shown below.

```
X = InputBox(TextMessage, Caption, DefaultResponse, Xpos, Ypos)
```

X is a variable used to hold the text string supplied by the user. TextMessage is a placeholder representing the text message you want to display in the pop-up windows. The text message can be up to 1,024 characters long, depending on the length of the letters used. Caption is another placeholder representing the text string you want displayed in the pop-up window's title bar. XPos and YPos are used to optional specify, in twips, the horizontal and vertical placement of the pop-up windows on the screen.

The following example shows the statements that were used to generate the example shown in Figure 3.23.

DEFINITION

A twip is a unit of measurement approximating a value of 1/1440th of an inch.

```
Private Sub Button1_Click(ByVal sender As System.Object, _
        ByVal e As System.EventArgs) Handles Button1.Click

        Dim UserResponse As String

        UserResponse = InputBox("What is your name?", _
            "Sample InputBox() Function Example")

End Sub
```

TRAP Once the user enters a response and clicks on the OK button, the text that was entered is assigned to the variable X. However, if the user clicks on the Cancel button without first entering text, an empty string ("") is returned.

CREATING A STAND-ALONE EXECUTABLE

Up to this point in the book, you have executed all the Visual Basic applications that you have worked on within the Visual Basic IDE. This version of your application is sometimes referred to as the design or debug version. However, what you really want to do is create a standalone program that can be run by itself, outside of the IDE. This requires that you generate a run-time or release version of your application.

To locate the debug version of your applications, click on the Show All Files icon in Solution Explorer and drill down into obj and then Debug, where you'll see the executable program that Visual Basic has created, as demonstrated in Figure 3.24.

TRICK The executable file that Visual Basic creates and stores in obj\Debug is not optimized for normal execution. It includes unnecessary code that Visual Basic used to debug your program. So while you can distribute this executable file, you would be a lot better off going through the following build procedure in order to create a more efficient and faster executing application.

FIGURE 3.24

Examining the
debug version of
your Visual Basic
application.

The release version is smaller in size and runs more efficiently than the debug version. The following process outlines the steps required to generate a release version of your Visual Basic application.

1. Finish creating and testing your Visual Basic application.

2. Click on File and select Save All.

3. Click on the Build menu and select the name of your application from the menu item list that will appear. In response, Visual Basic will automatically generate an executable file (.exe) for you, assigning it the name that you assigned to your solution file.

4. To locate this new file, click on the Show All Files icon in Solution Explorer. This will display additional file information. Drill down into obj and then Release to see the executable program that Visual Basic has created, as demonstrated in Figure 3.25.

You can run your new application by double-clicking on it in Windows Explorer or by clicking on Start and then selecting Run and specifying the name and path of your application's executable file, as demonstrated in Figure 3.26. At this point, if you wish to share your application with someone else, all that you have to do is provide the user with a copy of your executable file.

FIGURE 3.25

Examining the release build version of your Visual Basic application.

FIGURE 3.26

Locating and running the release build version of your Visual Basic application.

TRICK As a precaution, it is always a good idea to retest your standalone application once you have created it. In fact, it is also a good idea to let somebody else test it as well, before you begin passing it around.

PUBLISHING A VISUAL BASIC APPLICATION

While you can certainly make a copy of the release version of your Visual Basic application and distribute it as you see fit, Visual Basic 2005 Express provide a publishing feature that is designed to help automate the distribution of your application. Using this feature, you can automate the distribution of your Visual Basic applications to any of the following locations.

- **Disk path.** Select this option to save an executable copy of your application to a folder on your computer.

- **File share.** Select this option to save an executable copy of your application to a folder on a network server.

- **FTP server.** Select this option to save an executable copy of your application on a FRT server.
- **Web site.** Select this option to save an executable copy of your application to a folder on a web site.

If for example, you choose the option of publishing to a folder on your local computer, Visual Basic will automatically create all the files that are required to install the application on a user's computer, including a Setup.exe program. The following procedure outlines the steps involved in automating the publishing of a Visual Basic application.

1. Finish creating and testing your Visual Basic application.
2. Click on `File` and select `Save All`.
3. Click on the `Build` menu and then select `Publish`. In response, Visual Basic launches the Publish Wizard.
4. Specify the location where you wish to publish your application and then click on `Next`.
5. The Publish Wizard will collect the required information needed to automate the distribution of your application to the specified location.
6. Click on `Finish` to publish your application.

BACK TO THE SPEED TYPING GAME

Now, let's return our attention to this chapter's game project. You will create the Speed Typing game by following the same five steps that you have used to complete previous chapter projects. By the time you are done creating the Speed Typing game, you will have demonstrated your ability to implement many of the advanced design techniques that you learned about in this chapter.

Designing the Game

The Speed Typing game is played on a single window, comprised of one form and the 11 controls listed in Table 3.10.

TABLE 3.10: FORM CONTROLS FOR THE SPEED TYPING GAME

Control Type	Control Name	Description
Label	lblInstructions	Displays the game's instructions
Label	lblSourceText	Identifies the Textbox field that displays the source text that the player is to copy
Label	lblEntryText	Identifies the Textbox field where the player is to type game input
Textbox	txtDisplay	Name of the Textbox control where the game's source text string will be displayed
Textbox	txtEntry	Name of the Textbox control where the player will type game input
Button	btnGo	Name of the Button control that the player will click on to start the game
Button	btnDone	Name of the Button control that the player will click on to tell the game to check the player's game input
Button	btnExit	Name of the Button control that the player will click on to end the game
Timer	tmrControl	Name of the Timer control that controls the length of game play
ToolTip	tipControl	Name of the ToolTip control that allows the game to display ToolTip messages
StatusBar	stbControl	Name of the StatusBar control used to display informational messages as the game runs

Step 1: Creating a New Visual Basic Project

The first step in developing the Speed Typing game is to start Visual Basic and open a new project using the following procedure:

1. If you have not already done so, start up Visual Basic 2005 Express and then click on File and select New Project. The New Project dialog will appear.

2. Select Windows Application template.

3. Type Speed Typing as the name of your new application in the Name field located at the bottom of the New Project window.

4. Click on OK to close the New Project dialog.

Step 2: Creating the User Interface

Now, let's begin by adding all the controls required to put together the game's interface. Figure 3.27 shows the overall layout of the game's interface.

FIGURE 3.27

Completing the interface design for the Speed Typing game.

The following procedure outlines the steps involved in setting up the application's graphical user interface.

1. Add the ToolTip control to your form. By default, Visual Basic assigns the control a default name of ToolTip1. It will be displayed at the bottom of the form designer windows in a component tray.

2. Add the Timer control to your form. By default it is assigned a name of Timer1 and will also be displayed in the component tray.

3. Add a TextBox to the form. Its default name is TextBox1. Set its Multiline property equal to True and expand and reposition it right in the middle of the form, as shown in Figure 3.27.

4. Add a second TextBox to the form. Its default name is TextBox2. Set its Multiline property equal to True and expand and reposition it under the previous TextBox control, as shown in Figure 3.27.

5. Add a Label control to the upper left-hand corner of the form. Its default name is Label1.

6. Add a second Label control to the form just above the first TextBox control. Its default name is Label2.

7. Add a third `Label` control to the form just above the second `TextBox`. Its default name is `Label3`.

8. Add a `Button` control to the lower left-hand corner of the form. Its default name is `Button1`.

9. Add a second `Button` control to the lower right-hand side of the form. Its default name is `Button2`.

10. Add a third `Button` control to the upper right-hand corner of the form. Its default name is `Button3`.

11. Add a `StatusBar` control to your form. Its default name is `StatusBar1`.

Step 3: Customizing Form and Control Properties

The next step in completing the Speed Typing game is to customize properties associated with the form and the controls that you have added to it. Once this is done, you'll be ready to begin adding the program statements that will make the controls perform their required tasks.

IN THE REAL WORLD

Up to this point in the book, I have used the default names that Visual Basic has been assigning to controls. However, going forward, I am going to start implementing a naming convention to the controls and other programming elements within the chapter game projects. Naming conventions help to make program code easier to read and understand.

Before I explain the naming convention that I plan to follow going forward, you need to know about a few rules that Visual Basic strictly enforces regarding object names and programming elements. These rules include:

- Names must begin with either an alphabetic character or the underscore character (_).

- Names can only consist of alphabetic characters, numbers, and the underscore character (_).

- Names cannot match Visual Basic keywords.

When coming up with names to assign to controls, variables, and other objects in your applications, use a consistent naming scheme. For example, from this point forward, I'll try to use words that are descriptive and that help to identify what an element is. Also, I'll follow a consistent approach when creating names. For starters, I'll employ camelCase

continued

spelling. Using camelCase, you use one or more words or abbreviations to generate element names. The first word or abbreviation begins with a lowercase character, and the first letter of all remaining words or abbreviations is spelled with an uppercase character.

Working with the default names that Visual Basic assigned to form controls can be difficult, especially if you add a lot of controls to a form. Instead, I'll assign a descriptive name to form elements that describes their function. For example, I might assign a name of btnExit to a button that is responsible for exiting an application when clicked. Similarly, I might assign a name of txtInputName to a Textbox control intended to collect a user's name or txtInputAge to a Textbox intended to collect a user's age.

Let's begin customizing the form and the controls that you have added to it. Let's begin by modifying the Form1, changing the properties listed in Table 3.11.

TABLE 3.11: PROPERTY CHANGES FOR THE FORM

Property	Value
FormBorderStyle	FixedSingle
StartPosition	CenterScreen
Text	Speed Typing

Next, change the name property of the ToolTip control to tipControl. Then change the Name property of the Timer control to tmrControl and set its Interval property to 1000.

Now, modify the properties belonging to the two TextBox controls as shown in Table 3.12.

TABLE 3.12: PROPERTY CHANGES FOR THE TEXTBOX CONTROLS

Control	Property	Value
TextBox1	Name	txtDisplay
	ReadOnly	True
	ToolTip	Displays source text string
TextBox2	Name	txtEntry
	ReadOnly	True
	ToolTip	Type your text here

Modify the properties belonging to the three Label controls as shown in Table 3.13.

TABLE 3.13: PROPERTY CHANGES FOR THE LABEL CONTROLS

Control	Property	Value
Label1	Name	lblInstructions
	Text	Instructions: Click on Go to begin. You will have 15 seconds to type the text displayed in the Source Text field into the Enter Text Here field exactly as shown.
Label2	Name	lblSourceText
	Text	Source Text:
Label3	Name	lblEntryText
	Text	Enter Text Here:

Modify the properties belonging to the three Button controls as shown in Table 3.14.

TABLE 3.14: PROPERTY CHANGES FOR THE BUTTON CONTROLS

Control	Property	Value
Button1	Name	btnGo
	Text	Go
	ToolTip	Display new text string
Button2	Name	btnDone
	Text	Done
	ToolTip	Check typing
Button3	Name	btnExit
	Text	Exit
	ToolTip	Exit game

Finally, add a StatusBar control to your form, change its Name property to stbControl and clear out the default text stored in its Text property. These are all the control property modifications that are required for the Speed Typing game.

Step 4: Adding a Little Programming Logic

Now it is time to start writing code. To make the Speed Typing game work, you are going to need to add code to five places, including the btnGo, btnDone, btnExit, and tmrControl controls. In addition, you'll need to add a few lines of code to define a few variables.

 TRAP Because we haven't starting dissecting the statements that make up the Visual Basic programming language yet, you may not be able to understand everything that you'll see. So as with the previous two chapters, just key in what you see and follow along. We'll begin covering Visual Basic language elements in Chapter 5, "Storing and Retrieving Data in Memory," and by Chapter 8, "Enhancing Code Structure and Organization," you should be able to return to this chapter and fully understand all the details of the Speed Typing game.

For starters, double-click on the Code View icon in the Solution Explorer. The code editor will appear. The following two lines of code will already be displayed.

```
Public Class Form1

End Class
```

Add the following three statements between these two lines of code as shown below.

```
Public Class Form1

    Dim intWrong As Integer = 0
    Dim intCount As Integer = 0
    Dim intTimer As Integer = 0

End Class
```

These three statements define the variables that the game will use to track the number of strikes made by the player, the number of tries the player has made, and amount of time that has elapsed for each turn.

Next, switch back to the form designer and then double-click on the btnGo button. This will switch you back to the code editor, where the following new code will have been added.

```
Private Sub btnGo_Click(ByVal sender As System.Object, _
    ByVal e As System.EventArgs) Handles btnGo.Click

End Sub
```

This code identifies the beginning and ending of the program statements that execute when the user clicks on the btnGo button. Modify this portion of your application by adding the programming statements shown below in between these two statements.

```
Private Sub btnGo_Click(ByVal sender As System.Object, _
    ByVal e As System.EventArgs) Handles btnGo.Click

    If intCount = 0 Then txtDisplay.Text = _
      "Once upon a time there were three little pigs."
    If intCount = 1 Then txtDisplay.Text = _
      "In days gone by times were hard but the people were strong."
    If intCount = 2 Then txtDisplay.Text = _
      "Once in a while something special happens even to the " _
      & "worst of people."
    If intCount = 3 Then txtDisplay.Text = _
```

```
        "When injustice rears its head, it is the duty of all good " _
        & "citizens to object."
    If intCount = 4 Then txtDisplay.Text = _
        "It has been said that in the end there can be only one. " _
        & "Let that one be Mighty Molly."

    btnDone.Enabled = True
    btnGo.Enabled = False
    txtEntry.ReadOnly = False
    tmrControl.Enabled = True
    intTimer = 0
    txtEntry.Focus()

End Sub
```

The first five statements check to see what turn the game is currently executing (0 – 4) and displays the appropriate text in the txtDisplay control. For example, if this is the player's first turn then "Once upon a time there were three little pigs" will be displayed.

The next two statements enable the btnDone button and disable the btnGo button. Next, the txtEntry control's ReadOnly property is set equal to True in order to allow the player to begin typing text into it. Then the tmrControl is enabled and the value of intTimer is set equal to 0. This begins the 15-second countdown sequence. Finally, the cursor is automatically placed in the txtEntry field using the control's Focus() method.

TRICK The Focus method provides the ability to programmatically specify which control you wish to receive focus.

Return to the form designer windows and double-click on the btnDone button. This switches you back to the code editor, where code for the btnDone control's click event has been added, as shown below.

```
Private Sub btnDone_Click(ByVal sender As System.Object, _
        ByVal e As System.EventArgs) Handles btnDone.Click


End Sub
```

Add the following statements between these two statements:

```
stbControl.Text = ""
tmrControl.Enabled = False
```

The first statement clears out any text that might be displayed in the StatusBar. The second statement disables the game's Timer control so that it won't keep counting and eventually declare a strike at 15 seconds.

Next, add the following statements just beneath the previous statements.

```
If txtEntry.Text = "" Then
  MessageBox.Show("Error: You must enter something!")
  txtEntry.Text = ""
  txtDisplay.Text = ""
  btnDone.Enabled = False
  btnGo.Enabled = True
  txtEntry.ReadOnly = True
  intTimer = 0
  btnGo.Focus()
  Return
End If
```

This set of statements checks to make sure that the player has typed something into the txtEntry field. If the user has not typed anything, the indented statements contained within the opening If and closing End If statements will execute, displaying an error message and resetting all the controls back to their initial settings. Note the use of the Return statement in the preceding group of statements. The Return statement tells Visual Basic to stop processing any of the remaining statements in the btnDone control's click event. This is appropriate because there is no point to performing any further processing if the player has not typed anything.

Next, add the following statement just beneath the previous statements.

```
If txtEntry.Text = txtDisplay.Text Then
  MessageBox.Show("Match - You typed in the string correctly!")
  intCount = intCount + 1
  intTimer = 0
Else
```

```
MessageBox.Show("Strike " & intWrong + 1 _
    & " - You made at least one typo.")
  intWrong = intWrong + 1
  intTimer = 0
End If
```

These statements check to see if the text typed by the player exactly matches the text displayed by the game. In other words, does the text string currently stored in the txtEntry control match the text string stored in the txtDisplay control? If there is a match, the MessageBox.Show method is used to inform the player, and the game adds 1 to the number of turns of levels the player has completed and resets the variable used by the timer control (to track the number of seconds that a turn has lasted) back to 0. However, if the text stored in the two controls does not match, an error message is displayed, and the game adds 1 to the number of strikes made by the player before resetting the intTimer variable back to 0.

Now add the following statements just beneath the previous statements.

```
txtEntry.Text = ""
txtDisplay.Text = ""
btnDone.Enabled = False
btnGo.Enabled = True
txtEntry.ReadOnly = True
btnGo.Focus()
```

These statements reset the form's controls back to their default settings and sets the focus back to the btnGo control, in order to prepare the game for the player's next attempt.

Add the following statements just beneath the previous statements.

```
If intWrong = 3 Then

  If intCount < 2 Then
    MessageBox.Show("Game over. Your typing skill level " _
      & "is: Beginner. Please play again!")
    intCount = 0
    intWrong = 0
    Return
  End If
  If intCount < 4 Then
    MessageBox.Show("Game over. Your typing skill level " _
      & "is: Intermediate. Please play again!")
```

```
    intCount = 0
    intWrong = 0
    Return
  End If
  If intCount < 5 Then
    MessageBox.Show("Game over. Your typing skill level " _
      & "is: Advanced. Please play again!")
    intCount = 0
    intWrong = 0
    Return
  End If

End If

If intCount = 5 Then

  MessageBox.Show("Game complete. Your typing skill level " _
    & "is: Expert. Please play again!")
  intCount = 0
  intWrong = 0

End If
```

Each time the player clicks on the btnDone button, the game checks to see if the player has struck out or if all five levels have been completed. These statements are responsible for determining whether or not the player won the game and for assigning the player's typing skill level. If the player got three strikes, the game assigns a skill level rating of beginner, if the player was only able to complete the first level of the game. If the player managed to complete the second or third level, a skill level of intermediate is assigned. If the player manages to complete four levels, a skill level of advanced is assigned. Finally, if the player manages to complete all five levels, a skill level of expert is assigned.

Now its time to add code to the btnExit control as shown below.

```
Private Sub btnExit_Click(ByVal sender As System.Object, _
    ByVal e As System.EventArgs) Handles btnExit.Click

        Application.Exit()

End Sub
```

The last control that you need to provide code for is the game's Timer control. Switch back to the form designer and then double-click on the tmrControl control. This will switch you back to the code editor where the following new code will have been added.

```
Private Sub Timer1_Tick(ByVal sender As System.Object, _
      ByVal e As System.EventArgs) Handles tmrControl.Tick


End Sub
```

Modify this section of your application by adding the following statements inside these two statements.

```
intTimer = intTimer + 1
stbControl.Text = "Seconds remaining: " & (15 - intTimer)

If intTimer = 15 Then

  intWrong = intWrong + 1

  tmrControl.Enabled = False
  stbControl.Text = ""

  MessageBox.Show("Strike " & intWrong & " - Time is up. " _
    & "Please try again.")

  txtEntry.Text = ""
  txtDisplay.Text = ""
  btnDone.Enabled = False
  btnGo.Enabled = True
  txtEntry.ReadOnly = True
  btnGo.Focus()

  If intWrong = 3 Then

    If intCount < 2 Then
      MessageBox.Show("Game over. Your typing skill " _
        & "level is: Beginner. Please play again!")
      intCount = 0
      intWrong = 0
      Return
```

```
      End If
      If intCount < 4 Then
        MessageBox.Show("Game over. Your typing skill " _
          & "level is: Intermediate. Please play again!")
        intCount = 0
        intWrong = 0
        Return
      End If
      If intCount < 5 Then
        MessageBox.Show("Game over. Your typing skill " _
          & "level is: Advanced. Please play again!")
        intCount = 0
        intWrong = 0
        Return
      End If

    End If

    If intCount = 5 Then

      MessageBox.Show("Game complete. Your typing skill " _
        & "level is: Expert. Please play again!")
      intCount = 0
      intWrong = 0

    End If

  End If
```

The first statement adds 1 to the variable used by the Timer control to track the number of seconds that the current play has lasted. The second statement displays this information in the status bar located at the bottom of the window. The Timer control automatically executes every second. In its third statement, it checks to see if the 15 seconds have passed. If this is the case, it declares a strike by adding 1 to the variable used to track the number of failed attempts. The Timer control then disables itself, clears out any text displayed on the status bar, and uses the MessageBox.Show method to tell the player that time has expired.

The rest of the code that you added to the `tmrControl` control's click event checks to see if the game is over and assigns a skill level to the player using the same logic that you previously added to the `btnDone` control's click event.

Step 5: Testing the Execution of the Speed Typing Game

OK. That's it. The Speed Typing game should be ready to go. Press F5 to give it a try. If any errors occur, go back and double-check the code statements that you added to make sure that you did not make any typos.

SUMMARY

In this chapter, you learned a great deal about how to jazz up your Windows application interfaces. This included learning how to implement a number of standard Windows features, such as status bars, ToolTips, customized icons, and System Tray icons. You also learned how to control where Windows opens your applications and the border style of your application windows. On top of all this, you learned how to work with the `MessageBox.Show` method and the `InputBox` function as well as learning how to create splash screens.

Now, before you move on to Chapter 4, take a few minutes and enhance the Speed Typing game by implementing the following challenges.

CHALLENGES

1. For starters, add additional levels to the game, making sure that each additional level is more challenging that the one that precedes it.

2. Refine the game's skill level rating by assigning a different rating for each level the player successfully completes.

3. Modify the game so that it displays an icon in the System Tray whenever it is minimized. Provide the ability to redisplay the game when the player clicks on its System Tray icon.

4. Create a splash screen for the game and use the `PictureBox` control to include a suitable graphic image.

WORKING WITH MENUS AND TOOLBARS

In this chapter, you will learn how to enhance your Visual Basic applications by adding professional looking menus and toolbars. You will learn how to create menus and populate them with menu items. You will also learn how to create submenus and execute program code when users click on menu items. This chapter will show you how to make your menu systems easier to work with by adding shortcuts and access keys. You will also learn how to enable and disable menu items as well as how to make them appear and disappear. In addition to all this, this chapter will show you how to create context menus for specific controls and how to provide easy access to your application's most commonly used commands using toolbars. Finally, you will get the chance to get some hands-on experience with menus through the completion of this chapter's game project, the Lottery Assistant game.

Specifically, you will learn how to:

- Add a menu system to your application
- Add shortcuts and access keys to menu items
- Control when users can access menu items
- Create context menus for individual controls
- Add toolbars to your applications

PROJECT PREVIEW: THE LOTTERY ASSISTANT GAME

In this chapter, you will learn how to create a Visual Basic game called the Lottery Assistant that is designed to assist users in generating a list of randomly selected lottery numbers. Players will have control over a number of game settings, including the size font used to display game output and the game window's background color.

Different lottery games require the selection of numbers from various ranges. For example, one lottery game may require the selection of numbers in the range of 1 to 44, whereas another may set the range as 1 to 50. In addition, lottery games vary in the number of lottery numbers that must be selected to play. For example, for some games you may need to select five numbers, and for other games you might be required to pick six numbers. Therefore, the Lottery Assistant game provides players with the ability to specify:

- The range of numbers to select from
- The number of lottery numbers required to play the lottery game
- How many sets of lottery numbers they want generated

To play the game, the player must supply the information listed above into text fields. Then, to make the game run, the player will have to click on the appropriate menu item. Figures 4.1 through 4.6 demonstrate the overall execution of the Lottery Assistant game.

FIGURE 4.1

The Lottery Assistant game begins by collecting player input.

FIGURE 4.2

Players control the game using its menu system.

FIGURE 4.3

Up to 10 sets of lottery numbers can be generated at a time.

FIGURE 4.4

Players can
configure the
game's
background color.

FIGURE 4.5

Using the Font
Size submenu,
the user can
specify the font
size used to
display lottery
numbers.

FIGURE 4.6

By clicking on the
About menu item
located on the
Help menu,
players can learn
more about the
game and its
developer.

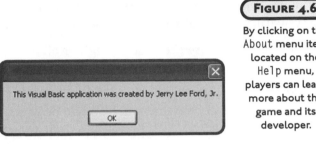

By the time you have created and run this game, you'll have learned how to create your own menu system, complete with menus, menu items, submenus, access keys, and shortcuts.

DESIGNING A MENU SYSTEM

One of the most basic features of any Windows application is its menu system. A menu system provides an intuitive and convenient means for organizing the commands that make your Visual Basic applications work.

A menu system is also a great space saver. It sits conveniently at the top of your application window and takes up very little space. In fact, it only takes up space when you access it, and then it closes back up automatically when you are done with it. A menu system frees up valuable space by allowing you to remove buttons and other types of controls that would otherwise be required.

Figure 4.7 shows a typical Windows application's menu system. As you can see, it consists of many different features.

FIGURE 4.7

Examining the
contents of the
Visual Basic
Express 2005 File
menu.

Windows application menu systems generally consist of one or more of the following six menu features, each of which is visible in Figure 4.7. These six menu features include:

- **Menus.** These are the first, or high level, menu items that are immediately visible from the menu bar (for example, File, Edit, Help, and so on).

- **Menu items.** These are additional menu items residing under menus, each of which represents a choice that can be made by users.

- **Submenus.** These are collections of menu items accessed through a parent menu item. Submenus can be identified by the black arrow on the right end of the menu item that provides access to them.

- **Shortcuts.** These are keyboard characters, such as the F1 key, that can be used to access menu items.

- **Access Keys.** These are keyboard keys that, when used in conjunction with the Alt key, activate a menu or menu item.

- **Separators.** These are horizontal lines used to organize menu items into logical groups.

IN THE REAL WORLD

Today, most users are sophisticated and experienced enough with Microsoft Windows that they have come to expect that all Windows applications work in certain ways. Any application that fails to meet these expectations, no matter how good it may be, runs the risk of disappointing its target audience. One expectation that most Windows users have is that all Windows application menus should follow a predictable formula. By this I mean that users expect to see menu headings such as File, Edit, and Help. For example, the File menu is generally listed first, and Help is listed last. Menu items for opening, closing, printing, exiting, and so on typically are located on the File menu. In addition, the last menu item on the File menu should be an Exit command. Unless you have a compelling reason for not following this formula, I strongly recommend against varying from it.

ADDING MENUS, MENU ITEMS, AND SUBMENUS

The first step in adding a menu system to a Visual Basic application is to add the MenuStrip control located in the Toolbox. Doing so adds an instance of the control to the component tray. Once you have done this, you can begin defining menus, as demonstrated in Figure 4.8.

FIGURE 4.8

Using the MenuStrip control to add a menu system to a Visual Basic application.

The following procedure outlines the steps involved in adding a menu system to your Visual Basic applications.

1. Open your Visual Basic application and select the form to which you wish to add a menu system.
2. Add the MenuStrip control to your form.
3. Click on the Type Here text that is displayed, and type the name of the first menu that you wish to define, as demonstrated in Figure 4.9.
4. To create an additional menu, click on the Type Here text shown just to the right of the first menu heading and type the name of the menu, as demonstrated in Figure 4.10.
5. To add a menu item under a particular menu, click on the menu, click on the Type Here text that appears just underneath it, and type in the name of the menu item, as demonstrated in Figure 4.11.
6. To create a submenu, select the menu item that will provide access to the submenu. Then click on the Type Here text located just to the right of the menu item and type in the name of the first menu item in the submenu. Then, to complete the submenu, continue clicking on the Type Here text displayed under each new menu item in the submenu, adding as many menu items as required, as demonstrated in Figure 4.12.
7. Repeat steps 4 through 6 as many times as necessary to assemble your application's menu system.

One important point to think about when adding menus and menu items is consistency in

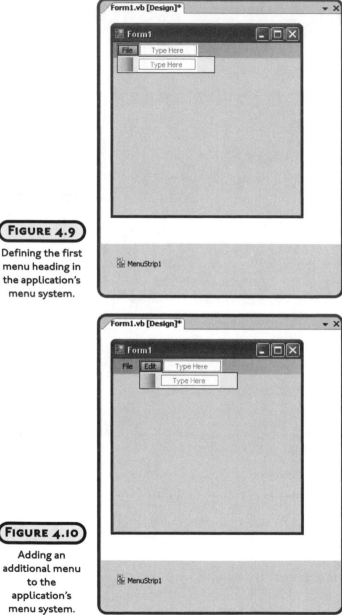

FIGURE 4.9

Defining the first
menu heading in
the application's
menu system.

FIGURE 4.10

Adding an
additional menu
to the
application's
menu system.

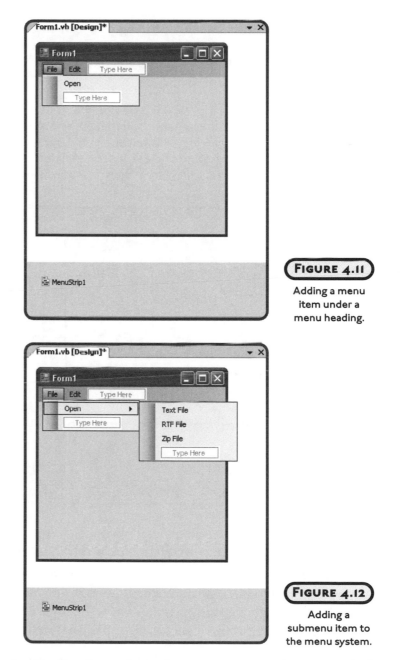

FIGURE 4.11

Adding a menu item under a menu heading.

FIGURE 4.12

Adding a submenu item to the menu system.

how you spell things. Always make the first letter in each menu or menu item a capital letter. Also, add three ellipses (...) to the end of any menu name that, when selected, will provide access to another window.

You can quickly rearrange the contents of your menu systems by using drag-and-drop to move a menu item to a new location. You can also select a menu item, right-click on it, and select Delete to remove it.

If you want, Visual Basic can help you start putting together a generic menu system that includes menus and menu items standard to most Windows applications. To take advantage of this feature, add the MenuStrip control to a form, right-click on the control, and select Insert standard items. In response, you'll end up with a preconfigured menu system like the one shown in Figure 4.13.

FIGURE 4.13

Inserting a preconfigured menu system to a forms.

Associating Code Statements with Menus and Menu Items

As you may have guessed, all that you have to do to associate Visual Basic programming statements with a given menu or menu item is to double-click on it. When you do this, the IDE opens up the code editor, creates a new Click event procedure for the selected menu or menu item, and positions the cursor so that you can begin entering your code statements.

For example, Figure 4.14 shows an example of the code associated with the Exit menu.

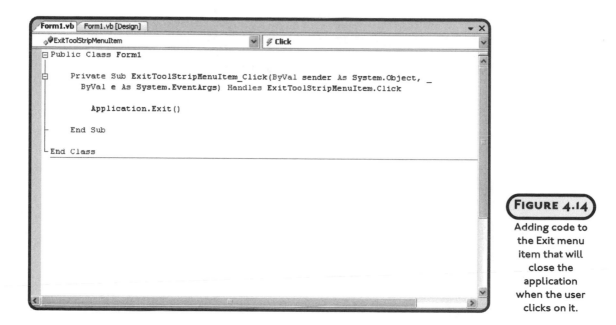

```vb
Public Class Form1

    Private Sub ExitToolStripMenuItem_Click(ByVal sender As System.Object, _
        ByVal e As System.EventArgs) Handles ExitToolStripMenuItem.Click

        Application.Exit()

    End Sub

End Class
```

FIGURE 4.14

Adding code to the Exit menu item that will close the application when the user clicks on it.

Enhancing Windows Menus

As shown in the following list, you can do a number of things to make your menu systems easier and more convenient for users:

- Adding shortcut keys
- Adding access keys
- Adding and removing check marks
- Organizing menu items using separator bars

Adding Shortcut Keys

Shortcut keys provide users with the ability to access menu items using only the keyboard. Shortcuts can be used to provide fast access to commonly used application commands. Examples of shortcut keys include all of the function keys (F1 to F12) and keystroke combinations such as Ctrl + N and Ctrl + O.

TRAP

A number of shortcut keys are so commonly used that they have become a de facto standard for Windows applications. Examples include Ctrl + S for saving and Ctrl + X for exiting an application. Make sure that you use these shortcuts when appropriate in your applications.

Adding a shortcut to a menu item is very straightforward, as outlined by the following procedure.

1. Select the menu containing the menu item that you wish to work with.

2. Select the appropriate menu item.

3. Click on the value field associated with the Shortcut property (in the Properties window) and select one of the shortcuts displayed in the drop-down list, as demonstrated in Figure 4.15.

FIGURE 4.15

Specifying the shortcut you wish to assign to a menu or menu item.

4. Once selected, the shortcut will be immediately visible, as demonstrated in Figure 4.16.

Adding Access Keys

Access keys also allow users to activate specific menu items using their keyboard. To set up an access key, you must designate one of the characters in a menu's or menu item's name as an access key. Access keys are identified by the presence of an underscore character under the letter in the menu or menu items name that represents the access key. For example, the letter F is generally used as the access key for the File menu.

To use an access key, all the user has to do is press and hold the Alt key while simultaneously pressing the appropriate letter key. For example, to active the File menu in Visual Basic Express 2005, all you have to do is press and hold Alt and F at the same time. While the File menu is displayed, you can release the Alt key and press the access key for any menu item located under the File menu to access it.

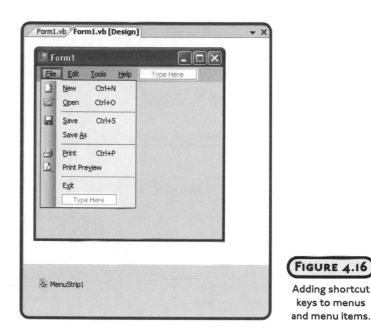

FIGURE 4.16

Adding shortcut keys to menus and menu items.

The following procedure outlines the steps involved in adding access keys to your Visual Basic menu and menu items.

1. Select the menu heading or menu item that you wish to work with.

2. Position the cursor in front of the letter in the menu or menu item name that you want to designate as the access key.

3. Add the ampersand (&) character just in front of the selected letter (for example &File or &Exit). The results will be immediately visible, as demonstrated in Figure 4.17.

Adding and Removing Check Marks

Another feature that you may want to implement when creating a menu system for your applications is the use of check marks. Check marks are used to identify the status of menu items that can be toggled on and off. The presence of a check mark indicates that the menu item has been selected or enabled. Similarly, the absence of a check mark indicates that the menu item has been deselected or disabled. For example, later in this chapter when you develop the Lottery Assistant game, you will use check marks to show the player which font and background colors have been selected.

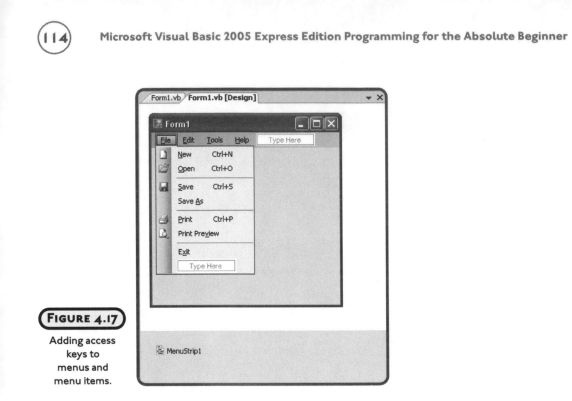

FIGURE 4.17

Adding access
keys to
menus and
menu items.

You can set an initial check mark setting at design time using the following procedure:

1. Select the menu item that you wish to work with.

2. Right-click on the menu item and select Checked from the popup menu that appears, as demonstrated in Figure 4.18.

FIGURE 4.18

Using a check
mark to indicate
when a menu
item has been
selected.

TRICK You can also set the check mark value by selecting the appropriate menu item and then setting the CheckState property in the Properties window to Checked.

Any menu item that can be checked can also be unchecked. When clicked, it is appropriate to switch the checked status of a menu item. Therefore, you will need to know how to programmatically change the checked status of your menu items at run time, as demonstrated in the following example.

```
Private Sub GrayToolStripMenuItem_Click(ByVal sender As System.Object, _
    ByVal e As System.EventArgs) Handles GrayToolStripMenuItem.Click

        GrayToolStripMenuItem.Checked = True
        YellowToolStripMenuItem.Checked = False
        WhiteToolStripMenuItem.Checked = False

End Sub
```

Here the statement marks the Gray menu item as checked whenever the user clicks on it and removes check marks from the Yellow and White menu items. Alternatively, if the user comes back later and clicks on the Yellow menu item, it's appropriate to remove the check mark from the Gray and White menu items and add it to the White menu item, as demonstrated below.

```
Private Sub YellowToolStripMenuItem_Click(ByVal sender As System.Object, _
    ByVal e As System.EventArgs) Handles YellowToolStripMenuItem.Click

        GrayToolStripMenuItem.Checked = False
        YellowToolStripMenuItem.Checked = True
        WhiteToolStripMenuItem.Checked = False
End Sub
```

Organizing Menu Items Using Separator Bars

To make a lengthy list of menu items easier for users to work with, you can visually group related menu items together. For example, in Microsoft Excel, menu items for opening and closing files, saving files, printing files, and closing the application are all grouped separately.

Of course, in order to use the separator bar to organize menu items, you must have grouped them together in the first place. The following procedure outlines the steps involved in adding a separator bar between your menu items.

1. Begin creating your menu items.
2. When you get to a point where you wish to insert a separator bar, add a temporary menu item at this location.
3. Right-click on the temporary menu item and select the Convert To option on the pop-up menu that appears. This displays a new list of available conversation items. Select the Separator option, as demonstrated in Figure 4.19.

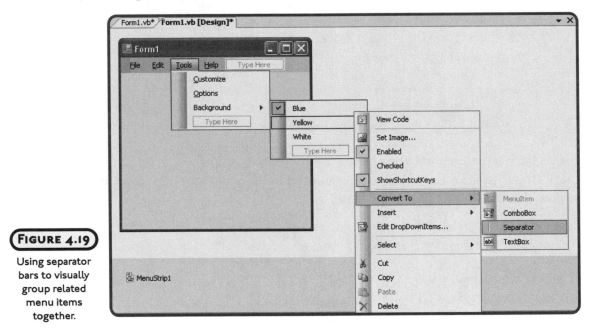

FIGURE 4.19

Using separator bars to visually group related menu items together.

Enabling and Disabling Menus and Menu Items

Based on the current status of your application, there may be times when you want to prevent a user from being able to click on a given menu item. For example, later in this chapter you will work on developing the Lottery Assistant game. This game will be controlled by its menu system, which will include Get Numbers and Clear Numbers menu items on its File menu. The game will enable and disable access to the Get Numbers menu item based on whether or not the user has entered all the data required to retrieve lottery numbers.

When a menu item is disabled, it will appear to the user to be grayed out and won't respond when clicked. By default, menu items are enabled. However, you can disable menu items at design time using the following procedure.

1. Select the menu or menu item that you wish to work with.

2. Using the Properties window, set the Enabled property for the menu or menu item to True to enable the menu or menu item (the default) or set it to False to disable it. The results will be immediately visible, as demonstrated in Figure 4.20.

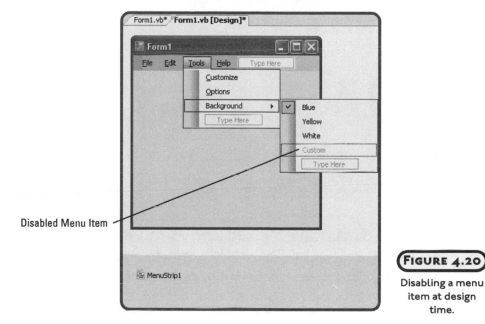

Disabled Menu Item

FIGURE 4.20

Disabling a menu item at design time.

Of course, for things to work, you need to add program statements to your code that enable your menu items at the appropriate time. Doing so is straightforward, as demonstrated below.

```
Private Sub Button1_Click(ByVal sender As System.Object, _
  ByVal e As System.EventArgs) Handles Button1.Click

      CustomToolStripMenuItem1.Enabled = True

End Sub
```

TRAP If you disable a menu heading or a menu item that provides access to a submenu, then all menu items and submenus underneath it will be hidden from view, as demonstrated in Figure 4.21.

FIGURE 4.21

Disabling a menu
item and its
associated
submenu.

Hiding and Displaying Menus and Menu Items

Depending on what your application is doing, there may be times where you feel that simply enabling and disabling menus and menu items is not enough. In these circumstances, you can go a step further by hiding and later redisplaying menus and menu items. The following procedure outlines the steps involved in hiding and displaying menus and menu items.

1. Select the menu or menu item that you wish to work with.

2. Using the Properties window, set the Visible property for the menu or menu item to True to enable its display (the default) or set it to False to disable it. The results will be immediately visible, as demonstrated in Figure 4.22.

FIGURE 4.22

Making the
Custom submenu
item invisible on
the Background
submenu.

TRAP If you hide a menu or a menu item that provides access to a submenu, then all menu items and submenus underneath it will be hidden from view.

Once hidden, you'll need to add program statements to your code that make menu or menu items visible later on. Doing so is straightforward, as demonstrated below.

```
Private Sub Button1_Click_1(ByVal sender As System.Object, _
  ByVal e As System.EventArgs) Handles Button1.Click

        CustomToolStripMenuItem1.Visible = True


End Sub
```

As Figure 4.23 demonstrates, the Custom menu item is once again visible once this above procedure as been executed.

FIGURE 4.23

You can also control user access to menu items by hiding and redisplaying them when appropriate.

CONTEXT MENUS

A second type of menu system that you may wish to add to your Visual Basic applications is a context menu. Context menus are hidden from view, only appearing when the user right-clicks on the form or control with which the context menu is associated.

DEFINITION

A context menu is a menu system that you can attach to a form or control to provide users with easy access to common commands or options made available by your application.

The following procedure outlines the steps involved in setting up a context menu.

1. Double-click on the ContextMenuStrip control located in the Toolbox to add it to the component tray.

2. Add menu items to it by keying in text on top of the Type Here text, as demonstrated in Figure 4.24.

3. Double-click on each of the menu items in the context list and add your program code, as demonstrated below. For example, you might add the following statement to the Click event for the first context menu:

```
Private Sub ExecuteCommand1ToolStripMenuItem_Click(ByVal sender _
     As System.Object, ByVal e As System.EventArgs) _
     Handles ExecuteCommand1ToolStripMenuItem.Click

        MessageBox.Show("Command 1 should execute now.")

End Sub
```

Similarly, you might add the following code to the Click event for the second context menu item:

```
Private Sub ExecuteCommand2ToolStripMenuItem_Click(ByVal sender _
        As System.Object, ByVal e As System.EventArgs) _
        Handles ExecuteCommand2ToolStripMenuItem.Click

    MessageBox.Show("Command 2 should execute now.")

End Sub
```

Finally, you could assign the following code to the Click event for the third context menu item as shown below.

```
Private Sub ExecuteCommand3ToolStripMenuItem_Click(ByVal sender As _
        System.Object, ByVal e As System.EventArgs) _
        Handles ExecuteCommand3ToolStripMenuItem.Click

    MessageBox.Show("Command 3 should execute now.")

End Sub
```

4. Select the control for which you created the context menu and set its ContextMenuStrip property equal to the name of the context menu that you just created.

Once you have finished configuring the form or control's ContextMenuStrip property, you can run your application and access the ContextMenu by right-clicking on the form or control, as demonstrated in Figure 4.25.

FIGURE 4.25

Examining the contents of Button control's associated context menu.

ADDING CONVENIENCE WITH TOOLBARS

Another feature commonly found on most Windows applications is toolbars. Toolbars display a collection of buttons, each of which when clicked executes a particular application command. By default, when you add a toolbar to a window, Visual Basic automatically places it at the top of the window, just below the menu, if one is present. However, you can move the toolbar to the bottom, right, or left side of the window if you prefer by setting the Dock property.

Typically, programmers use toolbars to give users single-click access to an application's most commonly used commands. Toolbar buttons can display either text, graphics, or both text and graphics.

The following procedure outlines the steps involved in adding a toolbar to a Visual Basic application and identifies various options that are available to you.

TRICK   The first step in adding a toolbar to a Visual Basic application is to add the ToolBar control located in the Toolbox to a form. However, by default, the ToolBar control is not found in the Toolbox window. But you can add it by right-clicking on the Toolbox window and selecting the Choose items option. This opens the Choose Toolbox Items dialog. Make sure that the .NET Framework Components property sheet is selected, and scroll down until you see ToolBar control. Select the ToolBar control and click on OK. The control will now be visible in the Toolbox window.

1. Drag and drop the ToolBar control onto your form.

2. Select the ToolBar control, locate the Buttons property in the Properties window, and click on the (Collection) ellipses button located in its property's value field. The Tool-BarButton Collection Editor appears as shown in Figure 4.26.

3. Click on the Add button to add as many buttons as you wish to the toolbar. Each time you click on the Add button, an entry for the button is displayed in the Members pane located on the left-hand side of the editor, as demonstrated in Figure 4.27.

4. To display a text string on the button, select the Text property and type in a string as its value.

5. To add a ToolTip to the button, select the ToolTipText property and type in the text that you want to be displayed.

FIGURE 4.26

Adding and removing buttons to a toolbar.

FIGURE 4.27

Use the up and down arrows to configure the order in which buttons are displayed on the toolbar.

6. Modify the `Style` property to specify the style that you wish to apply to the button. The following options are available:

- **PushButton.** Displays the three-dimensional button.
- **ToggleButton.** Toggles the button's appearance between a depressed and normal state each time the user clicks on it.
- **Separator.** Changes the button into a separator bar.
- **DropDownButton.** Modifies the button to behave as a drop-down control that displays menu items.

7. Click on OK to close the ToolBarButton Collection Editor.

TRICK If you are adding text to your toolbar buttons, you may need to specify toolbar button width, depending on the amount of text you plan on displaying. To change the width or height of toolbar buttons, select the ToolBar control's ButtonSize property and specify a new size for your toolbar buttons.

Adding Graphics to Your Toolbars

Instead of displaying text in your toolbar buttons, you can display graphic images. But to do so, you have to take a few extra steps before you can actually associate a graphic with a button. For starters, you must add an ImageList control from the Toolbox to your application. Using this control, you will identify all of the graphics images that you plan on adding to your toolbars. Once added to the ImageList, you can then configure each of your toolbar buttons to display one of the graphics images defined in the ImageList.

The following procedure identifies the steps that are involved in making all this work.

1. Add an ImageList control to your form.

2. In the Properties window, click on the (Collection) ellipses button located in the Images property's value field. The ImageCollection Collection Editor appears as shown in Figure 4.28.

FIGURE 4.28

Identifying the images that you plan on using to add graphics to your toolbar.

3. Click on the Add button and specify the name of an image to be added to the Image-List. Repeat this step as many times as necessary and make sure that you take note of the index number that is assigned to each image that you add.

4. Click on OK to close the ImageCollection Collection Editor.

Once you have finished adding images to the ImageList control, go back and select the ImageList property for your ToolBar control and specify the name of the ImageList that you just created. Then open the ToolBarButton Collection Editor by clicking on the Buttons property's (Collection) ellipses button. Modify the ImageIndex property for each button to associate the button with a given graphic image's index number within the ImageList control. For example, Figure 4.29 shows a toolbar under development with an image added to its first button.

FIGURE 4.29

Adding a graphic image to a ToolBar control button.

Associating Program Statements with Toolbar Buttons

Unfortunately, individual toolBar buttons do not have their own click event. There is just a single click event for the entire ToolBar control. Therefore, it is up to you to programmatically figure out which button the user clicked on and then to execute the appropriate program statements. Fortunately, it is not too hard to make this happen.

The ToolBarButtonClickEventArgs object's Button property is automatically passed to the ButtonClick event handler at run time. If you look back at Figure 4.27, you will see that just to the left of each toolbar button, there is a number that uniquely identifies the button's indexed position within the toolbar. By querying the Button property and comparing it to the button index numbers, you can identify which button was clicked.

To see how this all comes together, let's look at an example. For starters, access the toolbar's click event by double-clicking on it. The following code will appear in the code editor.

```
Private Sub ToolBar1_ButtonClick(ByVal sender As System.Object, _
      ByVal e As System.Windows.Forms.ToolBarButtonClickEventArgs) _
      Handles ToolBar1.ButtonClick


End Sub
```

In addition to defining the click event for the toolbar, this code automatically receives an argument that identifies the index number of the clicked button, which can then be accessed by your code as e.Button, as demonstrated in the following example.

```
Private Sub ToolBar1_ButtonClick(ByVal sender As System.Object, _
      ByVal e As System.Windows.Forms.ToolBarButtonClickEventArgs) _
      Handles ToolBar1.ButtonClick


        If ToolBar1.Buttons.IndexOf(e.Button) = 0 Then
            MessageBox.Show("You clicked on " & e.Button.Text)
        End If
        If ToolBar1.Buttons.IndexOf(e.Button) = 1 Then
            MessageBox.Show("You clicked on " & e.Button.Text)
        End If
        If ToolBar1.Buttons.IndexOf(e.Button) = 2 Then
            MessageBox.Show("You clicked on " & e.Button.Text)
        End If


End Sub
```

In this example, e.Button is an argument representing the index number of the button clicked by the user. The first three statements check to see if the first toolbar button was clicked. The next three statements check to see if the second toolbar button was clicked, and the last three statements check to see if the third toolbar button was clicked.

Figure 4.30 shows the output displayed when the previous example is executed and the user clicks on a button that is named Start.

FIGURE 4.30

Setting up programming logic to respond to button clicks.

Because toolbar buttons generally represent commonly used commands already found in a menu, you can speed up application development using the MenuItem object's PerformClick() method to set up the button so that it executes the corresponding menu's click event, just as if the user had clicked it. For example, the following statements execute the click event for a menu item named newToolStripMenuItem in the event the user clicks on the first toolbar button:

```
Private Sub ToolBar1_ButtonClick(ByVal sender As System.Object, _
    ByVal e As System.Windows.Forms.ToolBarButtonClickEventArgs) _
    Handles ToolBar1.ButtonClick

        If ToolBar1.Buttons.IndexOf(e.Button) = 0 Then
            newToolStripMenuItem.PerformClick()
        End If
        If ToolBar1.Buttons.IndexOf(e.Button) = 1 Then
            MessageBox.Show("You clicked on " & e.Button.Text)
        End If
        If ToolBar1.Buttons.IndexOf(e.Button) = 2 Then
            MessageBox.Show("You clicked on " & e.Button.Text)
        End If

End Sub
```

BACK TO THE LOTTERY ASSISTANT GAME

Now it is time to turn your attention back to this chapter's game project. You will create the Lottery Assistant game using the five development steps that you have followed in previous chapters. By the time you have finished creating this game, you will have demonstrated your ability to modify your Visual Basic applications by adding fully functional menu systems to your forms.

Designing the Game

The Lottery Assistant game is played on a single form. Therefore, it consists of a single form, upon which you add the nine controls listed in Table 4.1.

TABLE 4.1: FORM CONTROLS FOR THE LOTTERY ASSISTANT GAME

Control Type	Control Name	Description
Label	lblFullSet	Identifies the TextBox control where the player specifies how many numbers constitute a full set of lottery numbers
Label	lblNoPics	Identifies the TextBox control where the player specifies how many sets of lottery numbers the game should generate
Label	lblNoRange	Identifies the TextBox control where the player specifies the range of numbers from which the game should generate lottery numbers
Label	lblOutput	Identifies the TextBox control where the game displays the lottery numbers that it generates
TextBox	txtFullSet	The TextBox control where the player specifies how many numbers constitute a full set of lottery numbers
TextBox	txtNoPics	The TextBox control where the player specifies how many sets of lottery numbers the game should generate
TextBox	txtNoRange	The TextBox control where the player specifies the range of numbers from which the game should generate lottery numbers
TextBox	txtOutput	The TextBox control where the game displays the lottery numbers that it generates
MenuStrip	mnuStrip1	The name of the MenuStrip control that will be used to created the game's menu system

Step 1: Creating a New Visual Basic Project

The first step in developing the Lottery Assistant game is to start Visual Basic and open a new project, as outlined below.

1. If you have not already done so, start up Visual Basic 2005 Express and then click on File and select New Project. The New Project dialog will appear.

2. Select Windows Application template.

3. Type Lottery Assistant as the name of your new application in the Name field located at the bottom of the New Project window.

4. Click on OK to close the New Project dialog.

In response, Visual Basic creates a new project for you and displays a blank form on which you will design the game's user interface.

Step 2: Creating the User Interface

The next step in the creation of the Lottery Assistant game is to assemble the game's interface. To begin, let's review the overall layout of the game user interface, as shown in Figure 4.31.

FIGURE 4.31

Completing the interface design for the Lottery Assistant game.

1. Begin by adding a MenuStrip control to the form. By default, Visual Basic assigns the name MenuStrip1 to the control.

2. Add four Label controls to the form and line them up as shown in Figure 4.31. By default, Visual Basic names them Label1 to Label4.

3. Add three TextBox controls to the form and line them up horizontally with the first Label controls. By default, Visual Basic names these controls TextBox1 to TextBox3.

4. Finally, add a fourth TextBox control to the form just under the Label4 control. Set its Multiline property equal to True and resize it so that it covers most of the bottom half of the form, as shown in Figure 4.31. By default, Visual Basic assigns this control the name TextBox4.

The layout of the Visual Basic form is now complete. All controls should be visible on the form except for the MenuStrip1 control, which is displayed in a Component Tray just below the form.

Step 3: Customizing Form and Control Properties

Before you start customizing the properties associated with the controls that you just added to the form, you need to modify a few properties belonging to the form itself. The properties that need to be changed, along with their new value assignments, are listed in Table 4.2.

TABLE 4.2: PROPERTY VALUE ASSIGNMENTS FOR THE LOTTERY ASSISTANT GAME'S FORM

Property	Value
Name	ltaForm
BackColor	White
FormBorderStyle	Fixed3D
StartPosition	CenterScreen
Text	Lottery Assistant

Next, let's set the Name and Text properties for each of the four Label controls as specified in Table 4.3.

TABLE 4.3: PROPERTY CHANGES FOR EACH OF THE LABEL CONTROLS		
Control	**Property**	**Value**
Label1	Name	lblFullSet
	Text	How many numbers make up a full set?
Label2	Name	lblNoPics
	Text	How many sets of lottery numbers do you want?
Label3	Name	lblNoRange
	Text	What is the highest number that can be picked?
Label4	Name	lblOutput
	ReadOnly	True
	Text	Your lottery numbers:

Note that you may need to adjust the location of the first three Textbox controls after you change the text properties associated with the first three label controls. Now let's make modifications belonging to each of the TextBox controls as listed in Table 4.4.

TABLE 4.4: PROPERTY CHANGES FOR EACH OF THE TEXTBOX CONTROLS		
Control	**Property**	**Value**
TextBox1	Name	txtFullSet
TextBox2	Name	txtNoPics
TextBox3	Name	txtNoRange
TextBox4	Name	txtOutput
	ReadOnly	True
	ScrollBars	Vertical
	TabStop	False

Setting the ReadOnly property to True for the fourth TextBox control prevents the player from attempting to enter text into it. Setting the ScrollBars property to Vertical adds a scrollbar to the text box in order to allow the player to scroll up and down when more sets of lottery numbers are generated than can be displayed at one time. Setting the TabStop property to False takes the fourth TextBox control out of the tab index.

The last control that requires property modification is the MenuStrip control. For starters, click on the control and change its name to mnuStrip. Next, configure the MenuStrip control to create a menu system composed of the menus outlined in Table 4.5.

TABLE 4.5: MENUS FOR THE LOTTERY ASSISTANT GAME

Text Property	Resulting Menu Name	Description
&File	FileToolStripMenuItem	Contains commands that control the game's execution
&Options	OptionsToolStripMenuItem	Contains commands that configure the game's display
&Help	HelpToolStripMenuItem	Provides access to additional information about the game

Once you have created each of the menus listed in Table 4.5, it is time to configure each menu by adding menu items. Table 4.6 lists the menu items that you'll need to add to the FileToolStripMenuItem menu.

TABLE 4.6: MENU ITEMS RESIDING UNDER THE FILE MENU

Text Property	Resulting Menu Name	Description
&Get Numbers	GetNumbersToolStripMenuItem	Retrieves randomly generated lottery numbers
&Clear Numbers	ClearToolStripMenuItem	Clears out any text displayed in the game's TextBox controls
&Exit	ExitToolStripMenuItem1	Terminates game execution

The Clear Number menu item will be used to execute programming statements that remove any text that may currently be stored in the form's TextBox controls. When the form is first displayed, there won't be any text displayed in the TextBox controls. Therefore, it is appropriate to initially disable this Clear Number menu item at design time. Later, when the application is running and the player begins to key in text, you'll add programming logic to enable this menu item. So, to disable the Clear Numbers menu item, select it and set its Enabled property (in the Properties window) to False.

Table 4.7 lists the menu items that you are to add to the OptionsToolStripMenuItem menu.

TABLE 4.7: MENU ITEMS RESIDING UNDER THE OPTIONS MENU

Text Property	Resulting Menu Name	Description
&Background	BackgroundToolStripMenuItem	Provides access to a submenu where the game's background color can be changed
&Font Size	FontSizeToolStripMenuItem	Provides access to a submenu where the font size used to control the display of lottery numbers can be changed

Table 4.8 lists the menu item that you are to add to the HelpToolStripMenuItem menu.

TABLE 4.8: MENU ITEMS RESIDING UNDER THE HELP MENU

Text Property	Resulting Menu Name	Description
&About	AboutToolStripMenuItem	Executes code that displays information about the game in a pop-up window

At this point, you have defined all three of the game's menus, as well as the menu items that reside underneath them. However, you are not done yet. Both the Background and Font Size menu items need to be set up to provide access to their own submenus. Table 4.9 outlines the contents of the Background submenu.

TABLE 4.9: MENU ITEMS RESIDING ON THE BACKGROUND SUBMENU

Text Property	Resulting Menu Name	Description
&White	WhiteToolStripMenuItem	Sets the form's background color to white
&Yellow	YellowToolStripMenuItem	Sets the form's background color to yellow
&Gray	GrayToolStripMenuItem	Sets the form's background color to gray

Table 4.10 outlines the contents of the Font Size submenu.

TABLE 4.10: MENU ITEMS RESIDING ON THE FONT SIZE SUBMENU

Text Property	Resulting Menu Name	Description
8	ToolStripMenuItem1	Sets the font size displayed in the txtOutput control to 8
10	ToolStripMenuItem2	Sets the font size displayed in the txtOutput control to 10
12	ToolStripMenuItem3	Sets the font size displayed in the txtOutput control to 12

Before you call it quits with the Lottery Assistant game's menu system, let's add just a few more bells and whistles. For starters, add the access key F1 to the Get Numbers menu item located under the File menu. Then add the access key F2 to the Clear Numbers menu item, which is also located under the File menu. Then set the Checked property for the White submenu item under the Options menu to True, indicating that it is the default menu item, and then do the same things for the Checked property belonging to the first menu item on the Font Size submenu.

That's all the property modifications that are required for the Lottery Assistant game's controls and menu system. Now it is time to add the program statements required to make the game work.

Step 4: Adding a Little Programming Logic

All of the Lottery Assistant game's program code is controlled by the game's menu system. Unlike the game projects that you worked on in previous chapters, there are no Button controls for the player to click on in this game. To keep things straightforward, let's begin by adding the programming statements for each menu item one by one, starting with the first menu item located on the File menu and finishing up with the last menu item under the Help menu.

Adding Code to the Get Numbers Menu Item

The easiest way to associate programming statements with a menu item is to double-click on the menu item. When you do, Visual Basic automatically opens the code editor and creates a couple lines of initial code for you. So, for starters, double-click on the Get Numbers menu item located under the File menu. The following code will be automatically generated and displayed in the code editor.

```
Private Sub GetNumbersToolStripMenuItem_Click(ByVal sender _
        As System.Object, ByVal e As System.EventArgs) _
        Handles GetNumbersToolStripMenuItem.Click


End Sub
```

You will key in all the programming statements that are to be executed when the Get Numbers menu item is clicked between these two statements. For starters, add the following statements. These statements define variables and an array used by the application to store and manipulate the data it needs to execute. For now, just key in these statements exactly as shown. In Chapter 5, "Storing and Retrieving Data in Memory," you will learn all about variables and arrays.

```
Dim intForLoopCtr As Integer = 0
Dim blnFullSetComplete As Boolean = False
Dim intRndNo As Integer = 0
Dim strDisplayString As String = ""
Dim intNoOfValidPics As Integer = 0
Dim aintLotteryArray(10) As Array
Dim intNumberCount As Integer = 0
Dim strTestString As String = "_"
```

Next add the following statements, which check to see if the player has supplied valid input into the first TextBox control and displays an error message if this is not the case. Note the Return statement, which prevents Visual Basic from processing any of the remaining statements associated with the Get Numbers menu item Click event.

```
If txtFullSet.Text = "" Then
    MessageBox.Show("You must specify how many numbers " & _
    "make up a full set.")
    Return
End If
```

The next set of statements checks to ensure that the player entered numeric data into the first TextBox control and displays an error message if this is not the case.

```
If IsNumeric(txtFullSet.Text) = False Then
    MessageBox.Show("You must specify numeric input when " & _
    "specifying how many numbers make up a full set.")
    Return
End If
```

TRICK You can use Visual Basic's IsNumeric function to test whether a value is numeric or not.

The next set of statements to be added check to see if the player entered a number greater than 10 in the first TextBox control and displays an error message if this is the case.

```
If Int32.Parse(txtFullSet.Text) > 10 Then
    MessageBox.Show("The maximum number of numbers in a full " & _
      "set is 10. Please enter a number between 3 - 10.")
    Return
End If
```

TRICK By default, anything the player types into a TextBox control is seen by Visual Basic as a text string. You can use Visual Basic's Int32.Parse method to convert a text string value to an integer.

Now add the following statements, which check to make sure that the user specified a number of no less than 3 in the first TextBox control.

```
If Int32.Parse(txtFullSet.Text) < 3 Then
    MessageBox.Show("The minimum number of numbers in a full " & _
      "set is 3. Please enter a number between 3 - 10.")
    Return
End If
```

Let's add program statements that validate the contents of the second TextBox control. These statements display error messages if the player fails to supply any text, if the player does not supply numeric input, or if the player tries to specify a number less than 1 or greater than 10.

```
If txtNoPics.Text = "" Then
    MessageBox.Show("You must specify how many sets of " & _
      "lottery numbers you want.")
    Return
End If


If IsNumeric(txtNoPics.Text) = False Then
    MessageBox.Show("You must specify numeric input when " & _
      "specifying how many sets of lottery numbers you want.")
    Return
End If


If Int32.Parse(txtNoPics.Text) > 10 Then
    MessageBox.Show("The maximum number of lottery tickets " & _
      "that can be generated is 10. Please enter a number " & _
      "between 1 - 10.")
    Return
End If


If Int32.Parse(txtNoPics.Text) < 1 Then
    MessageBox.Show("The minimum number of lottery tickets " & _
      "that can be generated is 1. Please enter a number " & _
      "between 1 - 10.")
    Return
End If
```

Now let's add program statements that validate the contents of the third TextBox control. These statements display error messages if the player fails to supply any text, if the player does not supply numeric input, or if the player tries to specify a number that is less than 9 or greater than 50.

```
If txtNoRange.Text = "" Then
    MessageBox.Show("You must specify the highest number " & _
      " that can be picked.")
    Return
End If


If IsNumeric(txtNoRange.Text) = False Then
    MessageBox.Show("You must specify numeric input when " & _
      "specifying the highest number that can be picked.")
    Return
End If


If Int32.Parse(txtNoRange.Text) > 50 Then
    MessageBox.Show("The maximum value for the highest number " & _
      "that can be picked is 50. Please enter a number between " & _
      "less than or equal to 50.")
    Return
End If


If Int32.Parse(txtNoRange.Text) < 9 Then
    MessageBox.Show("The minimum value for the highest number " & _
      "that can be picked is 9. Please enter a number greater " & _
      "than or equal to 9.")
    Return
End If
```

Next add the following statements. These statements include a For loop and a Do loop, which you will learn more about in Chapter 7, "Processing Lots of Data with Loops." The For loop executes once for each set of lottery numbers that the player wants generated. The Do loop executes repeatedly until a complete set of numbers has been generated.

```
For intForLoopCtr = 1 To CInt(txtNoPics.Text)

    Do Until blnFullSetComplete = True

        Randomize()

        intRndNo = _
            FormatNumber(Int((txtNoRange.Text * Rnd()) + 1))


        If InStr(strTestString, _
            Convert.ToString("_" & intRndNo & "_")) = 0 Then
            strDisplayString = strDisplayString & " " & _
                intRndNo & ControlChars.Tab
            intNoOfValidPics = intNoOfValidPics + 1
            strTestString = strTestString & intRndNo & "_"
        End If

        If intNoOfValidPics = Int32.Parse(txtFullSet.Text) Then
            blnFullSetComplete = True

            strDisplayString = strDisplayString & _
                ControlChars.NewLine & ControlChars.NewLine
            strTestString = "_"
        End If

    Loop

    blnFullSetComplete = False
    intNoOfValidPics = 0

Next
```

The basic logic used in the statements wrapped inside the Do loop is as follows:

- Get a randomly generated number.
- Add that number to a string representing a list of lottery numbers, but don't allow duplicate numbers to be added to the list.
- Format the display string so that a new line is generated for each set of lottery numbers.

The programming logic used in these statements is more than a little involved. I'll defer further discussion on this group of statements at this point until after you have had the chance to read Chapters 5 through 8.

The last program statements that you will add to the code that executes in response to the Get Numbers menu item's Click event is shown below.

```
txtOutput.Text = strDisplayString
GetNumbersToolStripMenuItem.Enabled = False
ClearToolStripMenuItem.Enabled = True
```

The first of these three statements assigns the list of randomly generated lottery numbers created by the two previous loops to the txtOutput control's Text property, thus making the numbers visible to the player. The last two statements disable the Get Numbers menu item and enable the Clear Numbers menu item.

Adding Code to the Clear Numbers Menu Item

Now, switch back to the designer view, drill down into the File menu, and try to double-click on the Clear Numbers menu item. You may be surprised to see that you cannot use this technique to access the menu item's Click event. This is because the menu item has been disabled. However, you can still access this menu item's click event by remaining in the code editor and selecting ClearToolStripMenuItem from the drop-down list located in the upper left-hand side of the code editor. Once selected, all the events associated with this menu item become accessible in the drop-down list located on the upper right-hand side of the code editor. Use this drop-down list to select the Click event. The code editor will respond by generating the following code for you.

```
Private Sub ClearToolStripMenuItem_Click(ByVal sender _
    As System.Object, ByVal e As System.EventArgs) _
    Handles ClearToolStripMenuItem.Click


End Sub
```

Add the following statement between the two statements shown above. The first four statements clear out any text displayed in the four TextBox controls. The next statement places the cursor in the first TextBox control, and the last statement enables the Get Numbers menu item.

```
txtFullSet.Text = ""
txtNoPics.Text = ""
txtNoRange.Text = ""
txtOutput.Text = ""
txtFullSet.Focus()
GetNumbersToolStripMenuItem.Enabled = True
```

Adding Code to the Exit Menu Item

Now return to the designer view and double-click on the Exit menu item located under the File menu. Modify the code that is generated for you by inserting the Application.Exit() statement as shown below.

```
Private Sub ExitToolStripMenuItem1_Click(ByVal sender _
        As System.Object, ByVal e As System.EventArgs) _
        Handles ExitToolStripMenuItem1.Click


        Application.Exit()


End Sub
```

Adding Code to the White Menu Item

Now it is time to start adding the program statements required to make the menu items on the Background submenu work. Start by accessing the click event for the White menu item and modify the code that is automatically generated as shown below.

```
Private Sub WhiteToolStripMenuItem_Click(ByVal sender _
        As System.Object, ByVal e As System.EventArgs) _
        Handles WhiteToolStripMenuItem.Click

        Me.BackColor = Color.White
        WhiteToolStripMenuItem.Checked = True
        YellowToolStripMenuItem.Checked = False
        GrayToolStripMenuItem.Checked = False

End Sub
```

As you can see, you are adding four statements. The first statement changes the background color of the parent object (the form) to white. The next statement places a check mark to the right of the White menu item. The last two statements make sure that the Yellow and Gray menu items do not display a check mark.

Adding Code to the Yellow Menu Item

Next access the click event for the yellow submenu item and modify the code that is automatically generated as shown below.

```
Private Sub YellowToolStripMenuItem_Click(ByVal sender _
      As System.Object, ByVal e As System.EventArgs) _
      Handles YellowToolStripMenuItem.Click

         Me.BackColor = Color.LightYellow
         WhiteToolStripMenuItem.Checked = False
         YellowToolStripMenuItem.Checked = True
         GrayToolStripMenuItem.Checked = False

End Sub
```

As you can see, the only difference between this and the code that you added to the White menu item is that this code changes the background color to yellow and sets the check mark for the Yellow menu item.

Adding Code to the Gray Menu Item

Now access the click event for the Gray menu item and modify the code that is automatically generated as shown below.

```
Private Sub GrayToolStripMenuItem_Click(ByVal sender _
      As System.Object, ByVal e As System.EventArgs) _
      Handles GrayToolStripMenuItem.Click

         Me.BackColor = Color.LightGray
         WhiteToolStripMenuItem.Checked = False
         YellowToolStripMenuItem.Checked = False
         GrayToolStripMenuItem.Checked = True

End Sub
```

Adding Code to the First Font Size Submenu Item

Let's add the code that will execute when the menu items on the Font Size submenu are clicked. For starters, access the click event for the first menu item in the Font Sizes submenu (the menu item that sets the font size to 8) and modify the code that is automatically generated as shown below.

```
Private Sub ToolStripMenuItem1_Click(ByVal sender _
     As System.Object, ByVal e As System.EventArgs) _
     Handles ToolStripMenuItem1.Click

         txtOutput.Font = New Font("Microsoft Sans Serif", 8)
         ToolStripMenuItem1.Checked = True
         ToolStripMenuItem2.Checked = False
         ToolStripMenuItem3.Checked = False

End Sub
```

As you can see, the first statement that you added sets the Font property or the txtOutput control to Microsoft Sans Serif and specifies a font size of 8. The next three statements control the placement of the check mark.

Adding Code to the Second Font Size Submenu Item

Now access the click event for the second menu item in the Font Size submenu (the menu item that sets the font size to 10) and modify the code that is automatically generated as shown below.

```
Private Sub ToolStripMenuItem2_Click(ByVal sender As System.Object, _
     ByVal e As System.EventArgs) Handles ToolStripMenuItem2.Click

         txtOutput.Font = New Font("Microsoft Sans Serif", 10)
         ToolStripMenuItem1.Checked = False
         ToolStripMenuItem2.Checked = True
         ToolStripMenuItem3.Checked = False

End Sub
```

Adding Code to the Third Font Size Submenu Item

Finally, access the click event for the third menu item in the Font Size submenu (the menu item that sets the font size to 12) and modify the code that is automatically generated as shown below.

```
Private Sub ToolStripMenuItem3_Click(ByVal sender As System.Object, _
     ByVal e As System.EventArgs) Handles ToolStripMenuItem3.Click

        txtOutput.Font = New Font("Microsoft Sans Serif", 12)
        ToolStripMenuItem1.Checked = False
        ToolStripMenuItem2.Checked = False
        ToolStripMenuItem3.Checked = True

End Sub
```

Adding Code to the About Menu Item

Now let's add the program statements for the last remaining menu item by accessing the click event for the About menu item located under the Help menu. Modify the code that is automatically generated as shown below.

```
Private Sub AboutToolStripMenuItem_Click(ByVal sender _
     As System.Object, ByVal e As System.EventArgs) _
     Handles AboutToolStripMenuItem.Click

        MessageBox.Show("This Visual Basic application was created " & _
        "by Jerry Lee Ford, Jr.")

End Sub
```

As you can see, the MessageBox.Show method is executed whenever the player clicks on the About menu item, displaying information about the application and its author.

That's the last of this application's program statements. In the next four chapters, you will learn about the programming statements that make up the Visual Basic programming language. So if there is anything in this project that you had trouble understanding, bookmark it and then come back and look over the example again once you have gotten through Chapters 5 through 8.

Step 5: Testing the Execution of the Lottery Assistant Game

OK. That's it. It's time to test your newest creation. Press F5 and see how it runs. If you run into any errors, go back and check your typing and fix any typos that you may have made. Once you think you have the game running smoothly, share it with friends and ask them to test it out as well.

SUMMARY

In this chapter, you learned how to put finishing touches on your Visual Basic application's interfaces through the addition of a menu and toolbars. This included learning how to create menus, menu items, and submenus. You also learned how to enhance your menu system through the addition of shortcuts, access keys, and separator bars. On top of all this, you learned how to create context menus and how to associate them with controls. Finally, you learned how to provide single-click access to your Visual Basic application's most commonly used commands through the creation of toolbars.

Now, before you move on to Chapter 5, take a few minutes and enhance the Lottery Assistant game by implementing the following challenges.

CHALLENGES

1. Add a menu item under the Help menu that provides instructions for using the Lottery Game using the MessageBox.Show method.

2. Add a toolbar to the Lottery Assistant game and define buttons for each of the menu items found under the File and Options menus.

3. Going back to the material that you learned in Chapter 3, "Creating an Application Interface," create ToolTips for each TextBox and add a status bar to your application.

STORING AND RETRIEVING DATA IN MEMORY

When you interact with a computer application, the information that you provide and the actions that you take are processed by the application. In order to be able to work with this information, the application needs to be able to store data as it collects it so that it can later retrieve and modify the data. In this chapter, you will learn how to store and retrieve data in memory using constants, variables, structures, and arrays. I'll also cover a couple of extra items, including how to embed comments inside your program code and how to work with the ProgressBar control. In addition, you will get the chance to work on a new game project, the Story of Mighty Molly game.

Specifically, you will learn how to:

- Define constants, variables, structures, and arrays
- Properly specify data types
- Convert data from one data type to another
- Specify variable scope

PROJECT PREVIEW: THE STORY OF MIGHTY MOLLY

In this chapter, you will learn how to create a Visual Basic game called the Story of Mighty Molly. In this game, the player helps to tell the story by providing answers to questions that are designed to collect specific data that is then used to complete the story. Figures 5.1 through 5.5 provide a sneak preview of the Story of Mighty Molly and demonstrate the overall execution of the game.

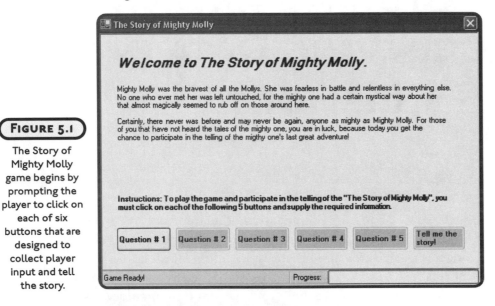

FIGURE 5.1

The Story of Mighty Molly game begins by prompting the player to click on each of six buttons that are designed to collect player input and tell the story.

FIGURE 5.2

Players' input is collected using the InputBox() function.

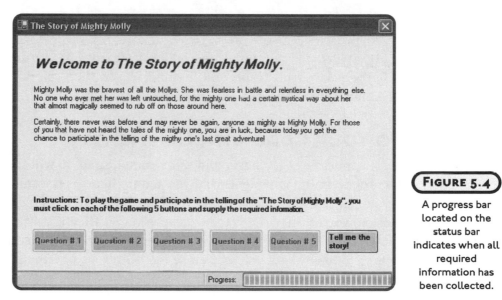

FIGURE 5.3

Buttons change colors to indicate that the player has already supplied their associated input.

FIGURE 5.4

A progress bar located on the status bar indicates when all required information has been collected.

FIGURE 5.5

Data input collected from the player is then plugged into the story line and displayed for the player to enjoy.

By the time you have created and run this game, you'll have learned how to declare variables and how to specify their data type, scope, and lifetime. In addition, you will have learned how to work with conversion functions and `String` constants.

ENHANCING YOUR CODE WITH COMMENTS

As your Visual Basic applications get bigger and more complicated, so will the number and complexity of the programming statements that you add to them. As the amount of code in an application grows, it becomes increasingly hard to follow along. Program code that makes perfect sense to you as you write it today may be very difficult for you to come back to a year or two later and try to work with again. It can be especially difficult for someone else who may have to follow behind you and make modifications or enhancements to the application.

So, like Hansel and Gretel, to make things easier on yourself or on someone who may have to follow up behind you, it's a good idea to leave a trail of breadcrumbs. You can leave this trail in the form of comments. By embedding comments at key points in your applications, you can leave behind notes that explain why you did things the way you did.

In Visual Basic, comments start with the ' character, as demonstrated below.

```
'Define an integer type variable named intCounter Dim intCounter As Integer = 0
```

DEFINITION

A comment is a statement embedded within an application that contains a text string that is visible to the programmer but ignored by the application.

You can also embed comments within your Visual Basic applications using the REM keyword. REM, which stands for remark, is a holdover from the earliest version of the BASIC programming language. Although still supported, you won't see it used by professional programmers.

As you can see, the first statement in the previous example documents what the following statement does. When executed, Visual Basic ignores the first statement, only executing the second line of code. Visual Basic also allows you to add comments to the end of other statements, as demonstrated below.

```
MessageBox.Show("The date is: " & Now())   'Display current date and time
```

Another good use of comments is to temporarily comment out statements when testing your application at development time. For example, you might develop an application that displays a message every time the application starts up, as demonstrated below.

```
Private Sub Form1_Load(ByVal sender As System.Object, _
    ByVal e As System.EventArgs) Handles MyBase.Load

        MessageBox.Show("Welcome to my application!")

End Sub
```

Seeing the pop-up window displayed by the MessageBox.Show method appear every time you test the execution of your application may get tiresome after a while, so to speed up your testing, you might choose to comment out the MessageBox.Show statement while you are working on your application. Once you are done making changes, all you have to do is remove the comment, and your application will resume displaying the pop-up dialog whenever it is loaded.

Storing and Retrieving Data

Like any programming language, Visual Basic requires the ability to store data and then later to retrieve and process it. You've seen numerous examples of this in game projects from earlier chapters. In this chapter, I'll explain your options for storing and retrieving data in Visual Basic.

DEFINITION

Data is information collected by your application that it stores, retrieves, and modifies during execution.

Alternative Ways of Storing Data

Visual Basic is an extremely flexible programming language, often offering you many different ways of performing a particular task. Such is the case when it comes to working with data. In fact, Visual Basic provides a number of different data management options, each of which is uniquely suited to different situations. The options that you decide to use will vary from situation to situation, because the best method for storing data varies based on the manner in which the data is used.

- **Constants.** There will be times when you develop applications that need to work with known values that do not change during the execution of the applications. A good example would be an application that performs various mathematical calculations, using known values such as pi. Because the value of pi does not change, you can assign it to a constant.

- **Variables.** Constants are fine for storing limited amounts of data. However, in most cases, the data that your applications process will change during program execution. In these situations, you will need to use variables to store the data.

- **Arrays.** Sometimes, you may find that you need to store and work with collections of related information, such as a list of user names. In these situations, you can load the entire list into an array, which is an indexed list of related information.

- **Structures.** A structure is a user-defined data type that allows you to group together related variables into a single entity. For example, if you were creating an application that needed to work with people's names, addresses, and phone numbers, you could define a structure containing variables representing each of these pieces of information. Then, later in your application, you could create an array based on that structure and use it to store and process all three pieces of data for each person at the same time.

Another option that is available to you for managing data is to define your own customized Class. This option is covered later in Chapter 9, "Getting Comfortable with Object-Oriented Programming."

Data Types

Visual Basic is capable of storing and working with many different data types. Table 5.1 lists each of the data types supported by Visual Basic.

TABLE 5.1: VISUAL BASIC SUPPORTED DATA TYPES		
Data Type	**Storage Requirements (in Bytes)**	**Value Range**
Boolean	2	True or False
Byte	1	0 to 255
Char	2	0 to 65535
Date	8	January 1, 0001 to December 31, 9999
Decimal	16	0 to +/- 79,228,162,514,264,337,593,543,950,335
Double	8	-1.79769313486231570E+308 to -4.94065645841246544E-324 for negative number and 4.94065645841246544E-324 to 1.79769313486231570E+308 for positive numbers
Integer	4	-2,147,483,648 to 2,147,483,647
Long	8	-2,147,483,648 to 2,147,483,647
Object	4	Any type of variable
Sbyte	1	-128 to 127
Short	2	-32,768 to 32,767
Single	4	-3.402823E+38 to -1.401298E-45 for negative numbers and 1.401298E-45 and 3.4028235E+E38 for positive numbers
String	Varies	Up to two billion characters
UInteger	4	0 to 4,294,967,295
Ulong	8	0 to 18,446,744,073,709,551,615
UShort	2	0 to 65,535

As Table 5.1 shows, Visual Basic supports a large collection of data types. Each data type, except the Object data type, is capable of storing a specific type of data. As Table 5.1 also shows, the amount of memory required to store data varies based on its data type. Visual Basic is very flexible. If you don't tell Visual Basic what the data type is for a particular piece of data, it assigns the data a default data type of Object.

Although convenient, using the Object data type is not the most efficient option and will cause your application to consume additional memory. Although a variable with a data type of Object can store any type of value, it cannot do so as efficiently as a variable that has been assigned the correct data type. Therefore, I strongly recommend that you always specify the data type for your variables. Just make sure when you do so that you specify a data type that accurately matches the type of data to be stored and that is capable of handling the size of the data to be stored.

When you specify the correct data types, you set up your Visual Basic programs to run faster by reducing the amount of memory used by the application and by eliminating the need to later convert data from one data type to another. However, I wouldn't invest too much time in analyzing the optimum data type for every variable that you ever need to create. In most cases, you can strike a good balance between program efficiency and memory usage versus your development time by using String, Integer, Double, Boolean, and Date.

By specifying a data type, you tell Visual Basic what range of values are allowable for a variable as well as what actions can be performed on the variable. For example, by specifying one of the numeric data types, you tell Visual Basic that it can perform mathematic calculations using the variable.

Working with Constants

When deciding whether to use a constant, variable, array, or structure to store a piece of data, it is best to first look at how the data is to be used. Data that is known at design time and that will not change during the execution of the application should be defined as a constant, allowing Visual Basic to more efficiently store and process the data.

Within Visual Basic, there are two sources of constants. You can define your own constants and assign data to them, or Visual Basic makes available to you a number of predefined constants.

Declaring Your Own Constants

By assigning data to a constant instead of to a variable, you eliminate the possibility that you might accidentally change the data later on in your application, which can happen in cases where you declare two very similarly named variables. If you try to change the data assigned to a constant, Visual Basic will flag it as an error when you test the execution of your application.

Constants make your application code easier to read. Your applications will also run faster because constants require less memory than variables.

To declare a constant within Visual Basic, you must use the Const keyword using the syntax outlined below.

```
Const ConstName As DataType = Expression
```

ConstName represents the name that you assign to the constant. DataType identifies the type of data that will be assigned to the constant, and Expression represents the value that is being assigned. To demonstrate how constants work, take a look at the following example:

```
Public Class Form1

    Const cTitleBarMsg As String = "The Story of Mighty Molly"

    Private Sub Form1_Load(ByVal sender As System.Object, _
      ByVal e As System.EventArgs) Handles MyBase.Load

        MessageBox.Show("Mighty Molly was the bravest of ......", _
          cTitleBarMsg)

    End Sub

End Class
```

In this example, a constant named cTitleBarMsg is declared with a date type of String and is assigned a value of "The Story of Mighty Molly". It is declared outside of any procedure and therefore can be accessed from anywhere within the Public Class Form1 and End Class statements. This is demonstrated when the MessageBox.Show method uses it as an argument specifying the pop-up window's title bar message, as shown in Figure 5.6.

FIGURE 5.6

By assigning a string to a constant, you can use it throughout your application to specify a title bar message in all pop-up windows.

TRICK

As you may have noticed in the previous example, I added the letter c to the beginning of the constant name to help identify the constant. I recommend this same naming convention for your constants. It will help make your constants stand out and make your code easier to read.

TRAP

When assigning data to constants or variables, it is important that you package it appropriately. The following example demonstrates how to define a constant for a numeric type value:

```
Const cMaxValue As Integer = 999
```

To assign a `String` data type value to a constant, you must enclose the string within a pair of matching quotation marks, as shown below.

```
Const cCompanyname = "Inner IV Enterprises, Inc."
```

Finally, to assign a `Date` data type value to a constant, you must enclose the string within a pair of matching pound signs, as shown below.

```
Const cBirthday = #November 20, 1964#
```

Using Visual Basic Built-in Constants

Visual Basic provides you with access to all sorts of predefined constants. For example, in Chapter 3, "Creating an Application Interface," you learned how to work with constants that specified what types of buttons and icons should appear in pop-up windows displayed by the `MessageBox.Show` method. Another example that you have seen of using Visual Basic built-in constants was in Chapter 4, "Working with Menus and Toolbars," where constants were used to format the output of text display by the Lottery Assistant game.

Table 5.2 lists a number of Visual Basic constants that you are likely to use over time to control the output of text strings.

TABLE 5.2: VISUAL BASIC CONSTANTS FOR FORMATTING STRINGS

Constant	Description
ControlCharsCr	Executes a carriage return
ControlCharsCrLf	Executes a carriage return and a line feed
ControlCharsFormFeed	Executes a form feed
ControlCharsLf	Executes a line feed
ControlCharsNewLine	Adds a newline character
ControlCharsTab	Executes a horizontal tab

You can see some of these string constants in action in the following example.

```
Private Sub Form1_Load(ByVal sender As System.Object, _
     ByVal e As System.EventArgs) Handles MyBase.Load


     Dim strStoryMsg As String = ""

     strStoryMsg &= "Once it was believed that the world was flat."
     strStoryMsg &= ControlChars.NewLine & "Later, it was found "
     strStoryMsg &= "that the world was round." & ControlChars.NewLine
     strStoryMsg &= "Who knew?" & ControlChars.NewLine
     strStoryMsg &= ControlChars.NewLine & ControlChars.Tab &

     MessageBox.Show(strStoryMsg)


End Sub
```

As you can see, the ControlCharsNewLine and ControlCharsTab constants were embedded within the string text in order to control when line breaks occurred and to execute a tab operation. When executed, the example displays the pop-up window shown in Figure 5.7.

FIGURE 5.7

Using string constants to specify the output format of a string.

WORKING WITH VARIABLES

Constants are great for storing data that does not change during program execution. However, most of the time, you will need to store data that may change as your application runs. In these situations, you will need to use variables to store the data.

A variable is a pointer or logical reference to a location in memory where a piece of data is stored. Therefore, a variable doesn't actually store the data, it only keeps track of where the data resides.

Variables provide your Visual Basic applications with the ability to process all kinds of data. For example, in previous chapter game projects, you have seen where applications have used text boxes to collect player input, which were then stored in variables and later processed.

DEFINITION

A variable stores data that may change during program execution.

There are two steps to working with variables, as listed below:

- **Variable declaration.** This involves the naming of a variable and the identification of the type of data that it will store.
- **Variable assignment.** This is the process of assigning a value to a variable.

Defining Variables

After working on the game projects in the first four chapters, you've probably figured out by now that one way to declare a variable is to use the Dim keyword, as demonstrated below.

```
Dim intCounter
```

The Dim keyword is used to reserve space in memory. In this example, I have declared a new variable named intCounter. A variable declared in this manner is considered to be *loosely typed*, meaning that because you did not tell Visual Basic what type of data it will store,

Visual Basic has, by default, assigned the variable and data type of Object. As a general rule, it's a good idea to *strongly type* variables. This is done by adding the As keyword to the end of a Dim statement and then specifying a data type, as demonstrated below.

```
Dim intCounter As Integer
```

In this example, I declared a variable named intCounter indicating that it will be used to store an Integer. By specifying a data type, I also told Visual Basic how much memory will be required to store the intCounter variable. If you refer back to Table 5.1, you'll see that an Integer type variable requires 4 bytes of memory.

TRICK Visual Basic provides a second way of declaring variables, known as implicit declaration. To implicitly declare a variable, all that you have to do is reference it as shown below, without previously declaring it.

```
strPlayerName = "Alexander Ford"
```

However, I strongly advise against implicitly declaring variables in your Visual Basic applications. Explicit variable declaration helps make your program code easier to read and is good programming practice.

If you wish, Visual Basic allows you to save space by declaring multiple variables of the same data type on a single line, as demonstrated below.

```
Dim strFirstname, strMiddleName, strLastName As String
```

Assigning Data to Variables

Once a variable has been declared, you can assign a value to it, as demonstrated below.

```
Dim dteMyBirthday As Date
dteMyBirthday = #November 20, 1964#
```

If you don't assign a value to your variables when you first declare them, Visual Basic automatically assigns them a default value. A zero is automatically assigned to variables with a numeric data type. A empty string ("") is automatically assigned to a variable with a data type of String, and a date of January 1, 0001 is automatically assigned to a variable with a data type of Date. Unless you want these default value assignments, you'll need to make sure that you remember to assign a value to your variables either when you first declare them or at least before the first time your application tries to use them.

To save space, you can also combine variable declaration and assignment into one statement, as demonstrated below.

```
Dim dteMyBirthday As Date = #November 20, 1964#
```

You can even declare and assign values to multiple variables in the same statement, as demonstrated below.

```
Dim intMinimumAge As Integer = 16, intMaximumAge As Integer = 21
```

You can also mix and match data types when declaring variables and making value assignments, as shown below.

```
Dim strPlayerName As String = "Alexander Ford", intPlayerAge As Integer = 7
```

Defining Local Variables

A local variable is one that is declared at the block or procedure level using the `Dim` keyword. Local variables can only be referenced within the block or procedure where they are defined and therefore are not accessible to other parts of a Visual Basic application.

DEFINITION

A block is a collection of statements that are processed as a unit. Blocks are created using the `If` statement and various looping statements.

For example, the following statements demonstrate how to declare and assign data to a local variable name `blnGameOver` within a block.

```
If intCounter > 10 Then
    Dim blnGameOver As Boolean
    blnGameOver = True
End If
```

Because the `blnGameOver` variable is defined within a block, it cannot be referenced from anywhere outside the block. Similarly, the following example demonstrates how to declare and assign data to a local variable named `strMessage` within a procedure.

```
Private Sub Button1_Click(ByVal sender As System.Object, _
    ByVal e As System.EventArgs) Handles Button1.Click

        Dim strMessage As String
        strMessage = "Hello World!"
        MessageBox.Show(strMessage)

End Sub
```

Local variables exist only while the block or procedure that declares them is executing. Once the block or procedure ends, Visual Basic destroys any local variables, freeing up the memory that they used. Thus, using local variables can help reduce the overall amount of memory used by your application when compared to static and module variables, which have a longer lifetime.

Defining Static Variables

A static variable is one that is declared at the block or procedure level using the Static keyword. Static variables can only be referenced within the block or procedure where they are defined and therefore cannot be accessed by other parts of a Visual Basic application. However, unlike local variables, a static variable continues to exist after the block or procedure that contains it has finished executing. In fact, a static variable exists as long as your application runs. The following example demonstrates how to use a static variable.

```
Private Sub Button1_Click(ByVal sender As System.Object, _
        ByVal e As System.EventArgs) Handles Button1.Click


        Static intCounter As Integer
        intCounter += 1


End Sub
```

One good use for static variables is to create a procedure that behaves differently based on the number of times it has been executed. You can accomplish this by declaring a static variable with a data type of Integer, incrementing its value by 1 each time the procedure executes and adding programming logic for the procedure to behave differently when the value of the static variable reaches a certain number.

Defining Variable Scope

A module variable is one that is declared inside a module, structure, or class but that is not inside a procedure. Module variables are declared using the following syntax:

```
Modifier VariableName As DataType
```

The ability to reference a module variable depends on which of the following modifiers is used to define it:

- **Private.** Accessible from within the module, structure, or class where it is declared
- **Public.** Accessible from anywhere within the project where it is declared
- **Friend.** Accessible from anywhere within the solution where it is defined

As an example, the following statements define a module variable name strMessage that can be accessed from anywhere within the Form1 class where it is defined. In this example, however, Form1 represents the form or window within the application. If the application consisted of more than one form and there was a need to be able to access the variable from either form, then you would need to use the Public or Friend keyword to redefine the variable's scope.

```
Public Class Form1

    Private strMessage As String = "Hello World!"

    Private Sub Form1_Load(ByVal sender As System.Object, _
        ByVal e As System.EventArgs) Handles MyBase.Load

        MessageBox.Show(strMessage)

    End Sub

End Class
```

 TRICK   As a general rule, it is considered to be a good programming practice to limit the scope of your variables as narrowly as possible. This helps conserve memory and reduces the chances of accidentally changing the value assigned to a variable from a location in a Visual Basic application.

Rules for Naming Variables

There are a few rules that you need to be aware of that govern the naming of variables. Failure to follow these rules, listed below, will result in an error.

- Variable names must begin with either an alphabetic character or the underscore character.
- Variable names cannot include spaces.
- Variable names cannot be reserved words.
- Variable names must be unique within their scope.

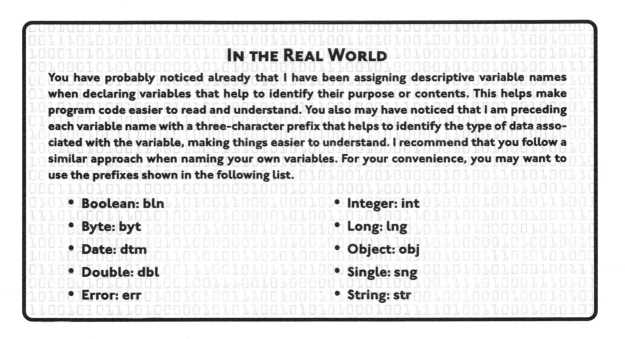

IN THE REAL WORLD

You have probably noticed already that I have been assigning descriptive variable names when declaring variables that help to identify their purpose or contents. This helps make program code easier to read and understand. You also may have noticed that I am preceding each variable name with a three-character prefix that helps to identify the type of data associated with the variable, making things easier to understand. I recommend that you follow a similar approach when naming your own variables. For your convenience, you may want to use the prefixes shown in the following list.

- **Boolean: bln**
- **Byte: byt**
- **Date: dtm**
- **Double: dbl**
- **Error: err**

- **Integer: int**
- **Long: lng**
- **Object: obj**
- **Single: sng**
- **String: str**

Recognizing Variables as Objects

As you may recall from Chapter 1, "An Introduction to Visual Basic 2005 Express," Visual Basic is an object-oriented programming language. The object-oriented programming design is so strongly integrated into Visual Basic that even variables are treated like objects. To see what I mean, perform the following exercise.

1. Start Visual Basic and create a new Visual Basic application.

2. Double-click on the default form (form1) to open the code editor and access the form's Load event procedure.

3. By default, Visual Basic will generate the following code to set up the application's response to the Load event for you.

```
Public Class Form1

    Private Sub Form1_Load(ByVal sender As System.Object, _
        ByVal e As System.EventArgs) Handles MyBase.Load

    End Sub

End Class
```

4. Declare a variable name `strUserAge` as an Integer and assign it a value of 55 as shown below.

```
Dim strUserAge As Integer = 55
```

5. Next, type the following partial statement exactly as shown below.

```
MessageBox.Show(strUserAge.
```

6. Because Visual Basic treats variables as objects, IntelliSense kicks in and displays all of the properties and methods available, as shown in Figure 5.8.

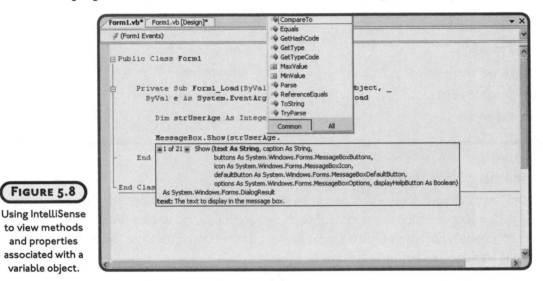

FIGURE 5.8

Using IntelliSense to view methods and properties associated with a variable object.

7. Click on `ToString` and press `Enter`. The statement should now look like the example shown below.

```
MessageBox.Show(strUserAge.Tostring)
```

TRICK You can use the ToString method to return a string showing the value for the specified variable, whether it is a number or a date.

Variable Conversion

Data typing is important because it tells Visual Basic how to store and handle the value that you assign. If you don't specify a variable's data type, Visual Basic assigns the variable a data type of `Object`. Then, later in your application when your program makes a change to the variable, Visual Basic takes its best guess as to how to convert the variable's data type assignment based on the action being taken. Most of the time, Visual Basic selects a data type that works just fine. However, it may not select the most efficient data type. And some-times, the data type it selects causes problems. For example, if you declare a variable as an Integer but then assign a number that includes a decimal point, such as 5.1, to it, Visual Basic automatically rounds 5.1 to 5, which can lead to all sorts of problems. Instead of Integer, a value type of Double would have been the right choice in this example.

 TRICK As with constants, Visual Basic gives you some control over the way that it iden-tifies variable data types. If you assign a value of 10 to a variable, Visual Basic automatically interprets the value as a number. But if you enclose the value inside matching double quotation marks, Visual Basic treats it as a string. Likewise, matching pound signs (##) are used to identify dates.

As you develop new Visual Basic applications, you are going to come across times when you will have to convert data from one type to another. There are two ways to convert a value's data type. One is to let Visual Basic do it for you automatically. However, as the following example demonstrates, sometimes Visual Basic gets things wrong.

```
Public Class Form1

    Private Sub Form1_Load(ByVal sender As System.Object, _
       ByVal e As System.EventArgs) Handles MyBase.Load

        Dim dblPI As Double = 3.14
        Dim intPI As Integer

        intPI = dblPI

        MessageBox.Show(intPI)

    Fnd Sub

End Class
```

If you key in and run this example, you see that Visual Basic truncates .14, displaying a value of 3. This occurs because variables of the data type Integer are not able to store decimal information. Most likely, a conversion of this type will cause a problem in your applications. One way to prevent this type of problem is to add an Option Strict On statement to your program, as demonstrated below.

```
Option Strict On

Public Class Form1

    Private Sub Form1_Load(ByVal sender As System.Object, _
        ByVal e As System.EventArgs) Handles MyBase.Load

        Dim dblPI As Double = 3.14
        Dim intPI As Integer

        intPI = dblPI

        MessageBox.Show(intPI)

    End Sub

End Class
```

TRAP Take note of the location of the `Option Strict On` statement. Visual Basic requires that you place it before any declaration statements; therefore, it had to go before the `Public Class Form1` statement. If you put it anywhere else in this example, you'll get an error.

Now, with the `Option Strict On` statement in place, press F5, and you see that Visual Basic displays a message indicating that an error has been detected. Visual Basic automatically displays the error message in the `Error List` window, as demonstrated in Figure 5.9.

FIGURE 5.9

Adding `Option Strict On` forces Visual Basic to alert you to variable conversion problems.

	Description	File	Line	Column	Project
1	Option Strict On disallows implicit conversions from 'Double' to 'Integer'.	Form1.vb	9	17	WindowsApplication1
2	Option Strict On disallows implicit conversions from 'Integer' to 'String'.	Form1.vb	10	25	WindowsApplication1

Error List — 2 Errors — 0 Warnings — 0 Messages

The first error displayed in the Error List window states that conversion from `Double` to `Integer` was disallowed. The following statement generated this conversion error when the example attempted to convert the value of pi from a data type of `Double` to a data type of `Integer`.

```
intPI = dblPI
```

The second error states that conversion from Integer to String was disallowed, as well. The following statement generated this conversion error, because the MessageBox.Show method can only display data of the String type.

```
MessageBox.Show(intPI)
```

Fortunately, Visual Basic supplies you with a large number of conversion methods and functions allowing you to tell it how you want to convert data from one type to another. To use the methods and functions, you must specify the data to be converted inside the opening and closing parentheses, as demonstrated in the following example.

```
Option Strict On

Public Class Form1

    Private Sub Form1_Load(ByVal sender As System.Object, _
      ByVal e As System.EventArgs) Handles MyBase.Load

        Dim dblPI As Double = 3.14
        Dim intPI As Integer

        intPI = CInt(dblPI)
        MessageBox.Show(Convert.ToString(intPI))

    End Sub

End Class
```

In this example, it is assumed that the truncation of .14 is acceptable. Therefore the value stored as a Double in the dblPI variable is converted to an Integer data type using the Cint() function. The Convert.ToString () method is used to convert the Integer data type associated with the intPI variable to a String so that it can be displayed by the MessageBox.Show method.

Functions and Methods for Manipulating Strings

A variable with a data type of String can be used to store up to 2 million characters. One of the many strengths of Visual Basic is the abundance of string manipulating functions and methods that it provides. In fact, Visual Basic provides so many different ways of manipulating strings that it is unlikely you will ever have to develop your own custom string handling functions.

In previous chapters, you have seen a number of examples of how to work with strings using the ampersand (&) operator, which joins or concatenates two strings together. Visual Basic provides a number of other string manipulation tools, including the properties and methods listed in Table 5.3.

DEFINITION

A string is a series of one or more characters, which may include alphabetic, numeric, and special characters, as well as spaces, that is defined by enclosing the characters within a pair of double quotation marks ("").

TABLE 5.3: STRING HANDLING PROPERTIES AND METHODS

String Object Methods	Description
String.ToLower	This method converts a string to all lowercase
String.ToUpper	This method converts a string to all uppercase
String.Length	This property is used to retrieve the length of a string
String.SubString	This method extracts a portion of a string
String.ConCat	This method combines two strings
String.Chars	This property is used to search for one string within another string
String.TrimStart	This method removes leading blank spaces from the left side of a string
String.TimeEnd	This method removes trailing blank spaces from the right side of a string

As a quick example of how to use these functions and methods, take a look at the following example.

```
Public Class Form1

    Private Sub Form1_Load(ByVal sender As System.Object, _
        ByVal e As System.EventArgs) Handles MyBase.Load
```

```
Dim strMsg As String = "Once upon a time in a far away land."


MessageBox.Show("String is " & strMsg.Length & " characters long.")


    End Sub


End Class
```

In this example, the Length property is used to display the number of characters that makes up the strMsg variable's value.

WORKING WITH ARRAYS

It can quickly become difficult to keep up with large numbers of variables. Many times, you'll find that the different pieces of data collected and processed by a Visual Basic program have a strong relationship to one another. For example, you might write an application that collects and processes a list of people's names. In this type of situation, you can organize and manage all the names collected by your application as a unit in an array.

Defining Arrays

You can use the Dim keyword to create a single-dimension array using the following syntax.

`Dim ArrayName(dimensions) As Integer`

Dimensions represents a comma-separated list of numbers that specify how many dimensions make up the array. For example, the following statement defines an array named strCustomerNamesArray that can hold up to five names:

`Dim strCustomerNamesArray(4) as String`

Because an array begins with an index number of 0, I specified the number 4 in order to set the array up to hold five entries (0 through 4).

> **DEFINITION**
>
> An array is an indexed list of data. The first piece of data stored in an array is assigned an index position of 0. The next piece of data is assigned an index position of 1, and so on. Any data stored in the array can be referenced based on its index position.

You may have noticed that in the previous example, I added the word Array to the end of the array name, thus identifying it as an array. I also added a three-character string to the beginning of the array name in order to identify the type of data that array will hold. I recommend that you employ a similar naming scheme when you define your own arrays.

Loading Array Elements

Once you have declared your array, you can populate it with data, as demonstrated below.

```
astrCustomerNamesArray(0) = "Markland B."
astrCustomerNamesArray(1) = "Mike M."
astrCustomerNamesArray(2) = "Nick C."
astrCustomerNamesArray(3) = "Jerry F."
astrCustomerNamesArray(4) = "Rocky B."
```

Once populated, you can reference pieces of data stored in the array by specifying the name of the array followed by an index number, as demonstrated below.

```
MessageBox.Show strCustomerNamesArray(2)
```

Retrieving Array Elements

Because data stored in an array is usually related, you can set up a loop to process the array contents using just a few lines of code. This is a lot faster and more efficient than trying to specify each piece of data in the array one at a time using its index number. For example, suppose you have an array that contains 1,000 names. It wouldn't be practical to reference each item in the array individually. Instead, a better way to process the contents of the array would be to set up a For…Next loop.

The syntax of the For...Next loop is outlined below.

```
For counter = begin To end
    statements
Next
```

Counter represents a variable that will be used to control the execution of the loop. Begin is a number specifying the starting value of the counter variable, and End specifies the ending value for the counter variable. To see how to use the For…Next loop to process the contents of an array, take a look at the following example.

```
Public Class Form1

    Private Sub Form1_Load(ByVal sender As System.Object, _
        ByVal e As System.EventArgs) Handles MyBase.Load

        Dim strMessage As String = ""
        Dim strCustomerNamesArray(4) As String
        Dim intCounter As Integer

        strCustomerNamesArray(0) = "Markland B."
        strCustomerNamesArray(1) = "Mike M."
        strCustomerNamesArray(2) = "Nick C."
        strCustomerNamesArray(3) = "Jerry F."
        strCustomerNamesArray(4) = "Rocky B."

        For intCounter = 0 To 4
            strMessage = strMessage & _
                strCustomerNamesArray(intCounter) & _
                ControlChars.NewLine
        Next intCounter

        MessageBox.Show(strMessage)

    End Sub

End Class
```

As you can see in this example, the For…Next loop was used to spin through each element in the strCustomerNamesArray and put together a display string, which was displayed by the MessageBox.Show method once the loop had finished running.

You will find additional information on the For..Next loop in Chapter 7, "Processing Lots of Data with Loops."

Resizing Arrays

There may be times when you need to increase the size of an array to accommodate additional data. When you think this might be the case, you should declare the array without specifying its initial size, as demonstrated below.

```
Dim strCustomerNamesArray() As String
```

Then later, perhaps after you have queried the user as to how much information will be provided, you can resize the array using the ReDim keyword, as shown below.

```
ReDim strCustomerNamesArray(9)
```

At this point, you can begin populating the array with data. If, however, you find that you have not made the array big enough, you can always resize it again, as shown below.

```
ReDim Preserve strCustomerNamesArray(19)
```

Note that this time I added the keyword Preserve just before the array name. This keyword tells Visual Basic not to delete any data already stored in the array when resizing it. If you forget to add the Preserve keyword when resizing an array, you'll lose any already populated data.

 TRAP In addition to increasing the size of an array, you can make it smaller. But if you do so, you'll lose data if you resize the array smaller than the number of elements already stored in it.

Erasing Arrays

Once your program has finished using the data stored in an array, it's a good idea to delete the array, thus freeing up memory. You can do this using the Erase keyword and the following syntax.

```
Erase ArrayName
```

For example, to delete strCustomerNamesArray, you would add the following statement at the appropriate location within your program code:

```
Erase strCustomerNamesArray
```

WORKING WITH STRUCTURES

As I stated earlier in this chapter, a structure is a user-defined entity. In other words, you name it, define the variables that make it up, and then populate it, usually by creating an array based on the structure. Structures can be declared within a module or class but not within a procedure. A Structure begins with the keyword Structure and ends with the End Structure statement. The basic syntax of a Structure is outlined below.

```
Structure StructureName
    Dim VariableName As DataType
    Dim VariableName As DataType
        .
        .
        .

End Structure
```

Once defined, every variable defined within a structure is treated as a method. To see how to really work with structures, let's look at an example.

1. Create a new Visual Basic project.

2. Double-click on form1. The code editor will appear, displaying code for the form's Load event.

3. Enter the following statements just below the Public Class Form1 statement. These statements define a Structure that will hold employee data. The Structure is made up of two variables that store employee names and numbers.

```
Structure EmployeeNames
    Dim EmployeeName As String
    Dim EmployeeNumber As Integer
End Structure
```

4. Enter the following statements inside the Load event procedure for the form. These statements declare two variables used later to control a For…Next loop and a display string.

```
Dim intCounter As Integer = 0
Dim strMessage As String = "Employee Name" & ControlChars.Tab & _
    "Employee #" & ControlChars.CrLf
```

5. Create a small array based on the EmployeeNames structure that can hold information for three employees, as shown below.

```
Dim EmployeeDataArray(2) As EmployeeNames
```

6. Now populate the array with data for three employees, as shown below.

```
EmployeeDataArray(0).EmployeeName = "Alexander Ford"
EmployeeDataArray(0).EmployeeNumber = 12345
EmployeeDataArray(1).EmployeeName = "William Ford"
EmployeeDataArray(1).EmployeeNumber = 23456
EmployeeDataArray(2).EmployeeName = "Mollisa Ford"
EmployeeDataArray(2).EmployeeNumber = 22335
```

7. Finally, add the following statements, which will loop through the EmployeeDataArray and display its contents.

```
For intCounter = 0 To UBound(EmployeeDataArray)
    strMessage = strMessage & _
        EmployeeDataArray(intCounter).EmployeeName & ControlChars.Tab & _
        EmployeeDataArray(intCounter).EmployeeNumber & ControlChars.CrLf
Next

MessageBox.Show(strMessage)
```

 Ubound() is a built-in Visual Basic function that returns the upper limit of an array.

8. Press F5 to run your application and you'll see, as demonstrated in Figure 5.10, that all of the employee names and numbers have been processed.

FIGURE 5.10

Managing large amounts of related data using an array based on a custom structure.

Employee Name	Employee #
Alexander Ford	12345
William Ford	23456
Mollisa Ford	22335

OK

RESERVED WORDS

The Visual Basic programming language is made up of a large number of keywords (also referred to as reserved words) that have very specific meanings. An example of a reserved word is Dim, which is used to declare variables and arrays. Because it is a reserved word, you can only use the Dim keyword in your Visual Basic applications when you follow its syntax rules. In other words, you cannot use Dim as a variable name or as a name for any other programming construction (constants, arrays, structures, procedures, and so on).

Table 5.4 provides a listing of Visual Basic reserved words for your review.

TABLE 5.4: VISUAL BASIC RESERVED WORDS

AddHandler	**AddressOf**	**Alias**	**And**
AndAlso	Ansi	As	Assembly
Auto	Boolean	ByRef	Byte
ByVal	Call	Case	Catch
Cbool	Cbyte	Cchar	Cdate
Cdec	CDbl	Char	Cint
Class	CLng	Cobj	Const
Cshort	CSng	CStr	Ctype
Date	Decimal	Declare	Default
Delegate	Dim	DirectCast	Do
Double	Each	Else	ElseIf
End	EndIf	Enum	Erase
Error	Event	Exit	False
Finally	For	Friend	Function
Get	GetType	Global	GoSub
GoTo	Handles	If	Implements
Imports	In	Inherits	Integer
Interface	Is	Let	Lib
Like	Long	Loop	Me

continued

TABLE 5.4: VISUAL BASIC RESERVED WORDS

Mod	Module	MustInherit	MustOverride
MyBase	MyClass	Namespace	New
Next	Not	Nothing	NotInheritable
NotOverridable	Object	On	Option
Optional	Or	OrElse	Overloads
Overridable	Overrides	ParamArray	Preserve
Private	Property	Protected	Public
RaiseEvent	ReadOnly	ReDim	REM
RemoveHandler	Resume	Return	Select
Set	Shadows	Shared	Short
Single	Static	Step	Stop
String	Structure	Sub	SyncLock
Then	Throw	To	True
Try	TryCast	TypeOf	Unicode
Until	Variant	Wend	When
While	With	WithEvents	WriteOnly
Xor	#Const	#ExternalSource	#If...Then...#Else
#Region	-	&	&=
*	*=	/	/=
\	\=	^	^=
+	+=	=	-=

BACK TO THE STORY OF MIGHTY MOLLY

Now it is time to turn your attention back to the development of this chapter's game project, the Story of Mighty Molly. To create this game, you will follow the same five development steps that you've used to create previous chapter projects.

Designing the Game

The Story of Mighty Molly will be played on a single window, although the InputBox() function and MessageBox.Show method will be used to collect and display stored input and output. The game will therefore be made up of one form and the 11 controls listed in Table 5.5.

TABLE 5.5: FORM CONTROLS FOR THE STORY OF MIGHTY MOLLY GAME

Control Type	Control Name	Description
Label	lblWelcomeMsg	Displays the game's welcome message
Label	lblIntroText	Displays a brief prologue to the Story of Mighty Molly
Label	lblInstructions	Displays instructions for playing the game
Button	btnquestion1	Controls access to the game's first question
Button	btnquestion2	Controls access to the game's second question
Button	btnquestion3	Controls access to the game's third question
Button	btnquestion4	Controls access to the game's fourth question
Button	btnquestion5	Controls access to the game's fifth question
Button	btnPlayGame	Displays the game story
StatusBar	stbControl	Displays status information as the game progresses
ProgressBar	prbControl	Provides a graphical indication of the game's progress

Step 1: Creating a New Visual Basic Project

The first step in creating the Story of Mighty Molly is to start Visual Basic and open a new project.

1. If you have not already done so, start up Visual Basic 2005 Express and then click on File and select New Project. The New Project dialog will appear.
2. Select Windows Application template.
3. Type The Story of Mighty Molly as the name of your new application in the Name field located at the bottom of the New Project window.
4. Click on OK to close the New Project dialog.

Visual Basic will now create a new project for you, including an empty form, which you'll use to create the game's user interface.

Step 2: Creating the User Interface

Let's continue by adding the controls required to set up the game's user interface. The overall design of the game's interface is shown in Figure 5.11.

FIGURE 5.11

Completing the interface design for the Story of Mighty Molly game.

1. Begin by adding three Label controls to the form. By default, Visual Basic assigns the names Label1 through Label3 to these controls.

2. Add six Button controls to the form and line them up horizontally beneath the last Label control. By default, Visual Basic names these controls Button1 through Button6.

4. Add a StatusBar control to the form. By default, Visual Basic assigns this control the name StatusBar1.

5. Add a ToolTip control to the form. By default Visual Basic assigns this control the name of ToolTip1.

6. Finally, add a ProgressBar control to the form and move it on top of the StatusBar control, as shown in Figure 5.11.

The overall layout for the application's form is now complete.

Step 3: Customizing Form and Control Properties

Now it is time to customize the form and its controls. By this point in the book, you should be comfortable with the steps involved in modifying form and control properties. So, instead of walking you through each step that is involved in modifying every control, I am going provide you with tables for each control that identify the property changes that need to be made and leave it up to you to go ahead and make the changes.

The property modifications that need to be made to form1 are listed in Table 5.6.

TABLE 5.6: PROPERTY CHANGES FOR FORM1

Property	Value
Name	frmMain
BackColor	White
Cursor	Hand
FormBorderStyle	Fixed3D
MaximizeBox	False
MinimizeBox	False
StartPosition	CenterScreen
Text	The Story of Mighty Molly

The property changes for each of the form's three Label controls are listed in Table 5.7.

TABLE 5.7: PROPERTY CHANGES FOR THE LABEL CONTROLS

Control	Property	Value
Label1	Name	lblWelcomeMsg
	ForeColor	DarkBlue
	Font.Bold	True
	Font.Italic	True
	Font.Size	16
	Text	Welcome to The Story of Mighty Molly.
Label2	Name	lblIntroText
	Text	Mighty Molly was the bravest of all the Mollys. She was fearless in battle and relentless in everything else. No one who ever met her was left untouched, for the mighty one had a certain mystical way about her that almost magically seemed to rub off on those around her.
		Certainly, there never was before and may never be again anyone as mighty as Mighty Molly. For those of you who have not heard the tales of the mighty one, you are in luck, because today you get the chance to participate in the telling of the mighty one's last great adventure!
Label3	Name	lblInstructions
	Font.Bold	True
	Text	Instructions: To play the game and participate in the telling of "The Story of Mighty Molly," you must click on each of the following 5 buttons and supply the required information.

The property changes for each of the six Button controls are listed in Table 5.8.

TABLE 5.8: PROPERTY CHANGES FOR THE BUTTON CONTROLS

Control	Property	Value
Button1	Name	btnQuestion1
	BackColor	LightYellow
	Font.Bold	True
	Text	**Question # 1**
	ToolTip	**Click on button to answer the first question.**
Button2	Name	btnQuestion2
	BackColor	LightGray
	Enabled	False
	Font.Bold	True
	Text	**Question # 2**
	ToolTip	**Click on button to answer the second question.**
Button3	Name	btnQuestion3
	BackColor	LightGray
	Enabled	False
	Font.Bold	True
	Text	Question # 3
	ToolTip	**Click on button to answer the third question.**
Button4	Name	btnQuestion4
	BackColor	LightGray
	Enabled	False
	Font.Bold	True
	Text	**Question # 4**
	ToolTip	**Click on button to answer the fourth question.**

continued

TABLE 5.8: PROPERTY CHANGES FOR THE BUTTON CONTROLS

Button5	Name	btnQuestion5
	BackColor	LightGray
	Enabled	False
	Font.Bold	True
	Text	**Question # 5**
	ToolTip	**Click on button to answer the fifth question.**
Button6	Name	btnPlayGame
	BackColor	LightGray
	Enabled	False
	Font.Bold	True
	Text	**Tell me the story!**
	ToolTip	**Click on button to see the story.**

The property changes for the StatusBar control are listed in Table 5.9.

TABLE 5.9: PROPERTY CHANGES FOR THE STATUSBAR CONTROL

Property	**Value**
Name	stbControl
Panels	StatusBarPanel1 (Text = **Game Ready!**)
	StatusBarPanel2 (Text = **Progress:**)
ShowPanels	True
Size.Height	24
SizingGrip	False

The property changes for the ProgressBar control are listed in Table 5.10.

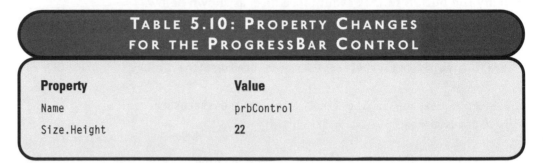

TABLE 5.10: PROPERTY CHANGES FOR THE PROGRESSBAR CONTROL	
Property	**Value**
Name	prbControl
Size.Height	22

Step 4: Adding a Little Programming Logic

Now that the game's user interface has been created and you have modified the appropriate form and control properties, it is time to begin coding. Start by double-clicking on form1. This will open the code editor and display code for the form's Load event. However, you don't need the code for the load event, so you can delete it, leaving just the opening and closing Class statements, as shown below.

```
Public Class frmMain


End Class
```

Now add the following statements in between these two statements.

```
'Declare constant used to specify titlebar message in pop-up Windows
Const cTitleBarMsg As String = "The Story of Mighty Molly"
'Declare variables used throughout the application
Private strCreature As String
Private strRoom As String
Private strColor As String
Private strWeapon As String
Private strFood As String
```

The first statement defines a constant that will be used to supply a title bar message for all the pop-up windows displayed by the game. The next five statements declare variables. Each variable will be used to store a piece of information supplied by the player. Notice that the Private keyword is used to limit the scope of each variable to the Class in which the variables were defined (such as form1). I could have just as easily used the Dim keyword and the application would have performed just the same. However, as a general rule, it is best to try and limit scope whenever possible.

Next, switch back to the form designer and double-click on the first button control. Then modify the button's Click event procedure, as shown below.

```
'This Sub procedure prompts the player to answer the 1st question
Private Sub btnQuestion1_Click(ByVal sender As System.Object, _
  ByVal e As System.EventArgs) Handles btnQuestion1.Click

      'Post message in the first panel on the statusbar
      StatusBarPanel1.Text = "Be Brave!"

      'Prompt player to answer the first question
      strCreature = InputBox("What scary creature scares you most?", _
        cTitleBarMsg)

      'Make sure the player entered something
      If strCreature = "" Then
        MessageBox.Show("You must answer all questions to " & _
        "continue.", cTitleBarMsg)
      Else
        strCreature = strCreature.ToLower 'Convert input to lowercase
        StatusBarPanel1.Text = ""   'Clear statusbar
        btnQuestion1.Enabled = False   'Disable the 1st button conrol
        btnQuestion2.Enabled = True   'Enable the 2nd Button control
        btnQuestion1.BackColor = Color.LightPink   'Turn button pink
        btnQuestion2.BackColor = Color.LightYellow 'Turn button yellow
        prbControl.Value = 20   'Update the ProgressBar control
      End If


End Sub
```

The first statement inside the procedure sets the Text property of the StatusBarPanel1 to "Be Brave!" The next statement uses the InputBox() function to prompt the user to provide the name of a scary monster. The player's input is stored in a variable named strCreature. The next statement checks to make sure that the player did not click on the

Cancel button or that the player did not click on the OK button without supplying any information. The MessageBox.Show method is used to display an error message if the player fails
to provide input. Otherwise the following actions are performed:

- The text string supplied by the player is converted to all lowercase using the ToLower
  method.
- The text displayed in the first Status Bar panel is cleared out.
- The btnQuestion1 button is disabled, preventing the player from clicking on it again.
- The btnQuestion2 button is enabled, allowing the player to click on it.
- The background color of the btnQuestion1 button is set to LightPink to indicate that
  the input collected from the player for the first question was accepted.
- The background color of the btnQuestion2 button is set to LightYellow to indicate that
  it is the currently active game button.
- The ProgressBar control is updated to show that the application has collected 20
  percent of the input that is required to tell the story.

Now, access the procedure of the btnQuestion2 control and modify it as shown below.

```
'This Sub procedure prompts the player to answer the 2nd question
Private Sub btnQuestion2_Click(ByVal sender As System.Object, _
  ByVal e As System.EventArgs) Handles btnQuestion2.Click

    'Post message in the first panel on the statusbar
    StatusBarPanel1.Text = "Any Room Will Do!"

  'Prompt player to answer the second question
  strRoom = InputBox("What's the worst room in a castle?", _
    cTitleBarMsg)

  'Make sure the player entered something
  If strRoom = "" Then
    MessageBox.Show("You must answer all questions to " & _
    "continue.", cTitleBarMsg)
  Else
    strRoom = strRoom.ToLower  'Convert input to lowercase
    StatusBarPanel1.Text = ""  'Clear statusbar
    btnQuestion2.Enabled = False  'Disable the 2nd button control
```

```
      btnQuestion3.Enabled = True 'Enable the 3rd Button control
      btnQuestion2.BackColor = Color.LightPink  'Turn button pink
      btnQuestion3.BackColor = Color.LightYellow 'Turn button yellow
      prbControl.Value = 40  'Update the ProgressBar control
   End If

End Sub
```

As you can see, the code for the btnQuestion2 control is almost identical to the code that you added to the btnQuestion1 control, the only differences being:

- A different status bar message is displayed.
- A different question is asked.
- The player's response is stored in a different variable.
- This time, btnQuestion2 is disabled and btnQuestion3 is enabled.
- This time, the background color of btnQuestion2 to set to LightPink and the background of btnQuestion3 is set to LightYellow.

Now, access the procedure of the btnQuestion3 control and modify it as shown below.

```
'This Sub procedure prompts the player to answer the 3rd question
Private Sub btnQuestion3_Click(ByVal sender As System.Object, _
  ByVal e As System.EventArgs) Handles btnQuestion3.Click

    'Post message in the first panel on the statusbar
    StatusBarPanel1.Text = "Any Color Will Do!"

    'Prompt player to answer the third question
    strColor = InputBox("What is your favorite color?", _
      cTitleBarMsg)

    'Make sure the player entered something
    If strColor = "" Then
      MessageBox.Show("You must answer all questions to " & _
        "continue.", cTitleBarMsg)
    Else
      strColor = strColor.ToLower  'Convert input to lowercase
      StatusBarPanel1.Text = ""   'Clear statusbar
      btnQuestion3.Enabled = False 'Disable the 3rd button control
```

```
            btnQuestion4.Enabled = True   'Enable the 4th Button control
            btnQuestion3.BackColor = Color.LightPink  'Turn button pink
            btnQuestion4.BackColor = Color.LightYellow 'Turn button yellow
            prbControl.Value = 60   'Update the ProgressBar control
        End If

End Sub
```

Next, access the procedure of the btnQuestion4 control and modify it as shown below.

```
'This Sub procedure prompts the player to answer the 4th question
Private Sub btnQuestion4_Click(ByVal sender As System.Object, _
  ByVal e As System.EventArgs) Handles btnQuestion4.Click

        'Post message in the first panel on the statusbar
        StatusBarPanel1.Text = "Better be enough to kill a " & _
            strCreature & "!"

        'Prompt player to answer the fourth question
        strWeapon = InputBox("Name something that can be used as " & _
          "weapon that you might find on the ground.", cTitleBarMsg)

        'Make sure the player entered something
        If strWeapon = "" Then
          MessageBox.Show("You must answer all questions to " & _
              "continue.", cTitleBarMsg)
        Else
          strWeapon = strWeapon.ToLower 'Convert input to lowercase
          StatusBarPanel1.Text = ""  'Clear statusbar
          btnQuestion4.Enabled = False 'Disable the 4th button control
          btnQuestion5.Enabled = True  'Enable the 5th Button control
          btnQuestion4.BackColor = Color.LightPink  'Turn button pink
          btnQuestion5.BackColor = Color.LightYellow 'Turn button yellow
          prbControl.Value = 80   'Update the ProgressBar control
        End If

End Sub
```

Access the procedure of the btnQuestion5 control and modify it as shown below.

```
'This Sub procedure prompts the player to answer the 5th question
Private Sub btnQuestion5_Click(ByVal sender As System.Object, _
  ByVal e As System.EventArgs) Handles btnQuestion5.Click

    'Post message in the first panel on the statusbar
    StatusBarPanel1.Text = "What's Your Preference?"

    'Prompt player to answer the fifth question
    strFood = InputBox("What is your favorite thing to eat?", _
      cTitleBarMsg)

    'Make sure the player entered something
    If strFood = "" Then
      MessageBox.Show("You must answer all questions to " & _
        "continue.", cTitleBarMsg)
    Else
      strFood = strFood.ToLower 'Convert input to lowercase
      StatusBarPanel1.Text = ""  'Clear statusbar
      btnQuestion5.Enabled = False 'Disable the 5th button control
      btnPlayGame.Enabled = True  'Enable the last Button control
      btnQuestion5.BackColor = Color.LightPink  'Turn button pink
      btnPlayGame.BackColor = Color.LightGreen 'Turn button green
      prbControl.Value = 100  'Update the ProgressBar control
    End If

End Sub
```

Finally, modify the code for the `btnPlayGame` control as shown below.

```
'This Sub procedure is responsible for displaying the game's story
Private Sub btnPlayGame_Click(ByVal sender As System.Object, _
  ByVal e As System.EventArgs) Handles btnPlayGame.Click
    'Declare local variable used to store the game's story
    Dim strText As String = ""

    'Post message in the first panel on the statusbar
    StatusBarPanel1.Text = "Let's Rock!"
```

```
'Assemble the game's story
strText &= "A long time ago in a land far away, there "
strText &= "was a castle where the great Prince William lived. "
strText &= "Prince William was a kindly boy who cared more for "
strText &= "his people than he did for himself. One day a storm "
strText &= "from out of nowhere swept upon the land where "
strText &= "Prince William lived. A mysterious " & strColor
strText &= " mist soon followed the storm. Out of this mist "
strText &= "appeared an evil " & strCreature & "."
strText &= ControlChars.NewLine & ControlChars.NewLine
strText &= "The " & strCreature & "'s heart was dark and cold. "
strText &= "The " & strCreature & " killed William's father, the "
strText &= "good King Stefford. So William became the new king. "
strText &= "Summoning up all his bravery, King William rode out "
strText &= "ahead of his armies to do battle with the fearsome "
strText &= strCreature & ". However, King William's army was "
strText &= "quickly crushed and King William was captured and "
strText &= "locked away in the castle's " & strRoom & "
strText &= ControlChars.NewLine & ControlChars.NewLine
strText &= "A call went out from far and wide for a great hero "
strText &= "to rescue King William. But no one dared answer "
strText &= "the call except for Mighty Molly, mightiest of all "
strText &= "the Mollys. Within a fortnight the mighty one "
strText &= "arrived in the land where King William once ruled. "
strText &= "Upon hearing of the mighty oneâ_™s arrival, the "
strText &= strCreature & " quickly rushed out to meet her."
strText &= ControlChars.NewLine & ControlChars.NewLine
strText &= "Mighty Molly and the dreaded " & strCreature
strText &= " fought for 4 days and 4 nights. As they did battle "
strText &= "a cloud of " & strColor & " dust gathered around "
strText &= "them, making them invisible to all who tried to "
strText &= "watch. Finally, at the end of the 4th day, the "
strText &= strCreature & " fell dead at the mighty oneâ_™s feet. "
strText &= "With her strength all but gone, Mighty Molly had "
strText &= "slain the " & strCreature & " with her final "
strText &= "blow, using a large " & strWeapon & " that she had "
strText &= "fallen on during the fight." & ControlChars.NewLine
strText &= ControlChars.NewLine & "When the fight was finally "
```

```
strText &= "over and the " & strColor & "mist finally cleared, "
strText &= "a great roar arose from the people who had gathered "
strText &= "around to watch. Happily, the people followed the "
strText &= "mighty one to King Williamâ_™s castle where she
strText &= "freed him. In gratitude, good King William declared "
strText &= "a holiday and ordered his cooks to prepare a great "
strText &= "feast of meat, wine and " & strFood & ". At the "
strText &= "feast, King William offered to give his kingdom over "
strText &= "to Mighty Molly and he knelt at her knees and "
strText &= "offered up his crown. But Mighty Molly turned down "
strText &= "his offer, for she knew that King William was the "
strText &= "true king and that as mighty as she was, she needed "
strText &= "to be mightier still to rule as wisely as King "
strText &= "William." & ControlChars.NewLine
strText &= ControlChars.NewLine & "The End."

'Display the fully assembled story
 MessageBox.Show(strText, cTitleBarMsg)

'Get the game ready to tell another story
StatusBarPanel1.Text = "Game Ready!" 'Update statusbar message
btnPlayGame.Enabled = False    'Disable the Button labeled Play

'Reset variables to prepare the game to allow the player to create
'a new story
strCreature = ""
strRoom = ""
strColor = ""
strWeapon = ""
strFood = ""

'Reset Button controls back to their original colors
btnQuestion1.BackColor = Color.LightYellow
btnQuestion2.BackColor = Color.LightGray
btnQuestion3.BackColor = Color.LightGray
btnQuestion4.BackColor = Color.LightGray
btnQuestion5.BackColor = Color.LightGray
btnPlayGame.BackColor = Color.LightGray
```

```
'Reset the ProgressBar control's value property to zero
prbControl.Value = 0

'Enable the first Button control
btnQuestion1.Enabled = True
```

End Sub

The first statement in this procedure declares a variable named strText, which will be used to hold the game's story line. The second statement posts a message of "Let's Rock!" in the left-hand status bar pane. The next series of statements builds the game's story line using the &= operator to append the lines of the story together. If you look closely at the text of the story, you see where the variables that contain the input provided by the player have been inserted throughout the story line. The MessageBox.Show method is then used to display the fully assembled story.

TRICK The &= operator can be used as a shortcut for concatenating a text string to a String variable. It can be use as shown below.

strText &= "Once upon a time..."

An alternative to using the &= operator is to take the String variable and set it equal to itself before using the & operator to append a text string as demonstrated below.

strText = strText & "Once upon a time..."

As you can see, using the &= operator is easier and reduces the length of your code statements.

• Display the string text "Game Ready!" in the left status bar pane
• Disable the btnPlayGame button
• Reset the value stored in each of the games variables to ""
• Set the background color of btnQuestion1 to LightYellow and the background of all the other buttons to LightGray
• Reset the Value property of the ProgressBar control to 0
• Enable the btnQuestion1 button

Step 5: Testing the Execution of the Story of Mighty Molly Game

OK. That's it. The Story of Mighty Molly should be ready to run. Press F5 and put the game through its paces. If you have any errors, double-check your typing. Once you think you have things working the way you want, try testing the game again, this time feeding data that the game doesn't expect to receive and see how it handles it.

SUMMARY

In this chapter, you learned how to store and retrieve data using a number of different programming constructs, including constants, variables, arrays, and structures. You learned how to specify data type, to convert data from one data type to another, and to control variable scope. You also learned how to add comments to your Visual Basic applications and to work with the ProgressBar control. Before you move on to Chapter 6, "Applying Conditional Logic," take a look at the following challenges and see if you can improve the Story of Mighty Molly.

CHALLENGES

1. Modify the story by providing players with the ability to change background colors and font types and sizes.

2. Create a unique looking icon for the game, display the icon on the application's title bar, and put an icon in the system tray when the game is running.

3. Modify the game so that the player can specify additional story inputs, including the name of the story's main character.

APPLYING CONDITIONAL LOGIC

In order to create truly effective applications, a programming language must be able to distinguish between two different situations and make a choice based on the results of that analysis. By examining user input, for example, you can use conditional logic to alter the execution flow of your Visual Basic applications. This allows you to develop applications that react dynamically and provide an interactive user experience. This chapter will provide you with instruction on how to apply conditional logic using variations of the If…Then and Select Case statements. In addition, you will get the chance to develop some advanced conditional logic of your own through the creation of the chapter's game project, the Guess a Number game.

Specifically, you will learn how to:

- Test two logical conditions
- Provide for alternative courses of action
- Embed conditional statements to create more complicated conditional logic tests
- Rest multiple conditions against a single value

PROJECT PREVIEW: THE GUESS A NUMBER GAME

In this chapter, you will learn how to create a Visual Basic game called the Guess a Number game. The development of this game will provide you with plenty of opportunities to apply your knowledge of conditional logic. Figures 6.1 through 6.4 provide a sneak preview of the Guess a Number game and demonstrate the game's overall execution.

FIGURE 6.1

The game begins by allowing the player to specify configuration options, including the range of numbers to pick from and the amount of information the game will display.

FIGURE 6.2

Once game play starts, the player's access to the configuration options is disabled and the player is prompted to take the first guess.

FIGURE 6.3

The game provides players with clues to help them hone in on the answer. It also displays a running count of the number of guesses made by the player.

FIGURE 6.4

At the end of each game, the player gets a chance to modify the game's configuration options and reset the score.

By the time you have created and run this game, you'll have learned how to develop some fairly complicated conditional logic tests. As a result, you should be ready to move on, having laid the foundation required to understand and develop the conditional logic required to complete the game projects in the remaining chapters.

APPLYING CONDITIONAL LOGIC

Conditional logic is something that we apply all the time in our everyday lives. For example, based on the sale price of a particular item, you may decide either to put it back on the shelf or to purchase it. Likewise, based on how cold it feels when you wake up in the morning, you may decide whether to get up or sleep in late. There is really not anything different between this type of logic and the conditional logic that you'll learn to apply in your Visual Basic applications.

At the core of any conditional logic test is a determination as to whether the condition being tested is true or false. Based on the results of this analysis, different actions may be taken. To help facilitate the development of conditional logic, Visual Basic provides you with two different statements, each of which is suited to different situations. These statements are:

- `If…Then`. This statement provides the ability to test a condition and then to alter the execution flow of your application based on the result of that test.
- `Select Case`. This statement provides you with the ability to perform a number of tests against a single value and to perform one of a series of possible actions based on the result.

THE IF...THEN STATEMENT

You have already seen various implementations of the `If…Then` statement in previous chapter game projects. It is practically impossible to develop a useful application without using the `If…Then` statement. For example, in the Click Race game that you created in Chapter 2 "Navigating the Visual Basic 2005 Express Development Environment", you set up an `If…Then` statement to terminate the game's execution once 30 seconds had passed, as shown below.

```
If intTimerCount = 30 Then
     Button1.Enabled = False
     Button2.Enabled = False
End If
```

In the Speed Typing game, which you created in Chapter 3, you used the `If…Then` statement numerous times. For example, you used five `If…Then` statements to determine which text statements the game should display, as shown below.

```
If intCount = 0 Then txtDisplay.Text = _
     "Once upon a time there were three little pigs."
If intCount = 1 Then txtDisplay.Text = _
```

```
        "In days gone by times were hard but the people were strong."
If intCount = 2 Then txtDisplay.Text = _
        "Once in a while something special happens even to the " _
        & "worst of people."
If intCount = 3 Then txtDisplay.Text = _
        "When injustice rears its head, it is the duty of all good " _
        & "citizens to object."
If intCount = 4 Then txtDisplay.Text = _
        "It has been said that in the end there can be only one. " _
        & "Let that one be Mighty Molly."
```

In the Lottery Assistant game that you created in Chapter 4 "Working with Menus and Tool-bars", you used the If…Then statement and the CInt() conversion function to determine when a full set of lottery numbers had been selected, as shown below.

```
If intNoOfValidPics = CInt(txtFullSet.Text) Then
    blnFullSetComplete = True
    strDisplayString = strDisplayString & vbNewLine & vbNewLine
    strTestString = "_"
End If
```

You used conditional logic extensively in the development of the Story of Mighty Molly game in Chapter 5 "Storing and Retrieving Data in Memory". For example, you used If…Then statements to validate player input, as shown below.

```
strColor = InputBox("What is your favorite color?", cTitleBarMsg)
If strColor = "" Then
    MessageBox.Show("You must answer all questions to " & _
    "continue.", cTitleBarMsg)
End If
```

To better understand how If…Then statements work, take at look at the following example.

```
If it is below 32 degrees outside
  Then I'll stay in bed another hour
Else
  I'll get up and read the newspaper
EndIf
```

This English-like or pseudocode outline demonstrates how to apply a variation of the If...Then statements to your everyday life. In this example, the first line sets up the conditional test. If the tested condition turns out to be true, then the actions specified by the second statement are executed. Otherwise, an alternative course of action is taken.

Now that you have seen several examples of the If...Then statement in action, let's spend some time dissecting it and exploring all its variations.

> **DEFINITION**
>
> Pseudocode is a rough, English-like outline or sketch of one or more program statements. By writing what you are trying to do in pseudocode and then translating that pseudocode into actual program statements, you can simplify application development. The pseudocode, in effect, becomes an initial-level draft version of your application.

If...Then Statement Syntax

The If...Then statement provides the ability to test two or more conditions and to alter program statement flow based on the outcome of those tests. The If...Then statement supports many variations, as demonstrated by the following syntax.

```
If condition Then
     statements
ElseIf condition Then
    statements
Else
    statements
End If
```

Within this overall structure, there are many variations of the If...Then statements. We'll explore these variations in the sections that follow.

The Single Line If...Then Statement

In its simplest form, the If...Then statement tests a single condition and performs a single command when the tested condition proves true, as demonstrated below.

```
Dim intCounter As Integer = 0
If intCounter = 0 Then MessageBox.Show("We have a match.")
```

Here the condition being tested is whether the value assigned to intCounter equals 0. If the value assigned to intCounter is equal to 0, the result of the conditional test is true and therefore the MessageBox.Show method will execute and display a message. However, if the test proves false, the MessageBox.Show method will not execute and the application continues on, processing any remaining programming statements.

The advantage of the single line If…Then statement is that it allows you to set up a simple conditional test and to perform a single action only if the test proves true. This allows you to keep your code simple and to place both the conditional test and the resulting action on the same line.

Multiline If…Then Statements

More often than not, the logic that you'll need to use when testing logical conditions will be too complicated or large to fit into a single statement. When this is the case, you'll need to use the If…Then statement in the format demonstrated below.

```
Dim intCounter As Integer = 0
If intCounter = 0 Then
    intCounter += 1
    MessageBox.Show("The value of intCounter is " & intCounter)
End If
```

In this example, the number of commands to be executed by the If…Then statement are too numerous to be placed in a single statement. Therefore, the If…Then statement had to be expanded into a code block by adding an End If statement to the end. When used in this manner, you can place any number of statements between the opening If…Then statement and the closing End If statement, and they will all be executed if the condition being tested proves true.

The If…Then…Else Statement

The two previous examples demonstrate how to execute one or more commands when a tested condition provides true. But what do you do when the tested condition proves false, and as a result, you want to execute an alternate set of commands? One option is to write a second If…Then statement. For example, suppose you created a small Visual Basic application as depicted in Figure 6.5.

Age Verification

How old are you? [   ]

Play

FIGURE 6.5

Validating player
age before
allowing the
game to be
played.

In this example, the application consists of a form with a Label, a TextBox, and a Button control. The application requires that the player types an age and clicks on the button labeled Play before being allowed to play the game. The following statements show the program code that has been added to the Button control's Click event.

```
Public Class Form1

    Private Sub Button1_Click(ByVal sender As System.Object, _
      ByVal e As System.EventArgs) Handles Button1.Click
        If Int32.Parse(TextBox1.Text) < 18 Then
            MessageBox.Show("Thanks for playing!")
        End If
        If Int32.Parse(TextBox1.Text) >= 18 Then
            MessageBox.Show("Sorry. You are too old to play this game!")
            Application.Exit()
        End If

    End Sub

End Class
```

TRICK Int32.Parse() is a method that is used to convert a String value to an Integer value. Since, in the previous example, the TextBox control was used to collect the user's input, I converted its contents to Integer before trying to it.

As you can see, two different If...Then statements have been set up. The first If...Then statement checks to see if the player is less than 18 years old. The second If...Then statement checks to see if the player is greater than or equal to 18 years of age. If the player is less than 18 years old a friendly greeting message is displayed. Otherwise, the player is told that he is too old and the game is terminated. Note that for this example to work correctly, the user is required to enter a numeric value. Otherwise, an error will occur. Later, in this chapter's game project, you'll see examples of how to perform input validation in order to prevent incorrect user input from causing errors.

Although these two sets of If...Then statements certainly get the job done, a better way to accomplish the same thing would be to set up an If...Then...Else statement, as demonstrated below.

```
Public Class Form1

    Private Sub Button1_Click(ByVal sender As System.Object, _
        ByVal e As System.EventArgs) Handles Button1.Click

        If Int32.Parse(TextBox1.Text) < 18 Then
            MessageBox.Show("Thanks for playing!")
        Else
            MessageBox.Show("Sorry. You are too old to play this game!")
            Application.Exit()
        End If

    End Sub

End Class
```

As you can see, the If...Then...Else version of this example is slightly smaller and requires one less conditional test, making the programming logic simpler and easier to follow. Graphically, Figure 6.6 provides you with a visual flowchart view of the logic used in this example.

DEFINITION

A flowchart is a graphical depiction of the logic flow in a computer application.

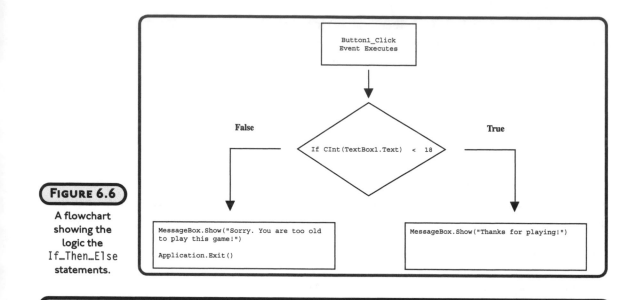

FIGURE 6.6

A flowchart showing the logic the If...Then...Else statements.

IN THE REAL WORLD

Professional programmers often develop flowcharts that outline the overall execution of an application that they are about to develop. This helps them by providing a visual map that lays out the application's overall design while also helping to organize the programmer's thoughts. Once the application is complete, the flowchart can also be used as supplemental documentation.

If an application is particularly large, a team of programmers, each of whom is assigned to work on a particular part of the application, may develop it. Using a flowchart, the team of programmers could divide up the work by each focusing on specific sections of the application as outlined in the flowchart.

The If...Then...ElseIf Statement

If you wish, you can add the ElseIf keyword one or more times to expand the If...Then statement. Each instance of the ElseIf keyword allows you to set up a test for another alternative condition. To better understand how the If...Then...ElseIf statement works, take a look at the following example, shown in Figure 6.7.

FIGURE 6.7

Using an If...Then...ElseIf statement to process the contents of a ComboBox control.

In this example, a new Visual Basic application has been created, consisting of a form with a Label, a Button, and a ComboBox control.

TRICK
The ComboBox control provides a drop-down list from which the user can select a single option. After adding a ComboBox to a form at design time, you can populate it with choices by locating its Items property in the Properties window and clicking on the (Collection) entry in the value column. This opens the String Collection Editor, as shown in Figure 6.8. All you have to do now is enter the choices that you want to display in the ComboBox control, making sure to type each option on its own line.

FIGURE 6.8

Using the String Collection Editor at design time to populate the contents of a ComboBox control.

To make a selection, the user must select one of the choices displayed in the ComboBox control and then click on the form's Button control. When this occurs, the code assigned to this control's Click event, shown below, will execute.

```
Public Class Form1

    Private Sub Button1_Click(ByVal sender As System.Object, _
        ByVal e As System.EventArgs) Handles Button1.Click

        If ComboBox1.Text = "1 - 12" Then
            MessageBox.Show("There is a skateboard park just " & _
                "down the street.")
        ElseIf ComboBox1.Text = "13 - 18" Then
            MessageBox.Show("There is a 99 cent movie theater " & _
                "2 blocks over.")
        ElseIf ComboBox1.Text = "19 - 21" Then
            MessageBox.Show("A new dance club has opened downtown " & _
                "on 3rd street.")
        Else
            MessageBox.Show("OH, You must be tired. How about a nap.")
        End If

    End Sub

End Class
```

As you can see, by adding multiple ElseIf keywords, you are able to set up a conditional logic that can test for multiple possible conditions.

NESTING CONDITIONAL LOGIC

Sometimes the logic that you are developing may be too complicated to be represented using the different variations of the If...Then statements. However, you can greatly extend the power of the If...Then statements by nesting them within one another. This enables you to develop logic that tests for one condition and then further tests other conditions based on the result of the previous test.

You've already seen examples of nested If statements in previous chapter game projects. For example, the following code comes from the btnDone_Click event belonging to the Speed Typing game that you worked on in Chapter 3.

DEFINITION

Nesting is the process of embedding one statement within another statement of the same type, such as when you embed If...Then statements in order to develop more complicated conditional logic.

```
If intWrong = 3 Then   'If intWrong equals three the player has struck out

    'Time to determine the player's typing skill level
    If intCount < 2 Then   'Set rank when less than 2 tests were passed
        MessageBox.Show("Game over. Your typing skill level " _
            & "is: Beginner. Please play again!")
        intCount = 0
        intWrong = 0
        Return   'Exit procedure immediately
    End If
    If intCount < 4 Then   'Set rank when less than 4 tests were passed
        MessageBox.Show("Game over. Your typing skill level " _
            & "is: Intermediate. Please play again!")
        intCount = 0
        intWrong = 0
        Return   'Exit procedure immediately
    End If
    If intCount < 5 Then   'Set rank when less than 5 tests were passed
        MessageBox.Show("Game over. Your typing skill level " _
            & "is: Advanced. Please play again!")
        intCount = 0
        intWrong = 0
        Return   'Exit procedure immediately
    End If

End If
```

In the Speed typing game, the game is set up to end if the player gets three strikes. The number of strikes made by the player is stored in the intWrong variable. The game also tracks the number of typing tests passed by the player by incrementing the value assigned to the intCounter variable.

In this example, the value of intWrong is first evaluated to see if it is equal to 3. If it is, then a series of three embedded If...Then statements are executed, each of which further refines the analysis by checking the value assigned to the intCount variable.

TRAP You can embed as many If…Then statements as you want within one another. However, the deeper you go, the more difficult your program code will be to read and maintain.

THE SELECT CASE STATEMENT

In many cases, you'll want to compare one value or expression to a whole series of possible values. One way to accomplish this is by setting up as many If…Then statements as are required to make all the comparisons. However, a better way to tackle this type of situation is to use the Select Case statement.

The syntax for the Select Case statement is shown below.

```
Select Case expression
  Case value
    statements
    .
    .
    .
  Case value
    statements
  Case Else
    statements
End Select
```

As you can see, you use the Select Case statement to set up a block of code that begins with a Select Case statement and ends with the End Select statement. Between these two statements, you insert one or more Case statements, each of which defines a value or expression to be tested. You can also include a Case Else statement as a sort of catchall. The Case Else statement will execute in the event that all of the previous Case statements failed to result in a match. To better understand how the Select Case statement works, take a look at the following pseudocode example.

```
Select Case Temperature
  Case If it is below 32 degrees stay in bed
  Case If it is exactly 32 degrees play the lottery
  Case Else Just read the newspaper
End Select
```

In this example, one value, the temperature, is compared to a number of different values. If any of the values, as defined by a Case statement, are equal to the value of the temperature, then the programming logic associated with that value is executed.

As you can see, functionally the Select Case and the If…Then…Else statements are fairly similar. However, the Select Case statement is easier to read and is perfect for performing multiple tests against a single value or expression.

In most cases, you'll be able to reduce the number of lines of code that you need to perform a conditional test when you use a Select Case code block in place of a series of If…Then statements. As an example, take a look at the following code, which represents a rewrite of the example presented earlier in this chapter in the section that covered the nesting If…Then statements.

```
Select Case intWrong = 3
    Case intCount < 2
        MessageBox.Show("Game over. Your typing skill level " _
            & "is: Beginner. Please play again!")
        intCount = 0
        intWrong = 0
        Return
    Case intCount < 4
        MessageBox.Show("Game over. Your typing skill level " _
            & "is: Intermediate. Please play again!")
        intCount = 0
        intWrong = 0
        Return
    Case intCount < 5
        MessageBox.Show("Game over. Your typing skill level " _
            & "is: Advanced. Please play again!")
        intCount = 0
        intWrong = 0
        Return
End Select
```

As you can see, this example is not only a few lines shorter than the previous example, but also easier to read and follow along.

COMPARISON OPERATORS

Up to this point in the book, most of the conditional tests that you have seen involved comparing two values or expressions to see if they were equal. Although this is certainly a powerful type of test, there are times when you need to test the relationship between values and expressions in different ways. For example, you may want to know if one value is less than, greater than, or equal to another value. To accomplish these types of comparisons, you can use any of the comparison operators listed in Table 6.1.

TABLE 6.1: VISUAL BASIC COMPARISON OPERATORS

Operator	Description
=	Equal
<>	Not equal
<	Less than
>	Greater than
<=	Less than or equal to
>=	Greater than or equal to

To get a better feel for how to use these operators, take a look at the following example.

```
Dim intSecretNumber As Integer = 6
Dim intPlayerGuess As Integer

intPlayerGuess = InputBox("Type a number between 1 and 10?")

If intPlayerGuess < intSecretNumber Then
    MessageBox.Show("Your guess is too low.")
End If
If intPlayerGuess = intSecretNumber Then
    MessageBox.Show("Your guess is correct.")
End If
If intPlayerGuess > intSecretNumber Then
    MessageBox.Show("Your guess is too high.")
End If
```

As you can see, three If…Then statements have been set up. The first If...Then statement uses the less than operator (<) to see if the value entered by the player is less than intSecretNumber (which is 6). Likewise, the second If…Then statement checks to see if the player's guess is equal to intSecretNumber. Finally, the third If…Then statement uses the greater than operator (>) to see if the number supplied by the user is greater than intSecretNumber.

BACK TO THE GUESS A NUMBER GAME

Let's get started on the development of this chapter's game project, the Guess a Number game. To create this game, you will follow the same five development steps that you've used to create previous chapter projects.

Designing the Game

The Guess a Number game is played on a single window. Unlike previous applications where data was collected from the user using the InputBox() function, this game will collect the player's input by adding radio buttons and a check box to the user interface. In addition, instead of displaying output using the MessageBox.Show method, the game will display information messages for the player to read in a TextBox control located on the user interface.

The advantage of collecting player input and displaying game output on the user interface is that it will make the game run smoother, meaning that the player won't have to constantly stop and respond to pop-up windows as the game runs. In order to create the user interface, you'll have to learn how to work with several new types of controls, including the GroupBox, RadioButton, and CheckBox controls.

The Guess a Number game is made up of one form and the 17 controls listed in Table 6.2.

TABLE 6.2: FORM CONTROLS FOR THE GUESS A NUMBER GAME

Control Type	Control Name	Description
GroupBox1	grpRange	Contains radio buttons, a check box and a button that control the game's configuration settings
GroupBox2	grpScore	Displays the number of games won by the player and contains a button that is used to reset the score
RadioButton1	rbnControl10	Sets the range of game numbers to 1 through 10
RadioButton2	rbnControl100	Sets the range of game numbers to 1 through 100
RadioButton3	rbnControl1000	Sets the range of game numbers to 1 through 1000
CheckBox1	chkVerbose	Determines the level of messaging displayed by the game
Label1	lblGamesWon	Identifies the TextBox control where the total number of games won is displayed
Label2	lblInstructions	Identifies the TextBox control where the player enters guesses
Label3	lblFeedback	Identifies the TextBox control where game output is displayed
Button1	btnDefaults	Resets default RadioButton and CheckBox control settings
Button2	btnReset	Resets the number of games won back to zero in order to start a new game session
Button3	btnCheckGuess	Processes the player's guess to see if the player guessed low, high, or won the game
Button4	btnNewGame	Start a new game
TextBox1	txtGamesWon	Displays the number of games that the player has won
TextBox2	txtInput	Collects and displays player guesses
TextBox3	txtOutput	Displays output messages generated during game play
StatusBar1	stbControl	Displays information messages during game play

Step 1: Creating a New Visual Basic Project

The first step in creating the Guess a Number game is to open up Visual Basic and create a new project as outlined below.

1. If you have not already done so, start up Visual Basic 2005 Express and then click on File and select New Project. The New Project dialog will appear.

2. Select Windows Application template.

3. Type Guess a Number as the name of your new application in the Name field located at the bottom of the New Project window.

4. Click on OK to close the New Project dialog.

Visual Basic will now create a new project for you and display a new form upon which you will design the game's user interface.

Step 2: Creating the User Interface

The first step in laying out the user interface is adding controls to the form and moving and resizing them to the appropriate locations. The following procedure outlines the overall steps involved in creating the game's user interface. As you go through each step, make sure that you reference Figure 6.9 so that you'll know where each control should be placed.

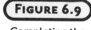

FIGURE 6.9

Completing the interface design for the Guess a Number game.

1. Start by adding two GroupBox controls to the form. Position and resize them as shown in Figure 6.9.

2. Add three RadioButton controls to the form and move them into the first GroupBox control, as shown in Figure 6.9.

3. Add a CheckBox control to the form and move it just underneath the last RadioButton control.

4. Add a Button control to the first GroupBox control and reduce its size as shown in Figure 6.9.

5. Now, add a Label, a TextBox, and a Button control to the second GroupBox and resize and position them as shown in Figure 6.9.

6. Add two additional Label controls and position them toward the middle of the form as shown in Figure 6.9.

7. Add a TextBox control to the right of the first Label control and increase its width by approximately 30 percent.

8. Add another TextBox control underneath the second Label control, set its Multiline property equal to True and resize it until it takes up most of the remaining space in the lower right-hand side of the form.

9. Add two more Button controls on the right-hand side of the form between the two Label and TextBox controls.

10. Lastly, add a StatusBar control to the bottom of the form.

The overall layout of your new application's form is now complete.

Step 3: Customizing Form and Control Properties

Now it is time for you to customize various properties belonging to the form and the controls that you have placed on it. Begin by changing the form properties listed in Table 6.3.

Property	Value
Name	frmMain
Cursor	Hand
FormBorderStyle	Fixed3D
StartPosition	CenterScreen
Text	**Guess a Number**

Table 6.3: Property Changes for Form1

Next, make changes shown in Table 6.4 to the GroupBox controls.

Table 6.4: Property Changes for the GroupBox Controls

Control	Property	Value
GroupBox1	Name	grpRange
	Font.Bold	True
	Text	**Select Range**
GroupBox2	Name	grpScore
	Font.Bold	True
	Text	**Score**

Make the changes shown in Table 6.5 to the RadioButton controls.

TABLE 6.5: PROPERTY CHANGES FOR THE RADIOBUTTON CONTROLS

Control	Property	Value
RadioButton1	Name	rbnControl10
	Font.Bold	True
	Text	**Range: 1 to 10**
RadioButton2	Name	rbnControl100
	Checked	True
	Font.Bold	True
	Text	**Range: 1 to 100**
RadioButton3	Name	rbnControl1000
	Font.Bold	True
	Text	**Range: 1 to 1000**

Make the changes shown in Table 6.6 to the CheckBox control.

TABLE 6.6: PROPERTY CHANGES FOR THE CHECKBOX CONTROL

Property	Value
Name	chkVerbose
Checked	True
CheckState	Checked
Font.Bold	True
Text	**Verbose Messaging**

Make the changes shown in Table 6.7 to the Button controls.

TABLE 6.7: PROPERTY CHANGES FOR THE BUTTON CONTROLS

Control	Property	Value
Button1	Name	btnDefaults
	Font.Bold	True
	Text	**Reset Defaults**
Button2	Name	btnReset
	Font.Bold	True
	Text	**Reset Score**
Button3	Name	btnCheckGuess
	Enabled	False
	Font.Bold	True
	Text	**Check Guess**
Button4	Name	btnNewGame
	Font.Bold	True
	Text	**New Game**

Make the changes shown in Table 6.8 to the Label controls.

TABLE 6.8: PROPERTY CHANGES FOR THE LABEL CONTROLS

Control	Property	Value
Label1	Name	lblGamesWon
	Font.Bold	True
	Text	No. of Games Won:
Label2	Name	lblInstructions
	Font.Bold	True
	Font.Size	10
	Text	Enter Your Guess:
Label3	Name	lblFeedback
	Font.Bold	True
	Text	Feedback and Results

Make the changes shown in Table 6.9 to the TextBox controls.

TABLE 6.9: PROPERTY CHANGES FOR THE TEXTBOX CONTROLS

Control	Property	Value
TextBox1	Name	txtGamesWon
	Font.Bold	True
	ReadOnly	True
	TabStop	False
TextBox2	Name	txtInput
	Enabled	False
	Font.Bold	True
TextBox3	Name	txtOutput
	Font.Bold	True
	ReadOnly	True
	TabStop	False

Make the changes shown in Table 6.10 to the StatusBar control.

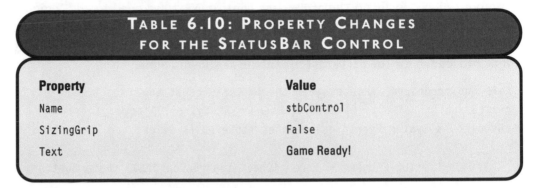

TABLE 6.10: PROPERTY CHANGES FOR THE STATUSBAR CONTROL

Property	Value
Name	stbControl
SizingGrip	False
Text	Game Ready!

That's it. At this point, you have configured all the form and control properties that need to be set at design time.

Step 4: Adding a Little Programming Logic

Let's begin by double-clicking on the form and adding the following statement just beneath the Public Class frmMain statement, as shown below.

```
Public Class frmMain

    'Declare variable used to store the game's randomly generated number
    Private intRandomNumber As Integer

End Class
```

The intRandomNumber variable will be used through the application to store the game's randomly generated secret number. Next, modify the form's Load event procedure as shown below.

```
'This Sub procedure executes when the game's interface is loaded
Private Sub Form1_Load(ByVal sender As System.Object, _
  ByVal e As System.EventArgs) Handles MyBase.Load

    txtGamesWon.Text = 0   'Set number of games won to zero
    btnNewGame.Focus()   'Set focus to the Button labeled New Game

End Sub
```

The first statement displays a value of 0 in the txtGamesWon control, and the second statement places focus on the btnNewGame control. Next, we need to add logic to the btnDefaults control that will reset the game's default settings, as controlled by the RadioButton and CheckBox controls located in the first GroupBox control. Do so by modifying the Click event procedure for the btnDefaults control, as shown below.

```
'This Sub procedure executes when the btnDefaults Button is clicked
Private Sub btnDefaults_Click(ByVal sender As System.Object, _
    ByVal e As System.EventArgs) Handles btnDefaults.Click

        rbnControl100.Checked = True  'Check the rbnConrol100 radio button
        chkVerbose.Checked = True   'Turn on verbose messaging
        txtInput.Focus()  'Set focus to txtInput

End Sub
```

The first statement selects the RadioButton that represents the range of 1 to 100. The second statement selects (by placing an x inside) the chkVerbose CheckBox control, and the third statement sets the focus to the txtInput control (to save the player the trouble of having to put it there before typing in the next guess).

Next, let's add logic to the btnReset control so that the player can reset the value that tracks the number of games won to 0. Also, take note that the value used to track the number of games won is not assigned to a variable. Instead, it is stored and managed within the txtGameWon control's Text property.

```
'This Sub procedure executes when the player clicks the Reset Defaults
Private Sub btnReset_Click(ByVal sender As System.Object, _
    ByVal e As System.EventArgs) Handles btnReset.Click

        txtGamesWon.Text = 0   'Set number of games won to zero

End Sub
```

Next, add the following statements to the TextChanged event for the txtInput control.

```
'This Sub procedure executes as soon as the player types in a guess
Private Sub txtInput_TextChanged(ByVal sender As System.Object, _
    ByVal e As System.EventArgs) Handles txtInput.TextChanged

        btnCheckGuess.Enabled = True 'Enable the Button labeled Check Guess
```

```
    btnNewGame.Enabled = False   'Disable the Button labeled New Game

End Sub
```

The `TextChanged` event is automatically triggered whenever the user keys something into the `TextBox` control associated with the event. It is used in the Guess a Number game to control when the `btnCheckGuess` button is enabled and when the `btnNewGame` is disabled.

Now we need to add logic to the application that randomly generates the game's secret number. To do so, I have decided to create a new procedure named `GetRandomNumber()` and place the logic to generate the random number in it. You won't be able to automatically generate this procedure by double-clicking on an object in the form designer. Instead, you'll need to key it in entirely by hand as shown below. You'll learn more about how to work with procedures in Chapter 8, "Enhancing Code Structure and Organization," including how to create your own custom procedures. For now, just key in the procedure as shown below.

```
'This Sub procedure retrieves the game's random number
Public Sub GetRandomNumber()

    'Declare variable representing the random number's maximum value
     Dim intUpperLimit As Integer

    'Instantiate a Random object
     Dim objRandom As New Random

    'If the 1st radio button is selected set the maximum value to 10
    If rbnControl10.Checked = True Then
        intUpperLimit = 10
    End If

    'If the 2nd radio button is selected set the maximum value to 100
    If rbnControl100.Checked = True Then
        intUpperLimit = 100
    End If

    'If the 3rd radio button is selected set the maximum value to 1000
    If rbnControl1000.Checked = True Then
        intUpperLimit = 1000
    End If
```

```
'Use the Random object's Next() method to generate a random number
intRandomNumber = objRandom.Next(intUpperLimit)
```

```
End Sub
```

When called by the `btnNewGame` control's `Click` event procedure, the `GetRandomNumber` procedure instantiates a new `Random` object called `objRandom` and checks to see which `RadioButton` control is currently selected so that it will know what range to use when generating the game's secret number. It then executes `Random` object's `Next()` method, in order to generate the random number. The `Next()` method is passed the value stored in the `intUpperLimit` variable, in order to specify the maximum range from which the random number should be selected (between 0 and the value of `intRandomNumber`).

TRICK The `Random` object's `Next()` method is used to generate a random number. If called without passing it any parameters, the `Next()` method generates a non-negative whole number. If passed a single integer value, the `Next()` method generates a random number between zero and the value of the integer argument. If passed two integer values, the `Next()` method will generate a random number within the specified range.

Now let's add the code required for the `Click` event belonging to the `btnCheckGuess` control, as shown below.

```
'This Sub procedure executes when the player clicks on the button
'labeled Check Guess
Private Sub btnCheckGuess_Click(ByVal sender As System.Object, _
   ByVal e As System.EventArgs) Handles btnCheckGuess.Click

      Dim intPlayerGuess As Integer 'Declare variable to store guess
      Static intNoOfGuesses As Integer 'Declare variable to keep track
                                 'of the number of guesses made

   If txtInput.Text.Length > 0 Then  'Make sure player typed something
        If IsNumeric(txtInput.Text) = True Then 'Ensure input is numeric

             'Convert String input to Integer data type
             intPlayerGuess = Int32.Parse(txtInput.Text)
             btnCheckGuess.Enabled = True 'Enable Check Guess button

             'See if player's guess is correct
```

```
If intPlayerGuess = intRandomNumber Then
    txtInput.Text = ""   'Clear the TextBox control

    intNoOfGuesses += 1   'Increment variable by one

    'See if player enabled verbose messaging
    If chkVerbose.Checked = True Then
        txtOutPut.Text = "Congratulations!" & _
          ControlChars.CrLf & ControlChars.CrLf & _
        "You have won the Guess a Number Game. " & _
        ControlChars.CrLf & ControlChars.CrLf & __
        "Number of guesses made = " & intNoOfGuesses
    Else
        txtOutPut.Text = "Congratulations! You Win."
    End If

    intNoOfGuesses = 0   'Reset variable to zero

    txtInput.Enabled = False   'Disable TextBox control

   'Update the display of the total number of games won
   txtGamesWon.Text = txtGamesWon.Text + 1
   'Disable the Button labeled Check Guess
   btnCheckGuess.Enabled = False
   'Enable the Button labeled New Game
   btnNewGame.Enabled = True '

    'Enable all Radio buttons
    rbnControl10.Enabled = True
    rbnControl100.Enabled = True
    rbnControl1000.Enabled = True

    'Enable the two reset buttons
    btnDefaults.Enabled = True
    btnReset.Enabled = True

    stbControl.Text = "Game Ready!"   'Post statusbar message
```

```
        End If

        'See if the player's guess was too low
        If intPlayerGuess < intRandomNumber Then
            txtInput.Text = ""  'Clear the TextBox control

            intNoOfGuesses += 1 'Increment variable by one

            'See if player enabled verbose messaging
            If chkVerbose.Checked = True Then
                txtOutPut.Text = "The number that you " & _
                "entered was too low. Enter higher number " & _
                "and try again." & _
                ControlChars.CrLf & ControlChars.CrLf & _
                "Number of guesses taken so far = " & _
                intNoOfGuesses
            Else
                txtOutPut.Text = "Too low."
            End If
        End If

        'See if the player's guess was too high
        If intPlayerGuess > intRandomNumber Then
            txtInput.Text = ""  'Clear the TextBox control

            intNoOfGuesses += 1  'Increment variable by one

            'See if player enabled verbose messaging
            If chkVerbose.Checked = True Then
                txtOutPut.Text = "The number that you " & _
                "entered was too high. Enter lower number " & _
                "and try again." & _
                ControlChars.CrLf & ControlChars.CrLf & _
                "Number of guesses taken so far = " & _
                intNoOfGuesses
            Else
                txtOutPut.Text = "Too high. Try again."
            End If
```

```
                End If

        Else
            txtInput.Text = ""   'Clear the TextBox control

            'Display message if player fails to provide numeric input
            If chkVerbose.Checked = True Then
                txtOutPut.Text = "Sorry but you entered a " & _
                "non-numeric guess. Please try again and be " & _
                "sure to enter a number this time."
            Else
                txtOutPut.Text = "Numeric input required. Try again."
            End If
        End If

    Else
        txtInput.Text = ""   'Clear the TextBox control

        'Display error if player fails to provide input
        If chkVerbose.Checked = True Then
            txtOutPut.Text = "Sorry but to play you must enter a " & _
            "number. Please enter a number and try again."
        Else
            txtOutPut.Text = "No input provided. try again."
        End If
    End If

    txtInput.Focus()   'Set focus to the TextBox control

End Sub
```

As you can see, this procedure is rather long and contains the bulk of the application's programming logic. It begins by declaring two variables. The first variable is `intPlayerGuess` and is used to store and process the input provided by the player. A new value will be assigned to this variable each time the player clicks on the `Button` control labeled Check Guess. Therefore, it is declared as a local variable. However, the second variable, which is named intNoOfGuesses, is defined as a Static variable, making its lifetime last for as long as the game runs, so that it can be used to maintain a count of the number of guesses that the player makes during each game.

Next, an If…Then…Else block is set up that determines what statements in the procedure will execute based on whether or not the player entered any input. If no input was provided, an error message is displayed in the txtOutput control. Otherwise a second nested If…Then…Else block executes and checks to see if the input supplied by the player is numeric. If the input is not numeric, an error message is displayed in the txtOutput control. Otherwise, one of three nested If…Then blocks execute. The first If…Then block checks to see if the player won the game by guessing the secret number. The second If…Then block checks to see if the player's guess was too low, and the third If…Then block checks to see if the player's guess was too high.

If the player's guess was too high or too low, an error message is displayed in the txtOutput control. The message that is displayed depends on whether the chkVerbose control is checked. If the player guesses correctly, she wins the game and a congratulatory message is displayed in the txtOutput control. In addition, the following actions are taken to prepare the game for another play:

- The value of intNoOfGuesses is reset to zero.
- The value indicating the number of games won is incremented by adding 1 to the value stored in the txtGamesWon control's text property.
- The Check Guess button is disabled and the New Game button is enabled.
- The game's RadioButton controls are enabled, allowing the player to make changes to them if desired.
- The game's Reset Default button is also enabled.
- The message displayed in the game's StatusBar control is updated.

Last but not least, it is time to add some code to the btnNewgame control's Click event procedure, as shown below.

```
'This Sub procedure executes when the New Game button is clicked
Private Sub btnNewGame_Click(ByVal sender As System.Object, _
  ByVal e As System.EventArgs) Handles btnNewGame.Click

    GetRandomNumber()  'Call the GetRandomNumber procedure

    txtOutPut.Text = ""  'Clear the TextBox control
    txtInput.Text = ""   'Clear the TextBox control
```

```
btnNewGame.Enabled = False  'Enable the New Game button
btnCheckGuess.Enabled = True  'Disable the Check Guess button

txtInput.Enabled = True   'Enabled the TextBox control

'Disable all Radio buttons
rbnControl10.Enabled = False
rbnControl100.Enabled = False
rbnControl1000.Enabled = False

'Disable the two reset buttons
btnDefaults.Enabled = False
btnReset.Enabled = False

stbControl.Text = "Enter your guess."  'Display instructions

txtInput.Focus()  'Set focus to the TextBox control
```

End Sub

When clicked, the code for the button labeled New Game clears out any text display in the txtInput and txtOutput controls. Next, the btnNewGame control is disabled, and the btnCheckGuess control is enabled. Then the txtInput control is enabled in order to allow the player to enter a guess, and the game's RadioButton control and btnReset control are all disabled, preventing the player from making configuration changes while a new game is being played. Lastly, an instructional message is displayed on the game's StatusBar control, and the cursor is placed in the txtInput control.

Step 5: Testing the Execution of the Guess a Number Game

That's it. The Guess a Number game is ready to run. Press F5 and see how it works. If you have any errors, double-check your typing. Otherwise, pass it on to your friends and ask them to play and to report any problems back to you if they run into one.

SUMMARY

In this chapter, you learned how to apply conditional logic to your Visual Basic applications using variations of the If…Then statement and the Select Case statement. This included learning how to set up conditional tests to test for one or more possible outcomes and developing alternative execution flows in the event that the conditional tests proved false. In addition, you learned how to work with the GroupBox, RadioButton, CheckBox, and ComboBox controls.

Before you jump into Chapter 7, "Processing Lots of Data with Loops," and learn how to apply advanced looping logic to your Visual Basic applications, take a few extra moments to review the following challenges and see if you can improve the Guess a Number game.

CHALLENGES

1. Modify the Guess a Number game by providing better clues as the player's guesses begin to get closer to the secret number. For example, you might add text that tells the player when they are getting "warm," "warmer," and "hot."

2. Add logic to the game to display the average number of guesses that it takes the player to guess the secret number and display this information in the grpScore control (GroupBox).

3. Modify the Guess a Number game so that the game ends if the player has not guessed the secret number after a certain number of tries and display the number of games lost in the grpScore control (GroupBox). Also, display the secret number in the txtOutput control (TextBox) when the player loses a game.

PROCESSING LOTS OF DATA WITH LOOPS

As you have already seen in previous chapter projects, there are times when you need to create loops within your applications in order to repeatedly perform a number of steps. Loops are also essential for processing large amounts of data without requiring a large number of programming statements. Loops are a great option for processing the contents of arrays and controls, such as the ComboBox and ListBox, which store collections of data. In this chapter, you will learn how to use a number of Visual Basic statements to create different kinds of loops. In addition, you will get the chance to apply what you'll learn through the development of the chapter's game project, the Dice Poker game.

Specifically, you will learn how to:

- Create Do...While and Do...Until loops
- Create For...Next and For...Each...Next loops
- Create While loops
- Use variations of the Exit keyword to break out of loops
- Guard against endless loops

PROJECT PREVIEW: THE DICE POKER GAME

In this chapter's project, you will apply your new knowledge of iterative processing to the development of the Dice Poker game. In addition, you'll get your first taste of working with and controlling graphics by learning how to work with the `ImageList` and `PictureBox` controls.

Figures 7.1 through 7.6 show examples from the Dice Poker game, demonstrating its functionality and overall execution flow.

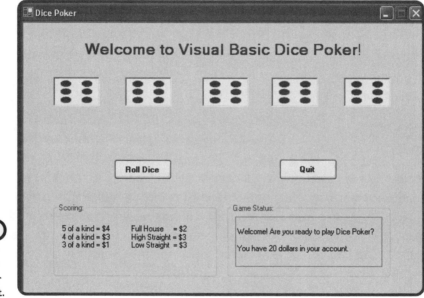

FIGURE 7.1

The Dice Poker game begins by giving the player $20 in an account.

Dice Poker

Welcome to Visual Basic Dice Poker!

☐ Keep ☑ Keep ☑ Keep ☐ Keep ☐ Keep

Roll Again   ☐ Keep All   **Quit**

Scoring:

5 of a kind = $4   Full House   = $2
4 of a kind = $3   High Straight = $3
3 of a kind = $1   Low Straight = $3

Game Status:

Welcome! Are you ready to play Dice Poker?

You have 20 dollars in your account.

FIGURE 7.2

Players can elect to hold onto specific dice before rolling the dice a second time.

Dice Poker

Welcome to Visual Basic Dice Poker!

Roll Dice   **Quit**

Scoring:

5 of a kind = $4   Full House   = $2
4 of a kind = $3   High Straight = $3
3 of a kind = $1   Low Straight = $3

Game Status:

Sorry, You lost this hand! You lose 2 dollars.

You have 18 dollars in your account.

FIGURE 7.3

Two dollars are deducted from the player's account for each losing hand.

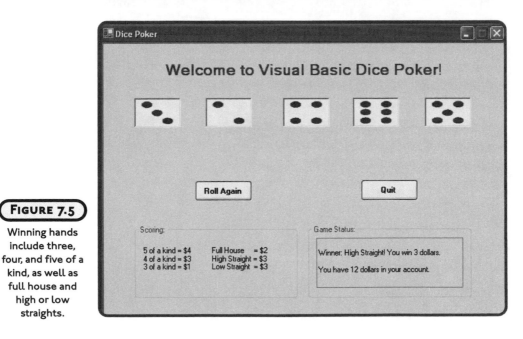

FIGURE 7.4

Winning hands are rewarded with additional credits to the player's account.

FIGURE 7.5

Winning hands include three, four, and five of a kind, as well as full house and high or low straights.

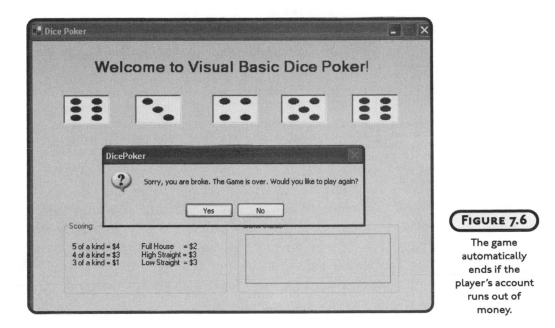

FIGURE 7.6

The game automatically ends if the player's account runs out of money.

By the time you have created and run this game, you'll have demonstrated your understanding of how to work with loops and will have received an introduction to working with graphics controls.

ITERATIVE PROCESSING

Loops provide programmers with the ability to do a lot of work with a little code. Thanks to loops, it is possible to process dozens, hundreds, or tens of thousands of elements using the same number of programming statements. Loops are especially adept at processing the contents of arrays and collections, such as the collection associated with the ListBox control. Loops can also be set up to drive any form or iterative logic, such as when you want to repeatedly prompt a user to supply additional information, or when you want to run a particular group of programming statements over and over again until a certain result is achieved.

Visual Basic provides you with a number of different ways to set up a loop, including:

- **Do...While.** Creates a loop that iterates as long as a condition remains true

- **Do...Until.** Creates a loop that iterates until a condition becomes true

DEFINITION

A loop is a group of programming statements that are executed repeatedly. Loops provide an effective tool for processing large amounts of data.

- **For…Next.** Creates a loop that iterates a specific number of times
- **For…Each…Next.** Creates a loop that iterates through every property belonging to an object, such as all the elements in an array or all the elements in a ListBox control
- **While.** Creates a loop that iterates as long as a condition remains true

Each of these different types of loops are discussed in greater detail in the sections that follow.

Do Loops

You can set up Do loops to iterate until or while a specific condition is true. Do loops are well suited to situations where you know in advance what specific condition must occur in order for the tested condition to become true. For example, you might set up a Do…Until or Do…While loop to allow a user to enter as much input as desired, terminating the loop's execution only when the user enters a trigger word such as "Quit" or "Exit."

Do…While

A Do…While loop iterates as long as a specified condition remains true. Visual Basic allows you to construct a Do…While loop in either of two formats. The syntax of the first format is shown below.

```
Do While condition
    statements
Loop
Dim intCounter As Integer = 0
Do While intCounter < 10
    intCounter += 1
Loop
```

DEFINITION

Condition represents an expression that is tested upon each iteration of the loop, as demonstrated in the following example.

In this example, an Integer type variable named intCounter is declared and then used to control the iteration of a Do…While loop. The loop iterates for as long as the value of int-Counter is less than 10. As you can see, the value of intCounter is increased by 1 at the end of each iteration, causing the loop to iterate 10 times.

However, if the value of intCounter had been set to a value greater than or equal to 10 at the beginning of the example, the loop would never have executed, because the While keyword and the tested expression have been placed on the same line as the Do keyword.

The syntax for the second format of the Do…While statement is shown below.

```
Do
    statements
Loop While condition
```

As you can see, the While keyword and the tested *condition* have been moved to the end of the loop and placed on the same line as the Loop keyword. The result is that the loop will always execute at least once, even if the tested condition is initially false.

To get a better feel for how to work with the Do…While loop, take a look at the following example.

```
Public Class Form1

    Private Sub Button1_Click(ByVal sender As System.Object, _
        ByVal e As System.EventArgs) Handles btnBooks.Click

        Dim strTitleAndAuthor As String = "", strInput As String = ""

        Do While strInput.ToLower <> "quit"
            strInput = InputBox("Enter a book title or type Quit to " & _
                "exit the application.", "Book Tracker")

            If strInput.ToLower <> "quit" Then
                strTitleAndAuthor = strTitleAndAuthor & strInput & _
                ControlChars.CrLf
            End If

        Loop

        MessageBox.Show(strTitleAndAuthor, "New Book Entries")

    End Sub

End Class
```

In this example, a Do…While loop was set up to collect names of books, using the InputBox() function. Each new book name is added to the end of a variable string, which is formatted so that it will display each book's title on its own line when later displayed. The loop has been set up to iterate until the user enters the word "Quit." Take note of the use of the ToLower method to translate the user's input to all lowercase letters when the example checks to see if the player entered the word "Quit." By converting the player's input to all lowercase like this, the example eliminates any concerns over the case the user might choose to use when typing in the word "Quit."

Figures 7.7 and 7.8 show the interaction between the above example and the user when executed.

FIGURE 7.7

Processing the names of books using a Do...While loop.

FIGURE 7.8

Displaying the information that was collected by the Do...While loop.

In this example, the first format of the Do...While loop was used. However, you could just as easily rewrite this example and move the While keyword and the tested expression to the end of the loop, as demonstrated below. Regardless, the results are the same.

```
Public Class Form1

    Private Sub Button1_Click(ByVal sender As System.Object, _
       ByVal e As System.EventArgs) Handles btnBooks.Click

        Dim strTitleAndAuthor As String = ""
        Dim strInput As String = ""
        Do

            strInput = InputBox("Enter a book title or type Quit to" & _
               "exit the application.", "Book Tracker")

            If strInput.ToLower <> "quit" Then
                strTitleAndAuthor = strTitleAndAuthor & strInput & -
                ControlChars.CrLf
```

```
        End If

    Loop While strInput.ToLower <> "quit"

    MessageBox.Show(strTitleAndAuthor, "New Book Entries")

    End Sub

End Class
```

Do...Until

The Do...Until loop iterates as long as a condition is false. In other words, it iterates until a condition becomes true. As with the Do...While loop, Visual Basic supports two different forms of the Do...Until loop. The syntax of the first format is shown below.

```
Do Until condition
    statements
Loop
```

To get a better feel for how the Do...Until loop works, take a look at the following example.

```
Public Class Form1

    Private Sub Button1_Click(ByVal sender As System.Object, _
        ByVal e As System.EventArgs) Handles Button1.Click

        Dim strPlayerInput As String = ""
        Dim blnStopGame As Boolean = False

        Do Until blnStopGame = True
            strPlayerInput = MessageBox.Show("Do you want to quit?", _
                "Continue?", MessageBoxButtons.YesNo, _
                MessageBoxIcon.Question)
            'Check to see if the user clicked on Yes when prompted to quit
            If Int32.Parse(strPlayerInput) = 6 Then
                blnStopGame = True
            Else
                MessageBox.Show("Oh, I see...")
```

```
        End If
    Loop

    Application.Exit()

    End Sub

End Class
```

In this example, a loop has been set up that requires the user to enter the word "Quit" in order to terminate the application. If the user enters the word "Quit," the application stops; otherwise, refusing to give up, this stubborn little example continues to prompt the user to type "Quit." Figures 7.9 and 7.10 demonstrate the interaction between the above example and the user when executed.

FIGURE 7.9

Using a Do...Until loop to prompt the player to terminate the game.

FIGURE 7.10

The game sarcastically responds to the player when he or she fails to enter the word "Quit."

The syntax for the second form of the Do...Until statement is outlined below.

```
Do
    statements
Loop Until condition
```

As you can see, the Until keyword and the condition to be tested have been placed on the third line just after the Loop keyword.

For...Next

The For...Next loop is an excellent choice when you know in advance how many times a loop will need to execute. The For...Next loop executes a specific number of times as determined by a counter, which can increase or decrease based on the logic you are implementing.

The syntax for the For...Next statement is shown below.

```
For counter [As DataType] = begin To end [Step StepValue]
    statements
Next
```

Counter is a variable that controls the execution of the loop. DataType is an optional parameter allowing you to define the loop's counter within the loop itself. If you choose not to supply the DataType here, you will still have to define it elsewhere in your application. Begin specifies the starting value of the counter variable, and end specifies its ending value. StepValue is optional. When supplied, StepValue specifies an increment value to be used by the For...Next statement when incrementing the value assigned to the counter variable. If you don't specify a value for StepValue, a value of 1 is assumed.

The following example, taken from Chapter 5, "Storing and Retrieving Data in Memory," demonstrates how to use a For...Next loop to iterate through the contents of an array.

```
Public Class Form1

    Private Sub Form1_Load(ByVal sender As System.Object, _
      ByVal e As System.EventArgs) Handles MyBase.Load

        Dim strMessage As String = ""
        Dim intCounter As Integer = 0

        Dim strCustomerNamesArray(4) As String

        strCustomerNamesArray(0) = "Markland B."
        strCustomerNamesArray(1) = "Mike M."
        strCustomerNamesArray(2) = "Nick C."
        strCustomerNamesArray(3) = "Jerry F."
        strCustomerNamesArray(4) = "Rocky B."
        For intCounter = 0 To 4
            strMessage &= strCustomerNamesArray(intCounter) & _
            ControlChars.NewLine
        Next intCounter
```

```
    MessageBox.Show(strMessage)

  End Sub

End Class
```

In this example, the For…Next loop is set up to iterate five times (from 0 to 4). Upon each iteration, the value assigned to intCounter is automatically incremented by 1. By plugging in the intCounter variable in place of a number (strCustomerNamesArray(intCounter)), a display string is assembled that shows all of the contents of the array.

It is important to understand that the value assigned to the StepValue can be something other than just 1. You could set it equal to 2 in the previous example to skip every other element stored in the array, or as the following example demonstrates, you could assign it a negative number in order to process the array in reverse order.

```
For intCounter = 4 To 0 Step -1
    strMessage &= strCustomerNamesArray(intCounter) & _
    ControlChars.NewLine
Next intCounter
```

You can also use the For…Next loop to work with Visual Basic controls that have collections, such as the ListBox control. The following example demonstrates how to use a For…Next loop to add elements to a ListBox control at run time.

TRICK

The first step in working with the ListBox control is to add an instance of the control from the ToolBox window to a form. Once added to a form, you can populate and access the contents of a ListBox using the methods and properties belonging to its Items property. The Items property is actually a collection and any items that you add to a ListBox are referenced by their index position within the Items collection. You can add items to a ListBox control using the Items collection's Add() method. You can then refer to any item in the Items collection using the Items collection's Items property.

DEFINITION

A *ListBox* is a control that displays a list of items from which a selection can be made.

```
Public Class frmMain

    Private Sub Button1_Click(ByVal sender As System.Object, _
        ByVal e As System.EventArgs) Handles Button1.Click

        Static intSheep As Integer = 0

        For intCounter As Integer = 0 To 9 Step 1
            intSheep += 1
            lbxNumbers.Items.Add(intSheep.ToString & " Sheep")
        Next

    End Sub

End Class
```

In this example, a Visual Basic application was created that consists of a Button control and a ListBox control. The application promises to help the user get to sleep by helping to count sheep, 10 at a time, whenever the user clicks on the Button control.

The For…Next loop in this example will iterate 10 times (0 to 9). Within the loop, the value of an Integer type variable named intSheep is incremented by 1, and the ListBox control's (lbxNumbers) Items property's (which itself is an object or collection) Add() method is used to load new items into the ListBox. Figure 7.11 shows output that is produced after this application is started and the user clicks on the button for the first time.

FIGURE 7.11

Using a For…Next loop to populate the contents of a ListBox.

 As is the case with this chapter's game project example, you will find a copy of the source code for the Sleep Aid application available for download on this book's companion Web site.

In addition to adding elements to a control's collection, you can use the For…Next loop to retrieve elements from a collection, as demonstrated in the next example.

```
Public Class Form1

    Private Sub Button2_Click(ByVal sender As System.Object, _
      ByVal e As System.EventArgs) Handles btnExit.Click

        Application.Exit()

    End Sub

    Private Sub Button1_Click(ByVal sender As System.Object, _
      ByVal e As System.EventArgs) Handles btnDisplay.Click

        Dim strMessage As String = ""
        Dim intCounter As Integer

        For intCounter = 1 To lbxCustomers.Items.Count - 1

            strMessage &= lbxCustomers.Items.Item(intCounter) & _
              ControlChars.CrLf
        Next

        MessageBox.Show("Customer List: " & ControlChars.CrLf & _
          ControlChars.CrLf & strMessage, "Customer Listing")

    End Sub

End Class
```

As you can see, this time, the For…Next loop uses the ListBox (lbxCustomers) control's Items collection's Item property to retrieve an element, using its index number from the ListBox control. Figures 7.12 and 7.13 demonstrate the operation of this application.

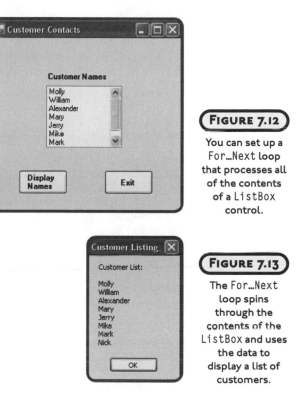

FIGURE 7.12

You can set up a For...Next loop that processes all of the contents of a ListBox control.

FIGURE 7.13

The For...Next loop spins through the contents of the ListBox and uses the data to display a list of customers.

 As is the case with this chapter's game project example, you will find a copy of the source code for the Customer Contacts application available for download on this book's companion Web site.

For...Each...Next

The For...Each...Next loop is perfect for processing the contents of arrays and collections when you don't know in advance the exact number of elements that are being stored. The For...Each...Next automatically iterates through each member and alleviates any concern regarding the tracking of index numbers.

The syntax of the For...Each...Next statement is shown below:

```
For Each element [As DataType] In collection
    statements
Next [element]
```

Element is a variable that represents a property (that is, a member) associated with the specified *collection*. The DataType parameter is optional. When used, it allows you to define the *element* variable's data type within the loop itself. If you choose not to supply the DataType parameter here, you still have to define it elsewhere in your application.

The following example demonstrates how to set up a For...Each...Next loop to process the contents of an array.

```
Public Class Form1

    Private Sub Form1_Load(ByVal sender As System.Object, _
    ByVal e As System.EventArgs) Handles MyBase.Load

        Dim strMessage As String = ""
        Dim strName As String = ""
        Dim strCustomerNamesArray(4) As String
        strCustomerNamesArray(0) = "Markland B."
        strCustomerNamesArray(1) = "Mike M."
        strCustomerNamesArray(2) = "Nick C."
        strCustomerNamesArray(3) = "Jerry F."
        strCustomerNamesArray(4) = "Rocky B."
        For Each strName In strCustomerNamesArray
            strMessage &= strName & ControlChars.NewLine
        Next strName

        MessageBox.Show(strMessage, "Customer Contact Names")

    End Sub

End Class
```

As you can see from this example, the For...Each...Next loop automatically iterates through each element in the array without requiring the use of a counter or any additional logic. Figure 7.14 shows the output that is generated when this example is executed.

FIGURE 7.14

Using a For...Each...Next loop to process the contents of an array.

While

One last type of loop that I want to introduce you to is the `While` loop. The `While` loop is designed to run as long as a stated condition is true. The `While` loop has the following syntax.

```
While condition

    statements
End While
```

Condition is expressed in the form of an expression, as demonstrated below.

```
Dim strUserResponse As String, blnTerminateFlag As Boolean = False

While blnTerminateFlag = False
    strUserResponse = InputBox("Enter Quit to stop the application.")
    If strUserResponse.ToLower = "quit" Then
        blnTerminateFlag = True
    Else
        MessageBox.Show("The current date and time is " & Now())
    End If
End While
```

In this example, the user is prompted to enter the word "Quit" in order to stop the application from continuing to execute. If the user enters anything other than the word "Quit," or if the user clicks on the pop-up window's `Cancel` button, the `While` loop displays the current date and time and then iterates and continues prompting the user to enter the word "Quit."

The previous example demonstrates that the `While` loop requires its tested condition to be checked at the beginning of the loop. Although useful, the `While` loop is not as flexible as the `Do…While` and `Do…Until` loops, which can test a condition before or after initial loop execution and provide the same capabilities as the `While` loop.

ENDLESS LOOPS

One of the concerns to be aware of when working with loops is an endless loop. Endless loops occur when you apply faulty logic in the creation of a loop that results in the loop running forever (or until you forcefully terminate your application).

DEFINITION

An *endless* loop is a loop that has no means for terminating, causing the loop to run forever and draining computer resources.

TRICK If, while testing the execution of your Visual Basic application during development, you think you may have an endless loop, you can stop the program from running by opening the Debug menu and clicking on the Stop Debug menu item.

If you are running a compiled Visual Basic application from the Windows desktop and you think it may be caught in an endless loop, you can forcefully terminate its execution by pressing the Ctrl + Alt + Delete keys simultaneously. This opens the Task Manager window, from which you can then select your application and click on the End Task button.

The following example demonstrates how easy it is to accidentally set up an endless loop.

```
Dim intCounter As Integer = 0
Do While intCounter < 5
  intCounter = intCounter - 1
  MessageBox.Show(intCounter)
Loop
```

In this example, a Do…While loop is set up to iterate as long as the value of intCounter is less than 5. However, instead of incrementing the value of intCounter by 1 upon each iteration of the loop, I accidentally decremented the value of intCounter by -1. As a result, the value of intCount will never reach 5 and the loop will never terminate on its own. The lesson here is to always double-check the way that you have set up your loops and to test your applications thoroughly so that if you do accidentally introduce a situation where an endless loop can occur, you'll catch it.

BREAKING OUT OF LOOPS

Sometimes you may find situations in which you will want to break out of a loop before it finishes processing, based on some condition that occurs. To deal with this type of situation, you can use either of two types of Exit statements to force an immediate termination of a loop. Once executed, the Exit statement transfers control to the next statement following the loop within the application.

Exit For

You can use the Exit statement to break out of any For…Next or For…Each…Next loop. The syntax for this form of the Exit statement is shown below.

```
Exit For
```

The following example demonstrates how to use the Exit For statement to break out of the processing of a loop.

```
Private Sub Form1_Load(ByVal sender As System.Object, _
      ByVal e As System.EventArgs) Handles MyBase.Load


      Dim intCounter As Integer
      Dim strResponce As String
      Dim UserArray(4) As String


      For intCounter = 0 To 4
          strResponce = InputBox("Enter a name or type Quit to exit.")
          If strResponce.ToLower = "quit" Then
              MessageBox.Show("Data collection has been terminated.")
              Exit For
          End If
          UserArray(intCounter) = strResponce
      Next


End Sub
```

In this example, a For…Next loop has been set up to collect five names that the user supplies by entering them into a pop-up window generated by an InputBox() function. However, if at any point during the collection process the user decides to enter the word "Quit," the Exit For statement executes and terminates the data collection process.

Exit Do

You can also use the Exit statement to break out of any Do…Until or Do…While loop. The syntax for this form of the Exit statement is shown below.

```
Exit Do
```

The following example demonstrates how to use the Exit Do statement to break out of the processing of a loop.

```
Private Sub Form1_Load(ByVal sender As System.Object, _
    ByVal e As System.EventArgs) Handles MyBase.Load


    Dim intCounter As Integer = 0
    Dim intOverFlow As Integer = 50
    Dim strResponce As String = ""
    Dim blnTerminate As Boolean = False
    Dim UserArray(49) As String
```

```
Do Until blnTerminate = True

    strResponce = InputBox("Enter a name or type Quit to exit.")
    If strResponce.ToLower = "quit" Then
        MessageBox.Show("Data collection has been terminated.")
        blnTerminate = True
    Else
        UserArray(intCounter) = strResponce
        intCounter += 1
        If intCounter = intOverFlow Then
            MessageBox.Show("Error: Array overflow, max size = 50")
            Exit Do
        End If
    End If

Loop

End Sub
```

BACK TO THE DICE POKER GAME

It is time to turn your attention back to the development of this chapter's game project, the Dice Poker game. You will create this game by following the five basic development steps that you've used to create all the previous chapter projects.

Designing the Game

The Dice Poker game is played on a single window and is made up of one form and the 20 controls listed in Table 7.1.

TABLE 7.1: FORM CONTROLS FOR THE DICE POKER GAME

Control Type	Control Name	Description
Label	lblWelcome	Displays the game's welcome message
PictureBox	pbxDie1	Displays the image for the first die
PictureBox	pbxDie2	Displays the image for the second die
PictureBox	pbxDie3	Displays the image for the third die
PictureBox	pbxDie4	Displays the image for the fourth die
PictureBox	pbxDie5	Displays the image for the fifth die
CheckBox	chkDie1	Determines whether the first die should be held at the end of the first roll
CheckBox	chkDie2	Determines whether the second die should be held at the end of the first roll
CheckBox	chkDie3	Determines whether the third die should be held at the end of the first roll
CheckBox	chkDie4	Determines whether the fourth die should be held at the end of the first roll
CheckBox	chkDie5	Determines whether the fifth die should be held at the end of the first roll
CheckBox	chkKeepAll	Determines whether the CheckBox controls representing all five dice should be checked
Button	btnRollDice	Controls the logic that rolls the dice for the game
Button	btnExit	Controls the termination of the game
GroupBox	grpScoring	Provides a container for storing the Label control that displays the game's scoring rules
GroupBox	grpOutput	Provides a container for storing the TextBox control that displays the output messages
Label	lblLegend	Displays the game's scoring rules
TextBox	txtOutput	Displays status messages during the game's execution
Imagelist	imlDiceList	Stores a list of bitmap images representing each of the six sides of a die
Timer	tmrRoll	Controls the logic that spins each of the game's five dice

Step 1: Creating a New Visual Basic Project

The first step in creating the Dice Poker game is to open up Visual Basic and create a new project, as outlined below.

1. If you have not already done so, start up Visual Basic 2005 Express and then click on File and select New Project. The New Project dialog will appear.

2. Select the Windows Application template.

3. Type Dice Poker as the name of your new application in the Name field located at the bottom of the New Project window.

4. Click on OK to close the New Project dialog.

Visual Basic will create a new project for you and display a new form upon which you will design the game's user interface.

Step 2: Creating the User Interface

The first step in laying out the user interface is to add controls to the form and move and resize them to the appropriate locations. As you go through each step, make sure that you reference Figure 7.15 so that you'll know where each control needs to be placed and what size it needs to be.

1. Begin by resizing form1 until it is about 7.25 inches wide and 5.5 inches tall.

2. Next, add a Label control near the top of the form. You'll use this control to display the game's welcome message.

3. Add five PictureBox controls to the form and space them out evenly just under the Label control.

4. Add six CheckBox controls to the form. Place each of the first five controls under one of the five PictureBox controls. Place the sixth CheckBox control in the middle of the form about .5 inch below the third Checkbox control.

5. Add two Button controls, one on each side of the sixth CheckBox control.

6. Next, add two GroupBox controls under the two Button controls and enlarge and resize each GroupBox control until they take up most of the space at the bottom of the form.

> ### DEFINITION
>
> A PictureBox control provides the ability to display a graphical image on a Visual Basic form. A PictureBox control can display graphic files stored in any of the following formats: .gif, .jpg, .jpeg, .bmp, .wmf, and .png.

FIGURE 7.15

Completing the interface design for the Dice Poker game.

7. The first GroupBox control displays a text string showing the player how winning hands are scored. Therefore, you need to add a Label inside the first GroupBox control.

8. The second GroupBox control displays informational messages that identify winning and losing hands and tells the player how many dollars are in the account. To display this text, you need to add a TextBox control inside the second GroupBox control. Set the Multiline property for the TextBox control equal to True and resize it until it almost fills the GroupBox control.

9. In order to control the rolls of each die, you need to add a Timer control to your application. Once added, the Timer control is displayed in a component tray.

10. Finally, you need to add an ImageList control to your application. Once added, the ImageList control is also displayed in the component tray.

DEFINITION

An *ImageList* control is used to store images, which can then be displayed by other controls, such as the PictureBox control.

At this point, the overall layout of the Dice Poker game's user interface is now complete and you can begin modifying form and control properties.

Step 3: Customizing Form and Control Properties

Let's begin by making the required changes to properties belonging to the form object as listed in Table 7.2.

TABLE 7.2: PROPERTY CHANGES FOR FORM1

Property	Value
Name	frmMain
Cursor	Hand
FormBorderStyle	Fixed3D
MaximizeBox	False
StartPosition	CenterScreen
Text	**Dice Poker**

Make the property changes shown in Table 7.3 to the Label controls.

TABLE 7.3: PROPERTY CHANGES FOR LABEL CONTROLS

Control	Property	Value
Label1	Name	lblWelcome
	ForeColor	Blue
	Font.Bold	True
	Font.Size	16
	Text	**Welcome to Visual Basic Dice Poker!**
Label2	Name	lblLegend
	Text	**5 of a kind = $4 Full House = $2**
		4 of a kind = $3 High Straight = $3
		3 of a kind = $1 Low Straight = $3

Make the property changes shown in Table 7.4 to the PictureBox controls.

TABLE 7.4: PROPERTY CHANGES FOR PICTUREBOX CONTROLS

Control	Property	Value
PictureBox1	Name	pbxDie1
	BorderStyle	Fixed3D
	Size Mode	StretchImage
PictureBox2	Name	pbxDie2
	BorderStyle	Fixed3D
	Size Mode	StretchImage
PictureBox3	Name	pbxDie3
	BorderStyle	Fixed3D
	Size Mode	StretchImage
PictureBox4	Name	pbxDie4
	BorderStyle	Fixed3D
	Size Mode	StretchImage
PictureBox5	Name	pbxDie5
	BorderStyle	Fixed3D
	Size Mode	StretchImage

Make the property changes shown in Table 7.5 to the CheckBox controls.

Control	Property	Value
TABLE 7.5: PROPERTY CHANGES FOR CHECKBOX CONTROLS		
CheckBox1	Name	chkDie1
	Text	Keep
	Visible	False
CheckBox2	Name	chkDie2
	Text	Keep
	Visible	False
CheckBox3	Name	chkDie3
	Text	Keep
	Visible	False
CheckBox4	Name	chkDie4
	Text	Keep
	Visible	False
CheckBox5	Name	chkDie5
	Text	Keep
	Visible	False
CheckBox6	Name	ChkKeepAll
	Text	Keep All
	Visible	False

Make the property changes shown in Table 7.6 to the Button controls.

Control	Property	Value
TABLE 7.6: PROPERTY CHANGES FOR BUTTON CONTROLS		
Control	Property	Value
Button1	Name	btnRollDice
	Font.Bold	True
	Text	Roll Dice
Button2	Name	btnExit
	Text	Quit
	Font.Bold	True

Make the property changes shown in Table 7.7 to the GroupBox controls.

Control	Property	Value
TABLE 7.7: PROPERTY CHANGES FOR GROUPBOX CONTROLS		
Control	Property	Value
GroupBox1	Name	grpScoring
	Text	Scoring:
GroupBox2	Name	grpOutput
	Text	Game Status:

Make the property changes shown in Table 7.8 to the TextBox control.

Property	Value
TABLE 7.8: PROPERTY CHANGES FOR TEXTBOX CONTROL	
Property	Value
Name	txtOutput
ReadOnly	True

Now, change the Name property for the Timer control to tmrRoll, and change the Name property of the ImageList control to imlDiceList. Change the ImageList control's ImageSize property to 48, 48. At this point, all that remains is to load the images representing each side of a die into the ImageList control's Images property (Collection) as outlined in Table 7.9. You'll find copies of each of the bitmap image files along with the source code for this chapter's game project at this book's companion Web site. The dice images were created using Microsoft Paint and saved as 24-bit color images.

Once you have loaded all of the application's bitmap images into the ImageList control, you'll be able to programmatically reference those images as demonstrated below.

```
PbxDie1.Image = imlDiceList.Images(3)
```

In this example, the fourth bitmap images stored in the ImageList control named imlDiceList is loaded into a PictureBox control named pbxDie1 using the PictureBox control's Image property.

TABLE 7.9: BITMAP IMAGES TO ADD TO THE IMAGELIST CONTROL'S IMAGES COLLECTION

Property	File	Index No.
Name	1.bmp	1
Name	2.bmp	2
Name	3.bmp	3
Name	4.bmp	4
Name	5.bmp	5
Name	6.bmp	6

You don't have to worry about packaging and distributing the six bitmap images of the game's dice. When you add the .bmp files to the Images property of the ImageList control, Visual Basic automatically saves copies of the bitmap files inside your application's binary file.

Step 4: Adding a Little Programming Logic

The first task to perform in putting together the program code for the Dice Poker game is to define class (or module) level constants and variables, as shown below.

```
'Declare constants and variables used throughout the application

'Controls the amount of time that it takes for the dice to roll
Private Const cintRollPeriod As Integer = 5

'Stores titlebar message
Private Const cTitleBarMsg As String = "DicePoker"

'Used to control display of Checkbox controls
Private blnExcludeList As Boolean
'Number of dollars in player's account
Private intTotalDollars As Integer = 20
Private intNoOfRolls As Integer   'Tracks the number of die rolls
Private intCounter As Integer   'Counter variable
Private intDice1 As Integer   'Number 1 die
Private intDice2 As Integer   'Number 2 die
Private intDice3 As Integer   'Number 3 die
Private intDice4 As Integer   'Number 4 die
Private intDice5 As Integer   'Number 5 die
```

Next, access the Load event procedure for the form and add the statements shown below.

```
'Load blank images at form load and display welcome message
Private Sub Form1_Load(ByVal sender As System.Object, _
   ByVal e As System.EventArgs) Handles MyBase.Load

    pbxDie1.Image = imlDiceList.Images(5)
    pbxDie2.Image = imlDiceList.Images(5)
    pbxDie3.Image = imlDiceList.Images(5)
    pbxDie4.Image = imlDiceList.Images(5)
    pbxDie5.Image = imlDiceList.Images(5)

    'Display greeting & the number of dollars in the player's account

    txtOutput.Text = ControlChars.CrLf & "Welcome! Are you ready " & _
```

```
"to play Dice Poker?" & ControlChars.CrLf & _
ControlChars.CrLf & "You have " & intTotalDollars & _
" dollars in your account."
```

End Sub

The first five statements load the image of the number 6 side of a die into the five PictureBox controls. The next statement displays a welcome message in the TextBox control and tells the player how many dollars are in the account.

Next, modify the Click event procedure for the form's first Button control, as shown below.

```
'This Sub procedure manages the first and second rolls of the die
Private Sub Button1_Click(ByVal sender As System.Object, _
  ByVal e As System.EventArgs) Handles btnRollDice.Click

    If intNoOfRolls = 2 Then   'See if the die have been rolled twice
        btnRollDice.Text = "Roll Dice"  'Change button's display text
        intNoOfRolls = 0   'Reset to 0 to get game ready for new hand
    End If

    'If the first roll has been made toggle the display of the
    'CheckBox control and keep track of the number of rolls
    If btnRollDice.Text = "Roll Dice" Then
        blnExcludeList = False
        intNoOfRolls += 1
    Else
        blnExcludeList = True
        intNoOfRolls += 1
    End If

    tmrRoll.Enabled = True   'Start the Timer control

End Sub
```

These statements use an Integer type variable named intNoOfRolls to keep track of whether the player is about to make the first or second roll. If the value of intNoOfRolls is equal to 2, then the text string "Roll Dice" is displayed on the first Button control and the value of int-NoOfRolls is reset back to 0. The following If…Else statement checks to see whether a Boolean type variable named blnExcludeList should be set to True or False based on the text displayed on the first Button control and increments the value of intNoOfRolls by 1. The btnExcludeList variable is used later in the application to determine whether or not to display the CheckBox controls that allow the player to hold on to dice before making the second roll. The last statement begins the dice rolling process by enabling the Timer control (tmrRoll).

Next, create the following subroutine procedure as shown below. Visual Basic won't create this procedure for you. You have to create this procedure from scratch.

```
'This Sub procedure controls the rolling of the die
Private Sub RollTheDice(ByVal x As Integer)
    'Stores randomly generated number representing the role of a die
    Dim intRoll As Integer
    'These variables are used to track which die the player chooses
    'to hold onto over his/her first roll
    Dim blnSkipCase1 As Boolean = False
    Dim blnSkipCase2 As Boolean = False
    Dim blnSkipCase3 As Boolean = False
    Dim blnSkipCase4 As Boolean = False
    Dim blnSkipCase5 As Boolean = False
    If blnExcludeList = True Then   'Flag die the player wants to hold
        If chkDie1.Checked = True Then blnSkipCase1 = True
        If chkDie2.Checked = True Then blnSkipCase2 = True
        If chkDie3.Checked = True Then blnSkipCase3 = True
        If chkDie4.Checked = True Then blnSkipCase4 = True
        If chkDie5.Checked = True Then blnSkipCase5 = True
    End If

    Randomize()  'Ensure a random number is generated
        intRoll = Int(Rnd() * 6) + 1  'Simulate a 6-sided die

    'Test the random value to determine what graphic to display
    Select Case intRoll

        Case 1 'Update image for the first die as it spins
            If blnSkipCase1 = False Then 'Player elected not to hold
```

```
            If x = 1 Then pbxDie1.Image = imlDiceList.Images(0)
            If x = 2 Then pbxDie1.Image = imlDiceList.Images(1)
            If x = 3 Then pbxDie1.Image = imlDiceList.Images(2)
            If x = 4 Then pbxDie1.Image = imlDiceList.Images(3)
            If x = 5 Then pbxDie1.Image = imlDiceList.Images(4)
            If x = 6 Then pbxDie1.Image = imlDiceList.Images(5)
            intDice1 = x
        End If

    Case 2 'Update image for the second die as it spins
        If blnSkipCase2 = False Then 'Player elected not to hold
            If x = 1 Then pbxDie2.Image = imlDiceList.Images(0)
            If x = 2 Then pbxDie2.Image = imlDiceList.Images(1)
            If x = 3 Then pbxDie2.Image = imlDiceList.Images(2)
            If x = 4 Then pbxDie2.Image = imlDiceList.Images(3)
            If x = 5 Then pbxDie2.Image = imlDiceList.Images(4)
            If x = 6 Then pbxDie2.Image = imlDiceList.Images(5)
            intDice2 = x
        End If

    Case 3 'Update image for the third die as it spins
        If blnSkipCase3 = False Then 'Player elected not to hold
            If x = 1 Then pbxDie3.Image = imlDiceList.Images(0)
            If x = 2 Then pbxDie3.Image = imlDiceList.Images(1)
            If x = 3 Then pbxDie3.Image = imlDiceList.Images(2)
            If x = 4 Then pbxDie3.Image = imlDiceList.Images(3)
            If x = 5 Then pbxDie3.Image = imlDiceList.Images(4)
            If x = 6 Then pbxDie3.Image = imlDiceList.Images(5)
            intDice3 = x
        End If

    Case 4 'Update image for the fourth die as it spins
        If blnSkipCase4 = False Then 'Player elected not to hold
            If x = 1 Then pbxDie4.Image = imlDiceList.Images(0)
            If x = 2 Then pbxDie4.Image = imlDiceList.Images(1)
            If x = 3 Then pbxDie4.Image = imlDiceList.Images(2)
            If x = 4 Then pbxDie4.Image = imlDiceList.Images(3)
            If x = 5 Then pbxDie4.Image = imlDiceList.Images(4)
```

```
            If x = 6 Then pbxDie4.Image = imlDiceList.Images(5)
            intDice4 = x
        End If

    Case 5 'Update image for the fifth die as it spins
        If blnSkipCase5 = False Then 'Player elected not to hold
            If x = 1 Then pbxDie5.Image = imlDiceList.Images(0)
            If x = 2 Then pbxDie5.Image = imlDiceList.Images(1)
            If x = 3 Then pbxDie5.Image = imlDiceList.Images(2)
            If x = 4 Then pbxDie5.Image = imlDiceList.Images(3)
            If x = 5 Then pbxDie5.Image = imlDiceList.Images(4)
            If x = 6 Then pbxDie5.Image = imlDiceList.Images(5)
            intDice5 = x
        End If

    End Select

End Sub
```

Note that when this procedure is called, it is passed a variable identifying which die (1 through 6) is being rolled, which it stores in a variable of its own named x. The procedure begins by defining local variables needed for the procedure's execution.

An If…Then statement that contains five embedded If…Then statements is then executed. All of these statements execute only if the value assigned to blnExcludeList is equal to True, indicating that the player has already taken the first roll. Each of the nested If…Then statements checks to see if the player has elected to hold on to any of the dice from the first roll (by selecting the CheckBox control for the associated die).

Next, the Randomize() function is executed, and a random number with a value between 1 and 6 is created and assigned to a variable named intRoll. A Select Case block is then used to associate the randomly generated number to the die passed to the procedure (represented by the variable named x). For example, if the randomly generated number is 2, then the program statements associated with Case 2 are executed. Then, if the value passed to the procedure is 3, indicating that the roll is for the third die, the third embedded If…Then statement executes and assigns the image of the number 2 die to the third PictureBox control.

Next, access the Tick event procedure for the Timer1 control and modify it as shown below.

```vbnet
'This Sub procedure controls the overall execution of the game
Private Sub Timer1_Tick(ByVal sender As System.Object, _
  ByVal e As System.EventArgs) Handles tmrRoll.Tick


    Dim I As Integer 'Declare variable used to control loop

    'Loop six times calling RollTheDice() upon each iteration
    For I = 1 To 6
        RollTheDice(I)
    Next

    intCounter += 1  'Increment counter by one

    'Disable timer & display CheckBox controls at the end of each roll
    If intCounter > cintRollPeriod Then
        intCounter = 0   'Reset counter
        tmrRoll.Enabled = False  'Disable timer control
        If intNoOfRolls = 1 Then   'Prepare game for second roll
            btnRollDice.Text = "Roll Again"
            chkDie1.Visible = True  'Enable Checkbox controls
            chkDie2.Visible = True
            chkDie3.Visible = True
            chkDie4.Visible = True
            chkDie5.Visible = True
            chkKeepAll.Visible = True
        End If

        If intNoOfRolls = 2 Then   'Prepare game for a new hand
            btnRollDice.Text = "Roll Dice"
            chkDie1.Checked = False  'Disable CheckBox controls
            chkDie2.Checked = False
            chkDie3.Checked = False
            chkDie4.Checked = False
            chkDie5.Checked = False
            chkKeepAll.Visible = False
            chkDie1.Visible = False  'Hide CheckBox controls
            chkDie2.Visible = False
```

```
            chkDie3.Visible = False
            chkDie4.Visible = False
            chkDie5.Visible = False
            chkKeepAll.Checked = False


        TotalTheScore() 'Call procedure that keeps track of score

        'Call procedure that displays the player's account status
        UpdateAccountStatus()

        If intTotalDollars <= 0 Then   'See if player has gone broke
              EndOfGame()   'Call procedure to see if game is over
        End If

      End If

    End IF

End Sub
```

This procedure begins by declaring a variable that will be used to control the execution of a For…Next loop. The loop iterates 6 times, calling the RollTheDice procedure and passing the procedure a number (e.g. I) representing one of the sides of the die. Next, the value assigned to the intCounter variable, which is used to control how long the Timer control is enabled, is incremented by 1.

An If…Then block is then executed in order to determine whether it's time to disable the Timer control. In addition, 2 embedded If…Then blocks execute, based on whether the player has made his or her first roll, enabling or disabling the display of the CheckBox controls.

Next the procedure calls on the TotalTheScore and UpdateAccountStatus procedures before checking the number of dollars in the player's account in order to determine whether the EndOfGame procedure should be called.

The next procedure that you'll work on is the TotalTheScore procedure. This is another procedure that you will have to create from scratch, as shown below.

```
'This Sub procedure keeps track of the player's score
Private Sub TotalTheScore()
```

```vb
'Declare array to be used to keep count of number in each hand
Dim intDieArray(6) As Integer

'Declare variable used to control loop execution
Dim intCounter As Integer = 1

'Iterate six times and keep count of the total number of
'1s, 2s, 3s, 4s, 5s and 6s that have been rolled
For intCounter = 1 To 6
    If intDice1 = intCounter Then intDieArray(intCounter) += 1
    If intDice2 = intCounter Then intDieArray(intCounter) += 1
    If intDice3 = intCounter Then intDieArray(intCounter) += 1
    If intDice4 = intCounter Then intDieArray(intCounter) += 1
    If intDice5 = intCounter Then intDieArray(intCounter) += 1
Next

'Iterate six times looking for winning hands
For intCounter = 1 To 6

    'See if the player has 5 of a kind
    If intDieArray(intCounter) = 5 Then
        intTotalDollars += 4  'Update player's account
        txtOutput.Text = ControlChars.CrLf & "Winner: 5 of " & _
          "a kind! You win 4 dollars."
        Return
    End If

    'See if the player has 4 of a kind
    If intDieArray(intCounter) = 4 Then
        intTotalDollars += 3  'Update player's account
        txtOutput.Text = ControlChars.CrLf & "Winner: 4 of " & _
          "a kind! You win 3 dollars."
        Return
    End If

    'See if the player has 3 of a kind or a full house
    If intDieArray(intCounter) = 3 Then 'Player has 3 of a kind
        Dim intCounter2 As Integer = 1
```

```
          For intCounter2 = 1 To 6 'See if player has a full house
              If intDieArray(intCounter2) = 2 Then
                  intTotalDollars += 2  'Update player's account
                txtOutput.Text = ControlChars.CrLf & "Winner:" & _
                    " Full house!  You win 2 dollars."
                  Return
              End If
          Next
          intTotalDollars += 1  'Update player's account
          txtOutput.Text = ControlChars.CrLf & "Winner: 3 of a " & _
            "kind! You win 1 dollar."
          Return
      End If

Next

'Iterate through die 2 - 6 looking for a High Straight
For intCounter = 2 To 6
    If intDieArray(intCounter) <> 1 Then
        Exit For  'No need to keep looking any further
    Else
        If intCounter = 6 Then
            intTotalDollars += 3  'Update player's account
            txtOutput.Text = ControlChars.CrLf & "Winner: " & _
                "High Straight! You win 3 dollars."
            Return
        End If
    End If
Next

'Iterate through die 1 - 5 looking for a Low Straight
For intCounter = 1 To 5
    If intDieArray(intCounter) <> 1 Then
        Exit For  'No need to keep looking any further
    Else
        If intCounter = 5 Then
            intTotalDollars += 3  'Update player's account
            txtOutput.Text = ControlChars.CrLf & "Winner: Low" & _
```

```
                      " Straight! You win 3 dollars."
                 Return
             End If
         End If
     Next

     intTotalDollars -= 2  'Update player's account
     txtOutput.Text = ControlChars.CrLf & "Sorry, You lost this " & _
       "hand! You lose 2 dollars."

End Sub
   End If
```

This procedure begins by defining an array that will be used to store the total number of 1s, 2s, 3s, 4s, 5s, and 6s in the player's hand. Then a local variable named intCounter is set up for use as a counter in the For...Next statement that follows. The For...Next loop iterates 6 times incrementing the appropriate array index value for each dice roll.

Next, another For...Next loop executes a series of embedded If...Then statements. The first If...Then code block checks to see if the player's hand is 5 of a kind by examining the value stored in each element of the intDieArray. The second If...Then code block looks for 4 of a kind and the third If...Then block first looks for 3 of a kind. If he or she does have 3 of a kind a second For...Next loop is executed to see if the player has a full house.

TRICK If you look closely at the code in the TotalTheScore procedure you'll see that even though the intDieArray has 6 elements, the procedure does not store any data in the first element of the array. I did this in order to simplify things by pairing up the index position 1 in the array with the die value of 1, the index position of 2 in the array with the die value of 2 and so on. Then, when I set up the procedure's For...Next loops, I made sure that I specified the correct starting and ending index numbers, so that the loops never processed the array's first index value (e.g. intDieArray(0)).

If the player does not have 3, 4 or 5 of a kind, the procedure checks to see if he or she has a High Straight (e.g. 2 – 6) using another For...Next loop to iterate through each of the values stored in the intDieArray. Next, if the player does not have a High Straight, another For...Next loop is set up to look for a Low Straight. Finally, if the player doesn't have a winning hand, 2 dollars are subtracted from his or her account. The logic used to develop this portion of code is fairly involved. To help make it easier to follow along, I have provided the flowchart shown in Figure 7.16, which shows the overall logical flow involved in analyzing the player's hand.

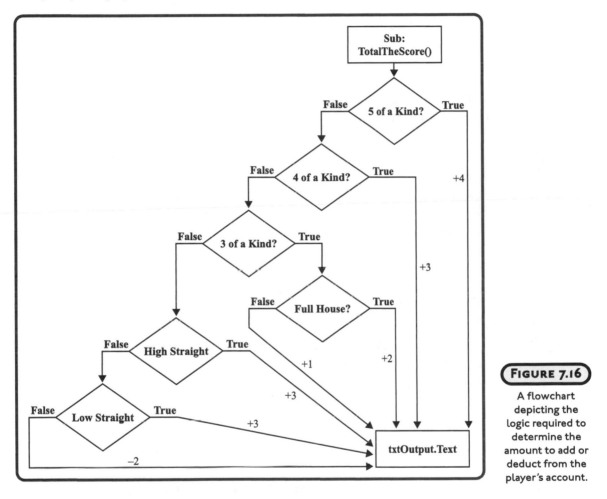

FIGURE 7.16

A flowchart depicting the logic required to determine the amount to add or deduct from the player's account.

The next procedure that you'll work on is the EndOfGame procedure. You'll have to create this procedure from scratch, as shown below.

```
'This Sub procedure prompts the player to play another hand and
'controls game termination
Private Sub EndOfGame()

    'Declare variable used to hold player response
```

```
Dim intPlayAgain As Integer

txtOutput.Text = ""  'Clear out any status messages

'Prompt player to try again
intPlayAgain = MessageBox.Show("Sorry, you are " & _
   "broke. The Game is over. Would you like to " & _
   "play again?", cTitleBarMsg, _
   MessageBoxButtons.YesNo, MessageBoxIcon.Question, _
   MessageBoxDefaultButton.Button1)

'If player clicks on Yes set up a new game
If intPlayAgain = 6 Then
    intTotalDollars = 20  'Reset the player's bank account
    pbxDie1.Image = imlDiceList.Images(5) 'Load blank images
    pbxDie2.Image = imlDiceList.Images(5)
    pbxDie3.Image = imlDiceList.Images(5)
    pbxDie4.Image = imlDiceList.Images(5)
    pbxDie5.Image = imlDiceList.Images(5)
    txtOutput.Text = ControlChars.CrLf & "Welcome! Are you " & _
       "ready to play Dice Poker?" & ControlChars.CrLf & _
       ControlChars.CrLf & "You have " & intTotalDollars & _
       " dollars in your account."
Else 'If player clicks on No end the game
    Application.Exit()
End If

End Sub
```

This procedure begins by declaring a variable used to hold the player's response when asked to play a new game. The player is prompted to play again using the MessageBox.Show method. If the player clicks on Yes, his or her bank account is reset to 20 dollars and an image of a blank die is loaded into each of the PictureBox controls. If the player clicks on No, the game is terminated.

The next procedure that you'll work on is the UpdateAccountStatus procedure which you will have to create from scratch, as shown below.

```
'This Sub procedure updates the display of the player's account status
Private Sub UpdateAccountStatus()

    txtOutput.Text &= ControlChars.CrLf & ControlChars.CrLf & _
        "You have " & intTotalDollars & " dollars in your account."

End Sub
```

This procedure is called from the Timer1_Tick procedure to append a string of text, showing the player's account balance, to the text displayed in the txtOutput TextBox control.

Next, access the Click event procedure for the game's Exit button and modify it as shown below.

```
Private Sub btnExit_Click(ByVal sender As System.Object, _
  ByVal e As System.EventArgs) Handles btnExit.Click

    Application.Exit()

End Sub
```

Lastly, access the CheckedChange event procedure for the chkKeepAll CheckBox control and modify it as shown below.

```
'This Sub procedure executes when the player selects the CheckBox
'control labeled KeepAll
Private Sub chkKeepAll_CheckedChanged(ByVal sender _
  As System.Object, ByVal e As System.EventArgs) _
  Handles chkKeepAll.CheckedChanged

    'If the player selects the CheckBox labeled KeepAll, select
    'the other CheckBox controls
    If chkKeepAll.Checked = True Then
        btnRollDice.Text = "Stick"
        chkDie1.Checked = True
        chkDie2.Checked = True
        chkDie3.Checked = True
        chkDie4.Checked = True
        chkDie5.Checked = True
    Else
```

```
'If the player clears the CheckBox labeled KeepAll, clear the
'other CheckBox controls
     btnRollDice.Text = "Roll Again"
     chkDie1.Checked = False
     chkDie2.Checked = False
     chkDie3.Checked = False
     chkDie4.Checked = False
     chkDie5.Checked = False
  End If

End Sub
```

This procedure provides the player with the ability to elect to hold on to all of the dice from the first roll, which makes sense in situations when the player gets a high or low straight or five of a kind on the first roll. The procedure also changes the text display on the first Button control to either "Stick" or "Roll Again" based on whether or not the player selected the chkKeepAll button.

Step 5: Testing the Execution of the Dice Poker Game

That's it. The Dice Poker game is now ready to run. Go ahead and run the game by pressing F5 and make sure that everything works like it is supposed to. If you run into any problems, go back and double-check your typing. Once things are in order, pass it around to a few of your friends and ask them what they think.

SUMMARY

In this chapter, you learned how to work with variations of the Do and For loops. You also learned how to set up a While loop. You learned how to use loops to collect and process user input and to process the contents of arrays and controls, such as the ListBox. In addition, you learned about endless loops and how to use variations of the Exit keyword to break out of loops. On top of all this, you created the Dice Poker game.

Now, before you move on to Chapter 8, "Enhancing Code Structure and Organization," and start learning how to work with procedures, take a few extra minutes and improve the Dice Poker game by completing the following challenges.

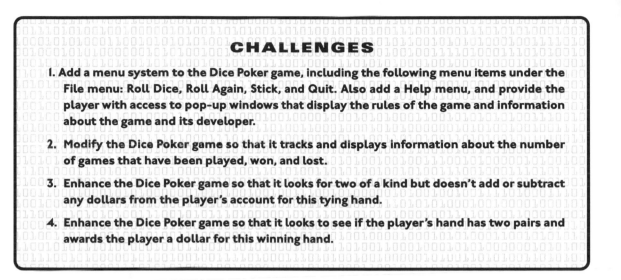

CHALLENGES

1. Add a menu system to the Dice Poker game, including the following menu items under the File menu: Roll Dice, Roll Again, Stick, and Quit. Also add a Help menu, and provide the player with access to pop-up windows that display the rules of the game and information about the game and its developer.

2. Modify the Dice Poker game so that it tracks and displays information about the number of games that have been played, won, and lost.

3. Enhance the Dice Poker game so that it looks for two of a kind but doesn't add or subtract any dollars from the player's account for this tying hand.

4. Enhance the Dice Poker game so that it looks to see if the player's hand has two pairs and awards the player a dollar for this winning hand.

ENHANCING CODE STRUCTURE AND ORGANIZATION

Whether you have realized it or not, every application that you have developed so far in this book has relied on procedures to organize and store program code. In this chapter, you will learn how to create your own custom procedures. You will learn how to create Sub and Function procedures and will understand the difference between the two. You will also learn how to pass data to your procedures for processing and how to return data from Function procedures. In addition, you will get plenty of chances to create and work with custom procedures when you create this chapter's game project, the Hangman game.

Specifically, you will learn how to:

- Organize the programming logic that makes up your applications into procedures in order to make them easier to develop and maintain
- Create custom procedures
- Pass and return data to and from procedures
- Streamline your applications by placing reusable code within procedures
- Develop procedures that can process optional data

PROJECT PREVIEW: THE HANGMAN GAME

In this chapter's project, you will apply your new knowledge of how to work with different types of procedures to the development of the Hangman game. Figures 8.1 to 8.7 show examples from the Hangman game, demonstrating its functionality and overall execution flow.

FIGURE 8.1

When first started, the game displays a graphic showing an empty hangman's gallows and a series of underscore characters representing the secret word.

FIGURE 8.2

As the game progresses, each correct guess is displayed at the top of the window, and a visual record of every letter guessed is displayed at the bottom of the window.

FIGURE 8.3

The game prevents the player from making the same letter guess more than once.

Error: Letter has already been guessed.

OK

FIGURE 8.4

The game only permits the player to enter one letter at a time.

Error: You may only enter one letter per guess.

OK

FIGURE 8.5

The game prevents the player from entering numeric input.

Error: Numeric entries are not valid.

OK

FIGURE 8.6

The game congratulates the player when the secret word has been successfully guessed.

HANGMAN

Congratulations. You have Won! Would you like to play again?

Yes   No

FIGURE 8.7

If the player fails to guess the secret word within six guesses, the game is lost and the picture of the hangman's gallows is updated to show a full hangman image.

HANGMAN

Sorry. You have lost. Would you like to play again?

Yes   No

By the time you have created and run this game, you will have demonstrated your understanding of how to create custom Sub and Function procedures and how to use them to improve the overall organization and maintenance of your Visual Basic applications.

CREATING PROCEDURES

In the previous chapter's project, the Dice Poker game, you were required to create two custom procedures in which you added code to manage the process of rolling the game's virtual die and totaling the game score. By creating these two procedures and assigning the code statements that performed specific tasks, you were able to simplify the logic in the Click procedure for the btnRollDice control. This made the overall development of the game a lot easier. As your applications continue to grow in size and complexity, it will become increasingly difficult to write them without using custom procedures.

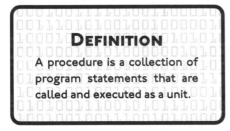

DEFINITION

A procedure is a collection of program statements that are called and executed as a unit.

Procedures make application development easier by providing you with the ability to break applications down into small pieces, which work together. This allows you to group related statements and to focus on writing your application one procedure at a time.

Because a procedure can be called and executed over and over again as needed, procedures also facilitate code reduction, which in turn makes your applications easier to develop and maintain. For example, anytime that you find yourself adding code to perform the same set of steps over again at various points in your applications, it's a good idea to create a single procedure that performs the task and then to call upon that procedure as needed.

IN THE REAL WORLD

In most cases, professional programmers try to develop procedures that perform one specific task. This streamlines application code and makes it modular. It also helps to reduce errors. For example, suppose you wrote a procedure that performed three or four separate tasks and then later decided that you needed to modify the code for one of the tasks. Because all the programming logic for all three or four tasks is grouped together, you significantly increase the chances that when you go to make a change to the code for one task, you might accidentally modify the code for the logic that performs a different task. Therefore, by putting the code for a specific task into its own procedure, you isolate its code from that stored in other procedures. This also has the added benefit of streamlining the code in each procedure, because no extraneous code unnecessary to performing its specific task is kept inside the procedure.

Sub and Function Procedures

Procedures begin with a declaration statement (Sub or Function) and end with an End statement. When called, program flow is transferred from the statement that calls the procedure to the procedure itself. Once the procedure finishes executing, program flow is returned back to the calling statement, as demonstrated in Figure 8.8.

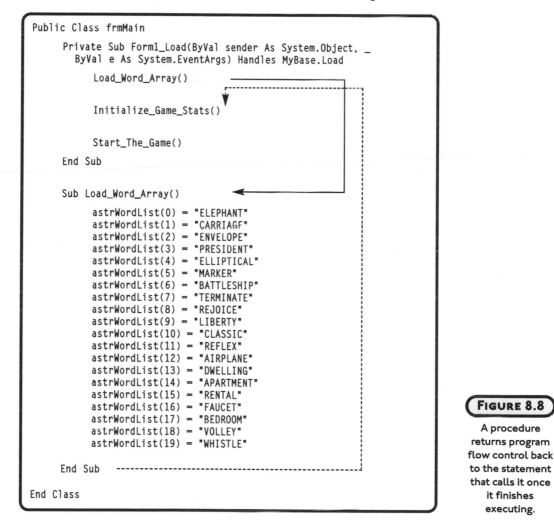

```
Public Class frmMain
        Private Sub Form1_Load(ByVal sender As System.Object, _
            ByVal e As System.EventArgs) Handles MyBase.Load

            Load_Word_Array()

            Initialize_Game_Stats()

            Start_The_Game()
        End Sub


        Sub Load_Word_Array()
            astrWordList(0) = "ELEPHANT"
            astrWordList(1) = "CARRIAGE"
            astrWordList(2) = "ENVELOPE"
            astrWordList(3) = "PRESIDENT"
            astrWordList(4) = "ELLIPTICAL"
            astrWordList(5) = "MARKER"
            astrWordList(6) = "BATTLESHIP"
            astrWordList(7) = "TERMINATE"
            astrWordList(8) = "REJOICE"
            astrWordList(9) = "LIBERTY"
            astrWordList(10) = "CLASSIC"
            astrWordList(11) = "REFLEX"
            astrWordList(12) = "AIRPLANE"
            astrWordList(13) = "DWELLING"
            astrWordList(14) = "APARTMENT"
            astrWordList(15) = "RENTAL"
            astrWordList(16) = "FAUCET"
            astrWordList(17) = "BEDROOM"
            astrWordList(18) = "VOLLEY"
            astrWordList(19) = "WHISTLE"

        End Sub
End Class
```

FIGURE 8.8

A procedure returns program flow control back to the statement that calls it once it finishes executing.

Procedures make for better organization of application logic by allowing you to group logical tasks together and to isolate those tasks from other tasks. Procedures also facilitate the development of smaller applications by providing a means of creating reusable tasks that you can call as many times as necessary. On top of all this, procedures help make code maintenance a lot easier by allowing you to isolate and streamline your code.

For example, you will find it a lot easier to make a change to a single procedure that performs a commonly called up task than it would be to make the same change over and over again to code that otherwise might be replicated at various points within an application.

Visual Basic allows you to organize your application into two primary types of procedures, as outlined below.

- **Sub.** A type of procedure that executes a set of embedded statements but does not return a value to the statement that called it
- **Function.** A type of procedure that executes a set of embedded statements and can optionally return a value to the statement that called it

Handling Events

With the exception of declaration statements, all Visual Basic code has to be stored inside a procedure. As I have already stated, you have been working with procedures in all of the chapter projects that you have completed so far in this book. For example, in many of the chapter game projects, you have added code to perform tasks that executed when the application was first loaded. Before adding this code, you double-clicked on the game project's form when viewing it in the form designer in order to get Visual Basic to automatically generate a Load event procedure for you, which was then displayed in the code editor. A good example of this can be taken from the Dice Poker game's form Load event procedure, which is shown below.

```
Private Sub Form1_Load(ByVal sender As System.Object, _
  ByVal e As System.EventArgs) Handles MyBase.Load


    pbxDie1.Image = imlDiceList.Images(5)
    pbxDie2.Image = imlDiceList.Images(5)
    pbxDie3.Image = imlDiceList.Images(5)
    pbxDie4.Image = imlDiceList.Images(5)
    pbxDie5.Image = imlDiceList.Images(5)
    txtOutput.Text = ControlChars.CrLf & "Welcome! Are you ready " & _
      "to play Dice Poker?" & ControlChars.CrLf & ControlChars.CrLf & _
      "You have " & intTotalDollars & " dollars in your account."


End Sub
```

If you go back and look at the rest of the code in the Dice Poker game, you'll see that it is all organized inside various procedures, most of which were generated automatically for you by Visual Basic.

Sub Procedures

Each procedure, whether it is a Sub or a Function procedure, must be assigned a unique name when it is declared. A Sub procedure is declared using the Sub and End Sub statements. Sub procedures are designed to group related statements together, which can then be executed as a unit. Sub procedures execute without returning any results back to the statement that calls them. Once its execution is completed, a Sub procedure returns processing control back to its calling statement.

The syntax that you'll use when defining your own custom Sub procedure is outlined below.

```
[Public | Private | Friend] Sub name [(arglist)]
    statements
End Sub
```

Private is an optional keyword that, when specified, limits access to the procedure to the class or module where it is declared. Public is an optional keyword that, when specified, makes the procedure available without restriction. Friend is an optional keyword that, when specified, makes the procedure available throughout an entire application. Name represents the name that you will assign to the Sub procedure. Arglist is a list made up of one or more comma-separated arguments that can be passed to the Sub procedure for processing. Statements represent one or more code statements that you insert inside the Sub procedure.

 Just like a variable name, a Sub procedure's name must be unique within its defined scope, otherwise an error will occur.

Defining a Custom Sub Procedure

Let's take a look at an example of a small Sub procedure named GoodBye().

```
Public Sub GoodBye()
    MessageBox.Show("Please play again soon.", "Good_Bye Demo")
End Sub
```

Because the Public keyword was added to the beginning of the Sub procedure declaration, the procedure is accessible from anywhere within the application. When called, the Sub procedure displays a message in a pop-up window and then returns control back to the statement that called it.

TRAP If you declare a procedure without specifying the Public, Private or Friendkeyword, Visual Basic automatically makes the procedure Public. Doing so is considered poor programming practice so be sure to always use the appropriate keyword when defining your own custom procedures.

Calling a Custom Sub Procedure

To execute a Sub procedure, you type the name of the procedure followed by a pair of parentheses. For example, the following statement can be used to call the GoodBye() Sub procedure defined above.

```
GoodBye()
```

TRICK You can also call on or execute a procedure using the Call keyword as demonstrated below.

```
Call GoodBye()
```

However, the Call keyword is considered to be a legacy statement, meaning that it is no longer required and seldom used anymore.

TRICK You can force the early termination of a Sub procedure using the following statement.

```
Exit Sub
```

Function Procedures

A Function procedure is declared using the Function and End Function statements. Function procedures work almost exactly like Sub procedures. Function procedures incorporate all the capabilities of Sub procedures. In addition, Function procedures are capable of returning a result (a value) back to their calling statement.

The syntax that you'll use when creating a custom Function procedure is outlined below.

```
[Public | Private | Friend] Function name [(arglist)] As DataType
    statements
    [Return]
End Function
```

Private is an optional keyword that, when specified, limits access to the procedure to the class or module where it is declared. Public is an optional keyword that, when specified, makes the procedure available without restriction. Friend is an optional keyword that, when specified, makes the procedure available throughout an entire application. Name represents the name that you will assign to the Function procedure. Arglist is a list made up of one or more comma-separated arguments that can be passed to the Function procedure for processing. Statements represent one or more code statements that you insert inside the Sub procedure. DataType specifies the data type of the value that the Function procedure will return to its calling statement. Return is a keyword used to specify a value that the Function is to pass back to the statement that called it.

The following example shows a Function procedure that displays a text message in a pop-up window without returning a result.

```
Public Function GoodBye() As String
    MessageBox.Show("Please play again soon.", "GoodBye Demo")
End Function
```

In this example, the Function procedure works exactly like the Sub procedure example you saw earlier. You can execute this procedure from anywhere in your application using the following statement.

```
GoodBye()
```

Function procedures can also return a result to their calling statements. This can be accomplished in two different ways. The first way is to create a variable with the same name as the Function procedure and to assign it the value that is to be returned, as demonstrated below.

```
Public Function GetUserName() As String
        GetUserName = InputBox("Please enter your first and last " & _
            "name.", "User Name")
End Function
```

You can call this Function procedure using the statements shown below.

```
Dim strUserName As String
strUserName = GetUserName()
```

In this example, the value returned by the Function procedure is assigned to a variable named strUserName.

TRICK If you have ever heard the expression "There is more than one way to skin a cat" and are used to working with Microsoft operating systems and applications, then you are probably used to being able to do things in several different ways. Retrieving data from procedures is no different. Instead of setting up your Function procedures so that they can return a value, you have the option of defining module or class-level variables, which you can then modify from within your Sub and Function procedures. This negates the need to return a value in order to make that value available to another part of the application. However, all things being equal, it is better to return a value using a Function procedure and to leave your variables scoped as tightly as possible.

Note that in this example the value stored in the strUserName variable is not returned until the function finishes executing.

TRICK You can force the early termination of a Function procedure using the following statement.

```
Exit Function
```

The Exit Function statement forces an immediate exit of the function and returns a value, if one has been specified.

The second way to set up a function to return a value is to use the Return statement to specify the value that you want returned, as demonstrated below.

```
Public Function GetUserName() As String
    Dim strUserName
    strUserName = InputBox("Please enter your first and last " & _
      "name.", "User Name")
    Return strUserName
End Function
```

Using the Return statement is the preferred method for returning a value back to a calling statement. It makes your code easier to read and I strongly recommend that you always use it.

TRAP If a Function procedure ends without setting a return value, Visual Basic will automatically supply a default value. For example, a 0 will be returned for a function with one of the numeric data types, and an empty string ("") will be returned for function with a String data type. Unless you want your functions to return default values, you need to be sure that you set them up to return the appropriate value. Otherwise, if no return value is required, change your Function procedure to a Sub procedure.

You can also call on functions by referring to them as part of another statement, as demonstrated in the following example.

```
MessageBox.Show("Hello " & GetUserName())
```

Passing Arguments

Procedures can be set up to process data that is passed to them in the form of arguments. These arguments are passed to a procedure and mapped to parameters that are defined as part of the procedure's declaration, as demonstrated below.

```
Public Sub DisplayMessage(ByVal strMessage As String)
    MessageBox.Show(strMessage, "Sample Message")
End Sub
```

 TRICK You can set up your Sub procedures to process as many arguments as you choose to pass to it, as long as you separate each corresponding argument definition with a comma.

In this example, a Sub type procedure named DisplayMessage is defined. The procedure defines a single variable, a parameter named strMessage with a data type of String. The argument passed to the Sub procedure is automatically assigned to the strMessage variable. The argument is passed by value (ByVal), meaning that any change made to the value of strMessage will have no effect on the value assigned to the argument passed to the procedure. You can also pass an argument by reference (ByRef). However, this is not the default option. In fact, if you fail to specify ByVal or ByRef when you define your procedure, Visual Basic will automatically insert ByVal for you.

DEFINITION

An argument is a value passed to a procedure for processing.

DEFINITION

A parameter is a declaration within a procedure that defines variables to be used to store copies of values passed to them as arguments.

You can pass as many arguments as required to a procedure, as long as you separate each argument by a comma when calling the procedure, as demonstrated below.

```
DisplayMessage("Click on Yes to accept.", "Sample Message", "question")
```

Like Sub procedures, you can set up Function procedures to process data that is passed to the procedures in the form of arguments. These arguments are passed to a procedure and mapped to parameters that are defined as part of the procedure's declaration, as demonstrated below.

```
Public Function DisplayMessage(ByVal strMessage As String, _
  ByVal strTitle As String) As String

    Dim intResult As Integer = 0

    intResult = MessageBox.Show(strMessage, strTitle, _
      MessageBoxButtons.YesNo)

    If intResult = 6 Then
        Return "Yes"
    Else
        Return "No"
    End If

End Function
```

Passing Optional Arguments

Visual Basic also provides you with the ability to set up procedures that can process optional arguments. There are a few rules that you need to be aware of when setting up a procedure to accept optional arguments. First of all, you must remember to define a default value for any Optional argument. The default value must be expressed as a constant value. In other words, you cannot use a variable or other type of value. Finally, any argument that follows an Optional argument must also be an Optional argument.

The following example demonstrates how to set up a procedure with an Optional argument.

```
Sub DisplayMessage(Optional ByVal strUserName As String = "")
        MessageBox.Show("Greetings " & strUserName)
End Sub
```

You can call the Sub procedure in the previous example without passing it an argument, as shown below.

```
DisplayMessage()
```

Alternatively, you can call the Sub procedure and pass it an argument, as demonstrated here.

```
DisplayMessage("Alexander Ford")
```

As mentioned above, you can set up your procedures to process more than one Optional argument at a time, as demonstrated below.

```
Public Sub DisplayMessage(ByVal strMessage As String, _
     Optional ByVal strTitleBarMessage As String = "", _
     Optional ByVal strIcon As String = "")

        If strIcon = "Exclamation" Then
           MessageBox.Show(strMessage, strTitleBarMessage, _
              MessageBoxButtons.OK, MessageBoxIcon.Exclamation)
        Else
           MessageBox.Show(strMessage, strTitleBarMessage, _
              MessageBoxButtons.OK, MessageBoxIcon.Information)
        End If

End Sub
```

You can call the previous Sub procedure in a number of different ways. For example, the following statement calls the procedure and passes it three arguments.

```
DisplayMessage("The current date and time are " & Now(), "Demo", _
  "Exclamation")
```

You can also call the procedure and pass it just two arguments, as shown below.

```
DisplayMessage("The current date and time are " & Now(), "Demo")
```

You can also call the procedure as shown below.

```
DisplayMessage("The current date and time are " & Now(), , _
  "Information")
```

In the last example, arguments representing the procedure's first and third parameters were passed. Notice that to make this work, I had to include a comma where the procedure's second parameter is defined.

Figure 8.9 shows how the pop-up windows produced by the three previous calling statements will look when displayed.

FIGURE 8.9

Using the `Optional` keyword, you can create flexible procedures that can process different numbers of arguments.

Pop-up window produced when three arguments are passed

Pop-up window produced when the first and second arguments are passed

Pop-up window produced when the first and third arguments are passed

LEVERAGING THE POWER OF VISUAL BASIC'S BUILT-IN FUNCTIONS AND .NET OBJECTS

Although the ability to create your own procedures is a very powerful programming tool, allowing you to perform all sorts of tasks, it is not always necessary for you to develop all of the programming logic required to perform a given task. Instead, you can often take advantage of Visual Basic's built-in collection of functions as well as properties and methods provided by .NET objects. By leveraging the functionality provided by these functions and objects, you can save a lot of development time.

You've already learned how to work with a number of built-in Visual Basic functions. One good example has been the use of the `InputBox()` function as a means of collecting input from the player during game play. This function allows you to display a text string and to collect and return text input provided by the player, as demonstrated in the following example.

```
Dim strUserReply As String = ""
strUserReply = InputBox("Please enter your first name.", _
   "Data Collection example")
```

The pop-up window produced by this example is shown in Figure 8.10.

FIGURE 8.10

Using the Visual Basic's InputBox() function to display a pop-up dialog that collects user input.

You could, of course, create your own custom InputBox()-like function by adding a new form to a Visual Basic project and then adding a Label, a TextBox, and two Button controls to it, followed by the programming logic required to tie everything together. However, unless the InputBox() function fails to provide you with a particular piece of functionality that you absolutely must have when prompting the user for input, there is no reason to take the extra time to create your own function.

Date-Related Objects

The .NET Framework provides numerous objects that assist you in working with the date and time. For example, the DateTime object's Now() method can be used to retrieve the current system date and time, as demonstrated below.

DEFINITION

The *DateTimeObject* is used to represent a moment in time. It's Now property retrieves the current date and time from the computer.

```
MessageBox.Show(DateTime.Now())
```

When executed, this statement produces the pop-up window shown in Figure 8.11.

You can also use the Convert object's ToDateTime method to convert a string value to a Date data type as demonstrated below.

FIGURE 8.11

Using the DateTime.Now() function to display the current date and time.

```
Dim strDate As String
Dim dteDate As Date

strDate = "12/01/05"
dteDate = Convert.ToDateTime(strDate)

MessageBox.Show(dteDate)
```

DEFINITION

The *Convert* object provides the ability to convert or change a data type from one type to another. It's ToDateTime method provides the ability to convert numerous data types to a Date data type.

The following example demonstrates how to use the TimeSpan object's Subtract method to determine the number of days that have elapsed from the specified date to the current date. In the case of this example the specified date is November 11, 1964.

```
Dim dteCurrentDate As Date = DateTime.Now
Dim dteBirthDate As Date = #11/20/1964#

Dim dteDateDiff As TimeSpan

dteDateDiff = dteCurrentDate.Subtract(dteBirthDate)

MessageBox.Show("I was born " & dteDateDiff.Days & " days ago.")
```

The first two statements in this example declare variables that store the current date and a date representing somebody's birthday. The third statement declares a variable named dteDateDiff as an instance of the TimeSpan object. The next statement uses the TimeSpan object's Subract method. The Subtract method is used to determine the amount of time that has

DEFINITION

The *TimeSpan* object is used to represent an interval of time.

passed between the two time periods. The value assigned to dteDateDiff is then displayed in the final statement which used the TimeSpan object's Days property to specify the unit of measurement to be used to represent the time span between the two time frames.

Figure 8.12 shows the output produced by the previous example when it is executed.

FIGURE 8.12

Using the TimeSpan object's Subtract method to count the number of days between two dates.

Before moving on, let's take a look at one last example of how to programmatically work with date and time values using the DateTime object's ToString method. The ToString method provides the ability to convert a date\time value to a specified string format. For example, using the DateTime object's ToString method you can create your own Visual Basic digital clock, as shown in Figure 8.13.

FIGURE 8.13

Using date-related functions to create a digital clock.

The code associated with the digital clock example is shown below and is available for download from this book's companion Web site.

```
Public Class Form1

    Private Sub Form1_Load(ByVal sender As System.Object, _
      ByVal e As System.EventArgs) Handles MyBase.Load

        txtDate.Text = DateTime.Now.ToString("D") 'Long Date pattern

    End Sub

    Private Sub Timer1_Tick(ByVal sender As System.Object, _
      ByVal e As System.EventArgs) Handles Timer1.Tick

        lblTime.Text = DateTime.Now.ToString("T")

        If DateTime.Now.ToString("T") = #12:00:00 AM# Then
            txtDate.Text = DateTime.Now.ToString("D")
        End If

    End Sub

End Class
```

In this example, the current date is displayed when the Form1_Load event procedure executes. The current date is collected using the DateTime object's Now method and then formatted using the object's `ToString` method. The `ToString` method is passed an argument of "D", specifying that the date be displayed in a long date format as shown in Figure 8.13.

The `Timer_Tick` event procedure updates the display of the current time every second by passing the `ToString` method an argument of "T", specifying a long time format. The `Timer` control that drives this procedure was enabled at design time, and its `Interval` property was set equal to 1000 so that the procedure starts executing the moment the application is loaded.

The `Timer_Tick` event procedure is also responsible for updating the display of the current date, which it changes automatically at 1 second past midnight.

String Manipulation Functions

Strings are a commonly used data type in Visual Basic applications. Applications need to work with string values in a number of different ways, including:

- Searching for one string within another
- Parsing string contents to extract a port of the string
- Formatting the contents of a string

The .NET Framework provides Visual Basic with an abundance of different `String` object methods for manipulating strings. For example, using the `ToString` method, you can convert a value to a `String` data type, as demonstrated below.

```
Dim intValue As Integer = 12345
Dim strSample As String = intValue.ToString()
```

In this example, the `String` object's `ToString` method is used to convert the number 12345 to a string, which is then assigned to a variable named `strSample`. The following list provides a sampling of different types of methods and properties provided by the `String` object.

- **Trim.** A method used to remove leading and trailing blank spaces from a value
- **ToUpper.** A method that retrieves an all upper case version of a string
- **ToLower.** A method that retrieves an all lower case version of a string
- **Length.** A property used to return the number of characters that make up a string
- **Substring.** A method used to return a value indicating the starting location of one string within another

The following example demonstrates how to use each of these `String` manipulation functions.

```
Dim strDataString As String = "   Once upon a time...    "
Dim strTestString As String = ""
Dim intLength As Integer = 0

'Assigns "Once upon a time..."
strTestString = strDataString.Trim

'Assigns "   ONCE UPON A TIME...    "
strTestString = strDataString.ToUpper

'Assigns "   once upon a time...    "
strTestString = strDataString.ToLower

'Assigns 25
intLength = strDataString.Length

'Displays "Once upon"
strTestString = strDataString.Substring(3, 9)
strDataString.Trim
```

Note that the value that is assigned or displayed by each statement in the above example is shown as a comment that precedes each statement.

BACK TO THE HANGMAN GAME

Now it is time to turn your attention back to this chapter's game project, the Hangman game. The Hangman game is based on a children's game in which the player attempts to guess a secret word. If the player guesses the word before making six incorrect guesses, the player wins. Otherwise, the game is lost.

You will create the Hangman game by following the same five basic development steps that you have followed when completing previous chapter projects.

Designing the Game

The Hangman game will be played within a single window. Therefore, it will be made up of one form and the 25 controls listed in Table 8.1.

TABLE 8.1: FORM CONTROLS FOR THE HANGMAN GAME

Control Type	Control Name	Description
Panel1	pnlLetters	A Panel control used to group Textbox controls that will be used to display guessed word letters
TextBox1	txtLetter1	Displays the first letter in the game's secret word
TextBox2	txtLetter2	Displays the second letter in the game's secret word
TextBox3	txtLetter3	Displays the third letter in the game's secret word
TextBox4	txtLetter4	Displays the fourth letter in the game's secret word
Textbox5	txtLetter5	Displays the fifth letter in the game's secret word
TextBox6	txtLetter6	Displays the sixth letter in the game's secret word
TextBox7	txtLetter7	Displays the seventh letter in the game's secret word
TextBox8	txtLetter8	Displays the eighth letter in the game's secret word
TextBox9	txtLetter9	Displays the ninth letter in the game's secret word
TextBox10	txtLetter10	Displays the tenth letter in the game's secret word
TextBox11	txtMisses	Displays the number of misses that the player has made
TextBox12	txtGuesses	Displays the letters that the player has already guessed (both right and wrong)
TextBox13	txtGamesWon	Displays the number of games that the player has won
TextBox14	txtGamesLost	Displays the number of games that the player has lost
GroupBox1	grpStatus	Contains Label and TextBox controls that display game statistics
Label1	lblInput	Identifies the TextBox control where the player enters a letter guess
Label2	lblNoMissed	Identifies the TextBox control that displays the number of misses that the player has made
Label3	lblGuessed	Identifies the TextBox control that displays the letters that the player has already guessed (both right and wrong)
Label4	lblGamesWon	Identifies the TextBox control that displays the number of games that the player has won
Label5	lblGamesLost	Identifies the TextBox control that displays the number of games that the player has lost

continued

TABLE 8.1: FORM CONTROLS FOR THE HANGMAN GAME		
Button1	btnSubmit	Executes code that checks to see if the player has guessed a letter in the secret word
PictureBox1	pbcHangmanBmp	Displays a graphic that visually shows how many letter guesses the player has missed
ImageList1	imlHangmanBmps	Stores an indexed collection of the hangman images that are displayed in the PictureBox control

Step 1: Creating a New Visual Basic Project

The first step in creating the Hangman game is to open up Visual Basic and create a new project as outlined below.

1. If you have not already done so, start up Visual Basic 2005 Express and then click on File and select New Project. The New Project dialog will appear.

2. Select Windows Application template.

3. Type Hangman as the name of your new application in the Name field located at the bottom of the New Project window.

4. Click on OK to close the New Project dialog.

Visual Basic will now create a new project for you and display a new form upon which you will design the game's user interface.

Step 2: Creating the User Interface

Now let's begin work on laying out the game's user interface by adding controls to the form and moving and resizing them in the appropriate locations. Refer to Figure 8.14 as you go through each step so that you'll know how to resize and place the controls.

1. Begin by clicking on the form and setting its Size property to 655, 412.

2. Add a Panel control to the form and resize as shown in Figure 8.14.

3. Add 10 TextBox controls inside the Panel control. Set the Multiline property for each TextBox control equal to True and resize them as shown in Figure 8.14.

DEFINITION

A Panel control is a control that stores and organizes other controls.

FIGURE 8.14

Examining the
layout of the
Hangman game's
user interface.

4. Add a Label control to the form. By default, Visual Basic will name it Label1.

5. Just to the right of the Label1 control, add a TextBox control and a Button control as shown in Figure 8.14. Set the Multiline property of the TextBox control equal to True.

6. Add a GroupBox control at the bottom of the form and resize it until it takes up the bottom 30 percent of the form.

7. Inside the GroupBox control, add four Label and four TextBox controls, as shown in Figure 8.14.

8. Add a PictureBox control to the upper right-hand corner of the form and resize it until it is approximately 2 inches tall by 2 inches wide.

9. Lastly, add an ImageList control, which will appear in a component tray, located at the bottom of the form designer.

Now that the overall layout for the Hangman game user interface has been laid out, you can begin form and control property customization.

Step 3: Customizing Form and Control Properties

Let's begin by modifying properties associated with the game's form, as shown in Table 8.2.

TABLE 8.2: PROPERTY CHANGES FOR FORM1

Property	Value
Name	frmMain
Cursor	Hand
FormBorderStyle	Fixed3D
MaximizeBox	False
MinimizeBox	False
Size	655, 412
StartPosition	CenterScreen
Text	**Hangman**

Next, modify the following properties associated with the Panel control, as shown in Table 8.3.

TABLE 8.3: PROPERTY CHANGES FOR THE PANEL CONTROL

Property	Value
Name	pnlLetters
BackColor	WhiteSmoke
BorderStyle	Fixed3D

Next, modify the following properties associated with the GroupBox control, as shown in Table 8.4.

TABLE 8.4: PROPERTY CHANGES FOR THE GROUPBOX CONTROL

Property	Value
Name	grpStatus
Text	Game Stats:

Now, modify the following properties associated with the TextBox controls, as shown in Table 8.5.

TABLE 8.5: PROPERTY CHANGES FOR THE TEXTBOX CONTROLS

Control	Property	Value
TextBox1	Name	txtLetter1
	BackColor	WhiteSmoke
	BorderStyle	None
	Font.Name	Courier New
	Font.Size	36
	Font.Bold	True
	ForeColor	DarkBlue
	ReadOnly	True
	TabStop	False
TextBox2	Name	txtLetter2
	BackColor	WhiteSmoke
	BorderStyle	None
	Font.Name	Courier New
	Font.Size	36
	Font.Bold	True
	ForeColor	DarkBlue
	ReadOnly	True
	TabStop	False
TextBox3	Name	txtLetter3
	BackColor	WhiteSmoke
	BorderStyle	None
	Font.Name	Courier New
	Font.Size	36
	Font.Bold	True

continued

TABLE 8.5: PROPERTY CHANGES FOR THE TEXTBOX CONTROLS

	Property	Value
	ForeColor	DarkBlue
	ReadOnly	True
	TabStop	False
TextBox4	Name	txtLetter4
	BackColor	WhiteSmoke
	BorderStyle	None
	Font.Name	Courier New
	Font.Size	36
	Font.Bold	True
	ForeColor	DarkBlue
	ReadOnly	True
	TabStop	False
TextBox5	Name	txtLetter5
	BackColor	WhiteSmoke
	BorderStyle	None
	Font.Name	Courier New
	Font.Size	36
	Font.Bold	True
	ForeColor	DarkBlue
	ReadOnly	True
	TabStop	False
TextBox6	Name	txtLetter6
	BackColor	WhiteSmoke
	BorderStyle	None
	Font.Name	Courier New
	Font.Size	36
	Font.Bold	True

continued

TABLE 8.5: PROPERTY CHANGES FOR THE TEXTBOX CONTROLS

	ForeColor	DarkBlue
	ReadOnly	True
	TabStop	False
TextBox7	Name	txtLetter7
	BackColor	WhiteSmoke
	BorderStyle	None
	Font.Name	Courier New
	Font.Size	36
	Font.Bold	True
	ForeColor	DarkBlue
	ReadOnly	True
	TabStop	False
TextBox8	Name	txtLetter8
	BackColor	WhiteSmoke
	BorderStyle	None
	Font.Name	Courier New
	Font.Size	36
	Font.Bold	True
	ForeColor	DarkBlue
	ReadOnly	True
	TabStop	False
TextBox9	Name	txtLetter9
	BackColor	WhiteSmoke
	BorderStyle	None
	Font.Name	Courier New
	Font.Size	36
	Font.Bold	True

continued

TABLE 8.5: PROPERTY CHANGES FOR THE TEXTBOX CONTROLS

	ForeColor	DarkBlue
	ReadOnly	True
	TabStop	False
TextBox10	Name	txtLetter10
	BackColor	WhiteSmoke
	BorderStyle	None
	Font.Name	Courier New
	Font.Size	36
	Font.Bold	True
	ForeColor	DarkBlue
	ReadOnly	True
	TabStop	False
TextBox11	Name	txtInput
	CharacterCasing	Upper
	Font.Size	18
	Font.Bold	True
TextBox12	Name	txtMisses
	ReadOnly	True
	TabStop	False
TextBox13	Name	txtGuesses
	ReadOnly	True
	TabStop	False
TextBox14	Name	txtGamesWon
	ReadOnly	True
	TabStop	False

continued

TABLE 8.5: PROPERTY CHANGES FOR THE TEXTBOX CONTROLS

TextBox15	Name	txtGamesLost
	ReadOnly	True
	TabStop	False

Now, modify the following properties associated with the Label controls, as shown in Table 8.6.

TABLE 8.6: PROPERTY CHANGES FOR THE LABEL CONTROLS

Control	Property	Value
Label1	Name	lblInput
	Text	Enter A Letter Guess:
	Font.Bold	True
Label2	Name	lblNoMissed
	Text	No. Of Misses:
	Font.Bold	True
Label3	Name	lblGuesses
	Text	Letters Guessed:
	Font.Bold	True
Label4	Name	lblGamesWon
	Text	No. Of Games Won:
	Font.Bold	True
Label5	Name	lblGamesLost
	Text	No. Of Games Lost:
	Font.Bold	True

Now, modify the following properties associated with the Button control, as shown in Table 8.7.

TABLE 8.7: PROPERTY CHANGES FOR THE BUTTON CONTROL

Property	Value
Name	btnSubmit
Font.Bold	True
Text	Submit

Now, modify the following properties associated with the PictureBox control, as shown in Table 8.8.

TABLE 8.8: PROPERTY CHANGES FOR THE PICTUREBOX CONTROL

Property	Value
Name	pbcHangmanBmp
BorderStyle	Fixed3D
SizeMode	StretchImage

Finally, change the name property of the ImageList control to imlHangmanBmps. Next change the ImageSize property to 80, 80 and add the following bitmap images to the Images property (collection) as shown in Table 8.9. Don't worry about having to create these bitmap images yourself. I have included copies of them with the source for the game project on the book's companion Web site.

TABLE 8.9: BITMAP IMAGES TO ADD TO THE IMAGELIST CONTROL'S IMAGES COLLECTION		
Property	**File**	**Index No.**
Name	100.bmp	0
Name	80.bmp	1
Name	60.bmp	2
Name	40.bmp	3
Name	20.bmp	4
Name	10.bmp	5
Name	0.bmp	6

Step 4: Adding a Little Programming Logic

Begin coding the Hangman game by double-clicking on the game's form, thus opening the code editor and creating the form's Load event procedure as shown below.

```
Public Class frmMain

End Class
```

Just above the Load event procedure, add the following statements

```
Const cTitleBarMsg As String = "HANGMAN"  'Titlebar message

Private astrWordList(19) As String  'Stores a list of game words

Private strGameWord As String = ""  'Stores the word currently in play
Private strWrong As String = ""   'Stores a list of missed guesses

Private intMisses As Integer = 0  'Keeps count of missed guesses
Private intNoRight As Integer = 0  'Keeps count of correct guesses
Private intPlayAgain As Integer = 0  'Track the player's response
Private intHangmanNo As Integer = 6 'Controls display of hangman image
```

These declaration statements define a constant, an array, and variables that are used by two or more procedures in the application. The array, strWordListArray, will be used to store secret words used to play the game. The rest of the variables will be used to hold the currently selected secret word and game statistics and to display a string of letters that have been guessed by the player.

Now, add the following statements to the Form1_Load procedure.

```
'This procedure executes when the game first starts
Private Sub Form1_Load(ByVal sender As System.Object, _
  ByVal e As System.EventArgs) Handles MyBase.Load

    LoadWordArray()  'Populate the array with words

    InitializeGameStats()  'Set up the game's starting values

    StartTheGame()  'Start the game

End Sub
```

The three statements inside the Form1_Load procedure set up game play by calling three custom procedures. The LoadWordArray procedure populates the strWordListArray array with 20 secret words. To create it, scroll down below the Form1_Load procedure and enter the following statements.

```
'This procedure loads words into the game's array
Sub LoadWordArray()

End Sub
```

Next, add the following statements inside the LoadWordArray procedure in order to populate each element of the array.

```
strWordListArray(0) = "ELEPHANT"
strWordListArray(1) = "CARRIAGE"
strWordListArray(2) = "ENVELOPE"
strWordListArray(3) = "PRESIDENT"
strWordListArray(4) = "ELLIPTICAL"
strWordListArray(5) = "MARKER"
strWordListArray(6) = "BATTLESHIP"
strWordListArray(7) = "TERMINATE"
```

```
strWordListArray(8) = "REJOICE"
strWordListArray(9) = "LIBERTY"
strWordListArray(10) = "CLASSIC"
strWordListArray(11) = "REFLEX"
strWordListArray(12) = "AIRPLANE"
strWordListArray(13) = "DWELLING"
strWordListArray(14) = "APARTMENT"
strWordListArray(15) = "RENTAL"
strWordListArray(16) = "FAUCET"
strWordListArray(17) = "BEDROOM"
strWordListArray(18) = "VOLLEY"
strWordListArray(19) = "WHISTLE"
```

The `InitializeGameStats` Sub procedure will set the game statistics displayed in the `GroupBox` control to zeroes. You'll need to create this Sub procedure from scratch by inserting it just under the `LoadWordArray` procedure. Once created, you will need to modify it as shown below.

```
'This procedure resets values stored in the game's TextBox controls
Sub InitializeGameStats()

    txtGamesWon.Text = 0
    txtGamesLost.Text = 0


End Sub
```

The `StartTheGame` Sub procedure is responsible for setting up the game to play a new round. It does so by making three Sub procedure calls, which reset variable defaults, retrieve a secret game word, and format the word for display. The procedure ends by setting focus to the `txtInput` control in order to ready the game for the player input.

```
'This procedure preps the game for a new round of play
Sub StartTheGame()

    ResetDefaultSettings()  'Call procedure to reset game settings

    strGameWord = RetrieveWord()  'Get a word for the player to guess

    FormatGameWord()  'Format the display of the mystery word
```

```
    txtInput.Focus()  'Prepare the game to accept the player's guess
```

End Sub

Next, create the `ResetDefaultSettings` `Sub` procedure, shown below, in order to prepare the game to play a new round.

```
'This procedure resets variables and TextBox control values back to
'their starting values
Sub ResetDefaultSettings()

    intMisses = 0
    intNoRight = 0
    txtGuesses.Text = ""
    txtMisses.Text = intMisses
    txtInput.Text = ""
    intHangmanNo = 6


    pbcHangmanBmp.Image = imlHangmanBmps.Images.Item(6)
```

End Sub

Note that in addition to resetting variable default values, the last statement in the previous procedure displays an empty hangman's gallows graphic in the `PictureBox` control.

Now, create the `RetrieveWord` procedure. The procedure will retrieve a random number, use that number to select a word from the `strWordListArray` array, and then return the secret word to the statement that called the procedure. Therefore, you will need to define this procedure as a `Function` and to return the secret word by assigning it to a variable that has the same name as the procedure.

```
'This procedure randomly retrieves a word for the player to guess
Function RetrieveWord() As String

    'Declare a variable to hold a randomly generated number
    Dim intRandomNo As Integer = 0
    Dim r As New Random  'Instantiate a Random object

    'Use the Random object's Next method to retrieve a number between
    'zero and the number of words in the array
    intRandomNo = r.Next(strWordListArray.Length)
```

```
'Use the random number to select a word from the array and pass
'the word back to the calling statement
Return strWordListArray(intRandomNo)

End Function
```

TRICK Note the use of the Random object and its Next method in the RetrieveWord procedure. In previous chapters you've seen me use Visual Basic's built-in Randomize and Rnd functions. The functionality provided by these two functions has been duplicated by the .NET Framework's Random object and its Next method.

Next, create the FormatGameWord Sub procedure as shown below. The procedure begins by declaring an Integer type variable named intCounter. It then assigns an empty string to each of the 10 TextBox controls that are used to display the letters that make up the game's secret word. The procedure then sets up a For…Next loop to display an underscore character for each letter in the secret word.

```
'This procedure formats the display of underscore characters
'representing the game's word
Sub FormatGameWord()

    'Define a variable to be used as a counter
    Dim intCounter As Integer = 1

    'Game words are limited to ten or less characters. Each letter is
    'stored in a separate Textbox control. Start by setting the value
    'stored in each Textbox control to a blank character
    txtLetter1.Text = ""
    txtLetter2.Text = ""
    txtLetter3.Text = ""
    txtLetter4.Text = ""
    txtLetter5.Text = ""
    txtLetter6.Text = ""
    txtLetter7.Text = ""
    txtLetter8.Text = ""
    txtLetter9.Text = ""
    txtLetter10.Text = ""
```

```
'Use a For…Next loop to display an underscore character for each
'letter that makes up the game's word
For intCounter = 1 To strGameWord.Length
      If intCounter = 1 Then txtLetter1.Text = "_"
      If intCounter = 2 Then txtLetter2.Text = "_"
      If intCounter = 3 Then txtLetter3.Text = "_"
      If intCounter = 4 Then txtLetter4.Text = "_"
      If intCounter = 5 Then txtLetter5.Text = "_"
      If intCounter = 6 Then txtLetter6.Text = "_"
      If intCounter = 7 Then txtLetter7.Text = "_"
      If intCounter = 8 Then txtLetter8.Text = "_"
      If intCounter = 9 Then txtLetter9.Text = "_"
      If intCounter = 10 Then txtLetter10.Text = "_"
Next
```

You can create the next procedure, shown below, by returning to the form designer and double-clicking on the btnSubmit control and then modifying the procedure as shown below.

```
'This procedure executes each time the player clicks on the button
'control labeled Submit
Private Sub btnSubmit_Click(ByVal sender As System.Object, _
  ByVal e As System.EventArgs) Handles btnSubmit.Click

    Dim intCounter As Integer = 0 'Variable to be used as a counter
    Dim strWordLetter As String = "" 'Store the player's guess
    Dim strInputOk As String = "" 'Used when validating player input

    strInputOk = ValidatePlayerInput() 'Call validation procedure
    If strInputOk = "Error" Then
        Exit Sub 'Exit procedure if player's guess is invalid
    End If

    'Display an error if the player has already guessed the letter
    If Strings.InStr(1, txtGuesses.Text, txtInput.Text.ToUpper, 1) _
      <> 0 Then
        MessageBox.Show("Error: Letter has already been guessed.")
    Else 'See if the player guessed a letter in the word

        'Add letter to list of letters that have already been guessed
```

```
txtGuesses.Text &= " " & txtInput.Text

'Look for the letter in the word
If Strings.InStr(1, strGameWord.ToUpper, _
  txtInput.Text.ToUpper, 1) = 0 _
  Then 'The player's guess was wrong

      'Append letter to the list of missed guesses
      strWrong &= " " & txtInput.Text.ToUpper
      intMisses += 1 'Add one to the number of missed guesses
      txtMisses.Text = intMisses 'Display # of missed guesses

      'Decrement variable used to keep track of which Hangman
      'graphic is to be displayed
      intHangmanNo -= 1
      pbcHangmanBmp.Image = _
        imlHangmanBmps.Images.Item(intHangmanNo) 'Display graphic

      If intMisses = 6 Then 'Game is over after 6 missed guesses
          txtGamesLost.Text += 1 'Increment counter
          'Call procedure to see if player wants to play again
          PromptForNewGame("Sorry. You have lost.")
      End If
End If

'Use For...Next loop to spin through each letter in the word
For intCounter = 1 To strGameWord.Length
    'Select one letter at a time
    strWordLetter = Mid(strGameWord, intCounter, 1)
    'See if the letter matches the player's guess
    If strWordLetter.ToUpper = txtInput.Text.ToUpper Then
        intNoRight += 1  'Increment counter
        'Execute procedure to display a guessed letter
        FlipGameLetter(intCounter)
    End If
Next
```

```
End If

'See if the player has guessed every letter in the word
If intNoRight = strGameWord.Length Then
    txtGamesWon.Text += 1
    'Call procedure to see if player wants to play again
    PromptForNewGame("Congratulations. You have Won!")
End If

txtInput.Text = ""
txtInput.Focus()

End Sub
```

The procedure begins by declaring three variables and then calls on the Validate-PlayerInput procedure to determine if the player's input is acceptable. If the input is OK, the procedure continues executing.

Next, the procedure uses an If…Then…Else statement to see if the player has entered a letter guess that has already been tried. If this is a new guess, the letter that is guessed is appended to the end of the test string displayed in the txtGuesses control.

An embedded If…Then statement then checks to see if the player's guess is wrong using the Strings object's Instr() function. If the player guesses incorrectly, the value stored in the txtMisses control is increased by 1 and the graphic displayed in the PictureBox control is changed to reflect the number of misses so far. A check is then made to see if the player has missed a total of six guesses, thus losing the game.

If the game has not been lost, a For…Next loop is used to spin through the secret word and display each letter that matches the player's guess. Finally, a check is made to see if the player has guessed all of the letters that make up the secret word, thus winning the game. If the game has not been won, the txtInput control is cleared and given focus, thus preparing the game for the player's next guess.

Next, you will need to manually create the Validate-PlayerInput procedure. This procedure will need to return a value, so you will need to define it as a Function, as shown below.

> **DEFINITION**
>
> The *Strings* object provides access to methods that can be used to perform string operations. The Strings object's InStr method retrieves an Integer specifying the start position of one string within another.

```vb
'This procedure validates the player's guess
Function ValidatePlayerInput() As String

    'See if the player clicked on Submit without entering a guess
    If txtInput.Text = "" Then
        MessageBox.Show("Error: You must enter a letter.")
        txtInput.Text = ""
        txtInput.Focus()
        Return "Error" 'Return a value indicating an invalid guess
    End If

    'See if the player entered more than one character
    If txtInput.Text.Length > 1 Then
        MessageBox.Show("Error: You may only enter one letter per" & _
            "guess.")
        txtInput.Text = ""
        txtInput.Focus()
        Return "Error" 'Return a value indicating an invalid guess
    End If

    'See if the player entered a number
    If IsNumeric(txtInput.Text) = True Then
        MessageBox.Show("Error: Numeric entries are not valid.")
        txtInput.Text = ""
        txtInput.Focus()
        Return "Error" 'Return a value indicating an invalid guess
    End If

    Return "Passed" 'Return a value indicating a valid guess

End Function
```

The procedure performs three input validation tests in order to make sure that the player has provided an acceptable guess. It accomplishes this using three If…Then statements. The first If…Then statement makes sure that the player enters something. The second If…Then statement makes sure that the player did not enter more than one character, and the third If…Then statement makes sure that the player didn't enter a number.

Each time the player correctly guesses a letter, the FlipGameLetter Sub procedure is executed. You'll need to manually create this procedure, as shown below.

```
'This procedure is responsible for displaying upper case letters in
'the appropriate Textbox controls
Sub FlipGameLetter(ByVal intLetterNumber As Integer)

      'Select the letter to be displayed based on the argument passed
      'to the procedure
      Select Case intLetterNumber
           Case 1
                txtLetter1.Text = txtInput.Text.ToUpper
           Case 2
                txtLetter2.Text = txtInput.Text.ToUpper
           Case 3
                txtLetter3.Text = txtInput.Text.ToUpper
           Case 4
                txtLetter4.Text = txtInput.Text.ToUpper
           Case 5
                txtLetter5.Text = txtInput.Text.ToUpper
           Case 6
                txtLetter6.Text = txtInput.Text.ToUpper
           Case 7
                txtLetter7.Text = txtInput.Text.ToUpper
           Case 8
                txtLetter8.Text = txtInput.Text.ToUpper
           Case 9
                txtLetter9.Text = txtInput.Text.ToUpper
           Case 10
                txtLetter10.Text = txtInput.Text.ToUpper
      End Select

End Sub
```

This procedure consists of a single `Select Case` statement, which compares the player's guess to each letter in the secret word and flips (that is, displays) any letters that match the guess.

The last procedure that you will need to create is the `PromptForNewGame` Sub procedure. You will need to manually define this procedure and then set it up as shown below.

```
'This procedure prompts the player to play again
Sub PromptForNewGame(ByVal strMessage As String)

        'Ask player to play again
        intPlayAgain = MessageBox.Show(strMessage & _
          " Would you like to play again?", _
          cTitleBarMsg, MessageBoxButtons.YesNo, MessageBoxIcon.Question)

        'The player clicked on Yes
        If intPlayAgain = 6 Then
            StartTheGame() 'Start a new game
        Else 'The player clicked on No
            Application.Exit() 'End the game
        End If

End Sub
        If intPlayAgain = 6 Then
```

The procedure uses the `MessageBox.Show` method to ask if the player would like to play another round. If the player clicks on the `Yes` button, the `StartTheGame` procedure is executed. Otherwise, the `Application.Exit` statement executes and terminates the application.

Step 5: Testing the Execution of the Hangman Game

The Hangman game is now complete. Press F5 and test out the game to make sure that everything is working properly. If you run into errors, then you have probably made one or more typing mistakes. Go back and double-check your code and see if you have made any errors. Before you pass the game along to your friends, make sure that you remember to test all aspects of the game, including feeding it good and bad input.

SUMMARY

In this chapter, you learned how to improve the overall organization and design of your Visual Basic applications using procedures. This included learning how to create your own custom Sub and Function procedures. You also learn how to pass arguments to your procedures and how to define optional parameters. In addition, you learned how to use the Panel control as a container for storing other controls. Before you move on to the next chapter, take a few extra minutes and see if you can improve on the Hangman game by implementing the following challenges

CHALLENGES

1. Improve the Hangman game by separating the display of letters correctly guessed from letters incorrectly guessed.

2. Increase the size of the game's array and make the required modifications to the program's code that references it so that you can add additional words to it and provide a bigger pool from which secret words will be randomly chosen.

3. Add a Checkbox control to the game just under the PictureBox control and use it to give the player the option of displaying or hiding the GroupBox control and its contents. Adjust the size of the form as appropriate.

GETTING COMFORTABLE WITH OBJECT-ORIENTED PROGRAMMING

In this chapter, you will learn about Visual Basic object-oriented programming. This will include learning about a number of new programming concepts, including abstraction, encapsulation, inheritance, and polymorphism. You will also learn more about working with objects. This will include a look at examples of objects provided by Visual Basic and the .NET Framework, as well as how to create your own objects by creating custom classes. You will also learn how to store and protect the data stored in your custom objects and to provide access to it through the implementation of properties and methods. In addition, you will get the chance to create another Visual Basic application based on the classic children's rock, paper, scissors game.

Specifically, you will learn:

- About object-oriented programming concepts and terms
- How to define custom classes
- How to instantiate objects based on your custom classes
- How to set up method overloading within custom classes
- How to provide controlled access to the data stored within objects

PROJECT PREVIEW: THE ROCK, PAPER AND SCISSORS GAME

This chapter's game project is the Rock, Paper and Scissors game, which you probably remember playing when you were a small child. The rules of the game haven't changed. Each player attempts to outplay an opponent (in this case, the computer) by consistently selecting superior choices. The rules for scoring the game are listed below.

- Rock crushes scissors to win.
- Paper covers rock to win.
- Scissors cuts paper to win.
- Everything else is a tie.

Figures 9.1 to 9.5 show examples of the Rock, Paper and Scissors game in action, showing its functionality and overall execution flow.

FIGURE 9.1

The Rock, Paper and Scissors game beings by displaying the game board.

FIGURE 9.2

When the player clicks on the Play button, a 1.5-second countdown begins.

FIGURE 9.3

The player gets a half-second at the end of the countdown to make a selection by choosing Rock, Paper, or Scissors.

FIGURE 9.4

As soon as both the computer and the player have made their choices, the game displays graphics showing each move and determines who won.

FIGURE 9.5

The Rock, Paper and Scissors game also keeps a running tally of the number of wins, losses, and ties.

OBJECT-ORIENTED PROGRAMMING

OOP (*object-oriented programming*) is a major feature of Visual Basic. In OOP, data and code are grouped together as objects. Objects are, in effect, self-contained entities. As an example, think about the Visual Basic forms and controls with which you have been working. Each of these represents a different type of object. Objects can store data and provide a carefully designed interface for accessing their data and exercising their functionality. This access is provided through object properties and methods. Objects also have the ability to validate any data that is passed to them and to reject it if it fails to meet certain predefined criteria. Thus, properly defined objects make applications more reliable.

Because objects control access to themselves and to their data, you can think of them as being like a black box, meaning that while you may know what a given object does and how to use it, you don't really know how it was put together or what makes it work. For example, think about the Form object. Every chapter game project that you have worked on has used one, yet you never had to create one. Visual Basic makes forms available to you as classes. Forms have their own properties, such as background color and foreground color, which you do not have to define or validate. Forms have methods associated with them, such as maximize and minimize, which you do not have to define. All you have to know is how to add new controls to your forms in order to modify them. Forms also have events, like the Load event, to which they automatically know how to respond.

OOP TERMS

In Visual Basic, objects are created from classes. A class provides a template that specifies data, properties, and methods that are available for working with the data.

DEFINITION

A class is a template that can be used to instantiate objects.

Visual Basic provides access to a large collection of classes. For example, the code behind a Form comes from the Form class, which is located in the System.Windows.Forms namespace. Examples of other classes include System.Windows.Forms.Button, where the Button class is defined, and System.Windows.Forms.CheckBox, where the CheckBox class is defined.

DEFINITION

A namespace is an organized collection of classes. The .NET Framework provides access to numerous namespaces, which it makes available in its class library.

Whether you realized it or not up to this point, you have been working with classes in all of the chapter game projects that you have worked on in this book. Every time that you have designed a new user interface, you have worked with classes provided by the .NET Framework. If you go back and look at your various chapter project applications, you'll notice that all of the code for the application is wrapped up inside an opening and closing Class statement. For example, the first and last statements in the Dice Poker game are shown below.

```
Public Class frmMain
```

```
End Class
```

As simple as these statements look, they deserve a little extra explanation. The opening statement publicly defines a new Class called frmMain, and the last statement defines the end of the class. However, there is more going on here than first meets the eye. Visual Basic 2005 Express makes things easy on you by hiding much of the work that it does behind the scenes on your behalf. To see what is really happening here, click on the Shall All Files button in Solution Explorer, expand the Form1.vb entry and click on the Form1.designer.VB entry. You'll see a whole bunch of behind-the-scenes code that Visual Basic has automatically generated on your behalf. You can learn a lot from studying the code that you see here, but it isn't necessary that you understand everything that you see. Take a look at the first two statements that are displayed, as shown below.

```
Partial Public Class frmMain
    Inherits System.Windows.Forms.Form
```

As you can now see, the form that Visual Basic has automatically provided you with is actually inherited (or cloned) from the Form class stored in the System.Windows.Forms namespace.

As should be obvious at this point, OOP simplifies the coding process by hiding many of the complexities of an application from the programmer. In addition, it promotes the reuse of code by making it possible to define a class once and then use it over and over again to create as many objects as required.

Visual Basic also allows you to create your own custom classes, which is much of the focus of this chapter. But before I get too deep into our discussion of OOP, let's stop for a minute and go over a few key terms and make sure that you understand the basic building blocks of OOP. These terms are abstraction, encapsulation, inheritance, and polymorphism.

Abstraction

Abstraction is a process by which you define in program code a logical representation of a class. This includes the specification of the base functionality belonging to the class and the definition of properties and methods that are required for the proper operation of the class. Returning to the Form class as an example, base properties include the Text, Size, BackColor, and ForeColor properties.

Encapsulation

Encapsulation is the process whereby you package the base functionality of a class and provide access to the features of the class through a collection of properties and methods. When an object is created from a particular class, the inner workings of the object are hidden from the programmer. Again, consider the Form class. You don't know what the code behind it looks like or how it is written. You cannot directly access its internal code or data. You only know that to work with the form, you modify its properties, execute its methods, and provide code for its events. How the Form class was designed to make all these things work is hidden from you. Thus, encapsulation helps simplify program development and hide complexity.

Encapsulation also includes data protection, meaning that code can be added to process and verify the validity of any data passed to an object to ensure that it meets certain criteria.

Inheritance

Inheritance is the process whereby one class is derived from another. When you define a new class in your program code, such as when you define a new class for a Visual Basic Form, the class that you create inherits its features from a base class, which in the case of this example is System.Windows.Forms.Form.

Polymorphism

Polymorphism is the ability to create something in different forms. Within Visual Basic, polymorphism is accomplished through a programming technique know as overloading. For example, using overloading, a programmer might develop multiple versions of the same procedure (with the same procedure name), each of which is designed to handle a different combination of arguments. For example, one version of a procedure might be set up to process a single Integer argument, whereas another version of

DEFINITION

Overloading is the process of defining the same method multiple times, each with a different argument list.

the procedure might be set up to process two arguments, one of which might be an Integer and the other of which might be a String.

TRICK One really good example of overloading that you have already seen and worked with is the MessageBox class's Show method. This method supports multiple overloads, allowing it to accept various combinations of arguments and data types. To view the various combinations of arguments and data that you can pass to the MessageBox.Show method, open the Visual Basic code editor and type MessageBox.Show. In response, IntelliSense will display a pop-up window showing the various options that are available to you. Click on the up and down arrows in the upper left-hand corner of the pop-up window to explore the various overload options that are available.

CLASSES AND OBJECTS

As I have already stated, a class is a template that defines all of the attributes, properties, methods, and events required to create an object. Using abstraction, programmers develop a design for a class. Using encapsulation, they implement a class structure. One class can be established by inheriting it from another class. Finally, using overloading, programmers can extend procedures within classes to handle different sets of arguments.

For example, you might analogize the relationship between a class and an object as being akin to the relationship between a mold and Jell-O. The mold defines an overall form and shape of the Jell-O. Once poured into the mold and solidified, the new instance of Jell-O takes on the basic qualities of the mold. As another, more specific, example, the Form object is an instance of the Form class and has access to all the features provided by that class.

In order to use a class, you must first instantiate it. The instantiation process varies depending on the class you are working with. For example, to instantiate a Button or CheckBox class (control), all that you have to do is place a copy of it on a form. However, if you create your own custom class as part of a Visual Basic application, you will create a new class instance using the New keyword.

Creating a New Class

There are a number of ways that you can create a new class. First, as you have already seen, anytime you create a new Visual Basic application, a new class is created for you based on the System.Windows.Forms.Form class. In the case of the Dice Poker game, the new class was named frmMain.

You can also add a new class to an application by simply inserting its declaration under the existing class definition in the code editor, as shown below.

```
Public Class frmMain

    Private Sub frmMain_Load(ByVal sender As System.Object, _
        ByVal e As System.EventArgs) Handles MyBase.Load

    End Sub

End Class

Public Class Greeting

End Class
```

In this example, a new class named Greeting has been defined. At the moment, the class does not have any data members, properties, or methods defined to it.

Let's continue on with the previous example, adding a little code to give the Greeting class a little functionality. Modify the example as shown below, starting with the code in the Greeting class and then adding the two statements inside the frmMain_Load event procedure.

DEFINITION

A data member is a variable that is defined within a class. Ordinarily, data members are hidden from the outside world and used only within the class. However, data members can be made directly accessible from outside the class using the Public keyword.

```
Public Class frmMain

    Private Sub frmMain_Load(ByVal sender As System.Object, _
        ByVal e As System.EventArgs) Handles MyBase.Load

        Dim SampleGreeting As New Greeting
        MessageBox.Show(SampleGreeting.Message)

    End Sub

End Class
```

```
Public Class Greeting

    Public Message As String = "Hello World!"

End Class
```

The statement that you added to the Greeting class sets up a data member. Data members are by default private, meaning that they cannot be accessed from outside of the class itself. However, in this example, I made the data member public just so that we could have a working example that does something.

By itself, the Greeting class does not do anything. You need to instantiate an object based on the class in order to be able to do something. The first statement in the frmMain_Load event procedure instantiates a new object named SampleGreeting using the New keyword, which follows the syntax shown below.

```
Dim ObjectName As New ClassName
```

Then the MessageBox.Show method is used to access and display the SampleGreeting object's Message data member.

Another way to add a new class to your application is to create it in its own code module, separate and distinct from the form's class code, as demonstrated in the following example.

1. Click on the Add Class option located on the Project menu. The Add New Item window appears, as shown in Figure 9.6.

Using the Class template to define a new class

Assigning a unique name to the class

FIGURE 9.6

Defining a new class in its own code module.

2. Select the Class icon and type a name for the class that you are about to define in the Name field, and then click on the Add button.

3. A new tab will appear in the code editor, and the opening and closing class statements for the new class will be displayed, as shown in Figure 9.7.

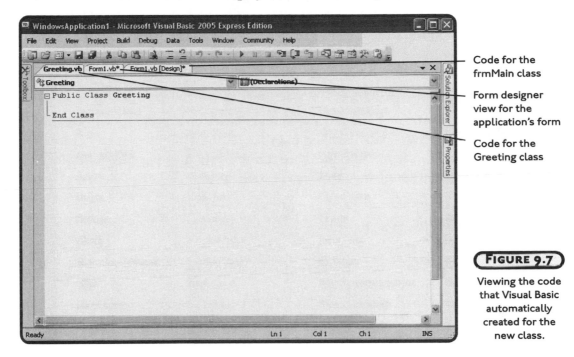

Code for the frmMain class

Form designer view for the application's form

Code for the Greeting class

FIGURE 9.7

Viewing the code that Visual Basic automatically created for the new class.

4. Modify the program code for the Greeting class as shown below.

```
Public Class Greeting

    Public Message As String = "Hello World!"

End Class
```

Now, if you run this example, you will find that it displays the same results as the example in which you embedded the Class definition beneath the bottom of the frmMain class.

Understanding Data Members

In the previous two examples that demonstrated how to create a new class, you learned how to define a new data member. By default, class data members are private, which means that they cannot be seen or accessed from outside the class. However, as the examples showed, you can make data members publicly available. You can also declare them as protected, in which case they can be accessed only by derived classes of the base class.

Although it is possible for data members to be accessed from outside the class, they are not properties of that class. However, when made publicly available, you lose the ability to restrict control over data members. Instead of making data members public, you should keep them private and set up properties to provide controlled access to any data stored in your classes.

Defining Class Properties

Properties can be used to set and retrieve values. To set up a property within a class, you start by declaring a private data member and then define a public property procedure that provides controlled access to the value stored in the data member. The following types of property procedures are supported by Visual Basic.

- **Get**. Retrieves the value assigned to a property
- **Set**. Assigns a value to a property

The following example demonstrates how to add a property to a class.

```
Public Class Greeting

    Private Message As String

    Public Property Text() As String
        Get
            Return Message
        End Get
        Set(ByVal Value As String)
            Message = Value
        End Set
    End property
End Class
```

As you have seen throughout this book, before you can use an object, you must instantiate it. You can then reference its properties by specifying the name of the object, followed by a period and the name of a particular property. When you assign a value to the Text property, the Set property procedure block executes. Note that the Set property procedure is automatically passed an argument named Value in which the data passed to the Set property procedure is stored. All you have to do to finish up the property assignment is to assign the data stored in Value to a private data member (Message). When you retrieve the value associated with the Text property, the Get procedure block is automatically executed.

The following statements demonstrate how to derive an object from the Greeting class and then set and retrieve the object's Text property. The first statement shown below instantiates a new object named SampleGreeting that is derived from the Greeting class. The next two statements assign a value to the object's Text property and then use the Message-Box.Show method to demonstrate that the property assignment was successful.

```
Dim objSample As New Greeting
objSample.Text = "Good Morning."
MessageBox.Show(objSample.Text)
```

As I mentioned earlier, the advantage of setting up properties, compared to simply making data members public, is that you can add code to your property procedures to perform data validation before allowing access to the data associated with a particular property. As a quick example of how this works, I have modified the previous example, shown below, to include such a check.

```
Public Property Text() As String
        Get
             Return Message
        End Get
        Set(ByVal Value As String)
            If Len(Value) > 2 Then
                 Message = Value
            End If
        End Set
End Property
```

This new example now requires that a property assignment for the Text property be at least two characters in length.

Adding Class Methods

In addition to defining data members and properties in your custom classes, you can add your own methods. To add a method to a class, all you have to do is add a Sub or Function procedure, as demonstrated below.

```
Public Class Greeting

    Private Message As String

    Public Property Text() As String
        Get
            Return Message
        End Get
        Set(ByVal Value As String)
            If Len(Value) > 2 Then
                Message = Value
            End If
        End Set
    End Property

    Public Sub PostWelcome()
        MessageBox.Show("Welcome to my Visual Basic application!")
    End Sub

End Class
```

In this example, the Greeting class has been modified by the addition of a method named PostWelcome(). When executed, this method uses the MessageBox.Show method to display a text message. Like all of the other object methods that you have worked with, you can call on this method by specifying the name of its object followed by a period and the name of the method, as shown below.

```
Dim objSample As New Greeting
objSample.PostWelcome()
```

One of Visual Basic's object-oriented programming features is polymorphism. Polymorphism is implemented in Visual Basic by providing the ability to overload class methods.

When you overload a method, as demonstrated below, Visual Basic makes sure that the correct method is executed based on the argument list that is passed.

```
Public Class DisplayMessage

    Public Overloads Sub Display(ByVal Message As String)
        MessageBox.Show(Message)
    End Sub
```

```
Public Overloads Sub Display(ByVal Message As String, Title As String)
    MessageBox.Show(Message, Title)
End Sub

End Class
```

In this example, two Sub procedures, both of which are named Display, are defined. Notice the use of the keyword Overloads in both Sub procedure definitions. The first Sub procedure is designed to process a single argument, whereas the second Sub procedure is designed to process two arguments.

 TRICK For overloading to work, you must provide each overloaded procedure with a unique set of arguments. You can vary the argument list by changing the number of arguments that are passed, by changing the types of argument passed, or a combination of both.

Inheriting from Another Class

Anytime Visual Basic provides you with a new form, behind the scenes the new instance of the form is created by specifying the Inherits keyword and the name of the class that is to be inherited from, as shown below.

```
Partial Public Class frmMain
    Inherits System.Windows.Forms.Form
```

The derived class inherits its features from the base class. Anytime you add a control to a form, Visual Basic automatically handles the setup of the new instance of the control (object). In addition to inheriting from classes provided to you by Visual Basic and the .NET Framework, you can derive new classes from classes that you create. The following example demonstrates how to create a new class named GreetingTwo using the Greeting class as the base class.

```
Public Class GreetingTwo
    Inherits Greeting

    Private Warning As String = "Action not allowed."

    Public ReadOnly Property ErrMsg() As String
        Get
            Return Warning
```

```
      End Get
  End Property
```

```
End Class
```

You'll notice that the GreetingTwo class not only inherits all of the properties and methods belonging to the Greeting class, but also extends this functionality by adding a new property of its own. In addition, you'll notice that the new ErrMsg property has been made read-only, meaning that it can be retrieved but not modified by calling statements.

Any objects created using the new GreetingTwo class automatically inherit all of the properties and methods from the GreetingTwo class, which itself includes methods and properties inherited from the Greeting class.

BACK TO THE ROCK, PAPER AND SCISSORS GAME

It is time to turn your attention back to the development of this chapter's game project, the Rock, Paper and Scissors game. You will create this game by following the five basic development steps that you've used to create all the previous chapter projects.

Designing the Game

The Rock, Paper and Scissors game is played on a single window and is made up of one form and the 22 controls listed in Table 9.1.

TABLE 9.1: FORM CONTROLS FOR THE ROCK, PAPER AND SCISSORS GAME

Control Type	Control Name	Description
PictureBox	pcbLeft	Displays an image showing the computer's selection
PictureBox	pcbRight	Displays an image showing the player's selection
Label	lblComputer	Identifies the PictureBox control where the player's computer's selection is displayed
Label	lblPlayer	Identifies the PictureBox control where the player's selection is displayed
Label	lblCountDown	Identifies the function of the ProgressBar control
ProgressBar	pgbCountDown	Displays a graphical 1.5-second countdown

continued

TABLE 9.1: FORM CONTROLS FOR THE ROCK, PAPER AND SCISSORS GAME

Button	btnPlay	Starts game play by enabling the Timer control
Button	btnRock	Allows the player to select Rock
Button	btnPaper	Allows the player to select Paper
Button	btnScissors	Allows the player to select Scissors
GroupBox	grpStatus	Contains Label and TextBox controls that identify and display game statistics
Label	lblWins	Identifies the TextBox control that displays the number of games won
Label	lblLosses	Identifies the TextBox control that displays the number of games lost
Label	lblTies	Identifies the TextBox control that displays the number of games tied
TextBox	txtWins	Displays the number of games the player has won
TextBox	txtLosses	Displays the number of games the player has lost
TextBox	txtTies	Displays the number of games the player has tied
Label	lblResults	Identifies the TextBox control where the results of each game are displayed
TextBox	lblOutput	Displays a test string detailing the results of each game
ToolTip	tltControl	Provides the ability to assign ToolTips to individual controls
Timer	tmrControl	Controls the 1.5-second countdown sequence and the half-second windows in which the player gets to make a selection
ImageList	imlHands	Stores the bitmap images that are displayed in the PictureBox controls during game play

Step 1: Creating a New Visual Basic Project

The first step in creating the Rock, Paper and Scissors game is to open up Visual Basic and create a new project as outlined below.

1. If you have not already done so, start up Visual Basic 2005 Express and then click on File and select New Project. The New Project dialog will appear.

2. Select Windows Application template.

3. Type `RockPaperScissors` as the name of your new application in the `Name` field located at the bottom of the New Project window.

4. Click on `OK` to close the New Project dialog.

Visual Basic will now create a new project for you and display a new form upon which you will design the game's user interface.

Step 2: Creating the User Interface

Let's begin the development of the Rock, Paper and Scissors game by laying out and resizing all of the controls that will be needed to set up the game's user interface. As you go about the job of configuring the game's user interface, refer to Figure 9.8 so that you'll know where to place each control and when and how to resize them.

FIGURE 9.8

Completing the interface design for the Rock, Paper and Scissors game.

1. Begin by clicking on the form and setting its `Size` property to `488, 456`.

2. Add two `PictureBox` controls, one in the upper left-hand corner of the form and the other in the upper right-hand corner. Set the `Size` property for both `PictureBox` controls to `129,103`.

3. Next, add a pair of `Label` controls to the form. Place the first one just under the first `PictureBox` control and the second one just under the second `PictureBox` control.

4. Add another Label control about an inch below the left-hand side of the first PictureBox control, and then add a ProgressBar control just beneath it, setting its Size property to 250, 34.

5. Add four Button controls to the form, as shown in Figure 9.8.

6. Add a GroupBox control to the lower left-hand corner of the form and set its Size property to 187, 108.

7. Add three Label controls and three TextBox controls inside the GroupBox control as shown in Figure 9.8.

8. Add another Label control just to the right of the GroupBox control and then add a TextBox underneath it. Set the TextBox control's Multiline property equal to True and set its Size property for the TextBox control to 229, 86.

9. Finally, add ToolTip, Timer, and ImageList controls.

At this point, you have added all of the controls that you will need in order to develop the Rock, Paper and Scissors game. In addition, you have completed the overall layout of the game's user interface and are ready to start making property modifications to the game's form and controls.

Step 3: Customizing Form and Control Properties

OK, let's get to work on making the required changes to the game's form and control properties as listed in Table 9.2.

TABLE 9.2: PROPERTY CHANGES FOR FORM1

Property	Value
Name	frmMain
BackColor	LightYellow
FormBorderStyle	Fixed3D
MaximizeBox	False
MinimizeBox	False
StartPosition	CenterScreen
Text	**Rock, Paper and Scissors**

Make the property changes shown in Table 9.3 to the PictureBox controls.

TABLE 9.3: PROPERTY CHANGES FOR PICTUREBOX CONTROLS

Control	Property	Value
PictureBox1	Name	pcbLeft
	BorderStyle	Fixed3D
	SizeMode	StretchImage
PictureBox2	Name	pcbRight
	BorderStyle	Fixed3D
	SizeMode	StretchImage

Make the property changes shown in Table 9.4 to the Label controls.

TABLE 9.4: PROPERTY CHANGES FOR LABEL CONTROLS

Control	Property	Value
Label1	Name	lblComputer
	Font.Bold	True
	Text	Computer's Pick
Label2	Name	lblPlayer
	Font.Bold	True
	Text	Player's Pick
Label3	Name	lblCountDown
	Font.Bold	True
	Text	Countdown
Label4	Name	lblWins
	Font.Bold	True
	Text	Wins :

continued

TABLE 9.4: PROPERTY CHANGES FOR LABEL CONTROLS

Label5	Name	lblLosses
	Font.Bold	True
	Text	**Losses :**
Label6	Name	lblTies
	Font.Bold	True
	Text	**Ties :**
Label7	Name	lblResults
	Font.Bold	True
	Text	**Game Results**

Next, change the name of the ProgressBar control to pgbCountDown. Then make the property changes shown in Table 9.5 to the four Button controls.

The ProgressBar control is used to display a visual indication of the status of a process. Once added to a form, you can update the ProgressBar control's appearance by setting its Value property to zero to represent a process that has not started. You can then set the Value property anywhere between 0 and 100 to represent the current status of a process. Finally, you can set the Value property to 100 to represent a process that has completed.

TABLE 9.5: PROPERTY CHANGES FOR BUTTON CONTROLS

Control	Property	Value
Button1	Name	btnPlay
	BackColor	ButtonFace
	Font.Bold	True
	Text	**Play**
	ToolTip	**Begin 1.5 second countdown**
Button2	Name	btnRock
	BackColor	ButtonFace
	Enabled	False
	Font.Bold	True
	Text	**Rock**
	ToolTip	**Select Rock**
Button3	Name	btnPaper
	BackColor	ButtonFace
	Enabled	False
	Font.Bold	True
	Text	**Rock**
	ToolTip	**Select Paper**
Button4	Name	btnScissors
	BackColor	ButtonFace
	Enabled	False
	Font.Bold	True
	Text	**Rock**
	ToolTip	**Select Scissors**

Make the property changes shown in Table 9.6 to the four TextBox controls.

Control	Property	Value
TABLE 9.6: PROPERTY CHANGES FOR TEXTBOX CONTROLS		
Control	Property	Value
TextBox1	Name	txtWins
	Font.Bold	True
	ReadOnly	True
	TextAlign	Right
TextBox2	Name	txtLosses
	Font.Bold	True
	ReadOnly	True
	TextAlign	Right
TextBox3	Name	txtTies
	Font.Bold	True
	ReadOnly	True
	TextAlign	Right
TextBox4	Name	txtOutput
	Font.Bold	True
	ReadOnly	True

Next, change the name of the ToolTip control to tltControl. Then make the property changes shown in Table 9.7 to the Timer control.

Control	Property	Value
TABLE 9.7: PROPERTY CHANGES FOR TIMER CONTROL		
Control	Property	Value
Timer1	Name	tmrControl
	Interval	500

Finally, change the name of the Name property for the ImageList control to imlHands. Change the ImageList control's ImageSize property to 96,96 and then add the following bitmap images to its Images property (collection) as shown in Table 9.8. You'll find copies of the Bitmap images required to complete this project, along with the source code, on this book's companion web site.

TABLE 9.8: BITMAP IMAGES TO ADD TO THE IMAGELIST CONTROLS IMAGES COLLECTION		
Property	**File**	**Index No.**
Name	Left-Paper.bmp	0
Name	Right-Paper.bmp	1
Name	Left-Rock.bmp	2
Name	Right-Rock.bmp	3
Name	Left-Scissors.bmp	4
Name	Right-Scissors.bmp	5
Name	Blank.bmp	6

That's it. The user interface for the Rock, Paper and Scissors game is now complete. Let's move on to the next step and begin adding program code.

Step 4: Adding a Little Programming Logic

The first task to perform in putting together the program code for the Rock, Paper and Scissors game is to double-click on the game's form in order to open the code editor. In response, Visual Basic automatically defines a new Class for you called frmMain (the name you assigned to Form1). This derived class will inherit properties, methods, and events associated with the System.Windows.Forms base class.

Once the frmMain class has been defined, you can begin adding the program code. For starters, define a variable named intCounter with a data type of Integer as shown below. This variable will be used later in the application to keep track of a 1.5-second countdown process that controls the tempo of the game.

```
Public Class frmMain

    'Declare a variable to be used as a counter
    Private intCounter As Integer

End Class
```

There are a few one-time activities that need to be performed when the Rock, Paper and Scissors game first starts up. These activities include loading a blank bitmap image into both of the game's PictureBox controls and setting all of the Text properties for the three Textbox controls located in the GroupBox control to zero. To accomplish these activities, add the following code statements to the form's Load event.

```
'This procedure loads default settings when the form first loads
Private Sub Form1_Load(ByVal sender As System.Object, _
   ByVal e As System.EventArgs) Handles MyBase.Load

    pcbLeft.Image = imlHands.Images.Item(6) 'Load a blank Bitmap
    pcbRight.Image = imlHands.Images.Item(6) 'Load a blank Bitmap

    'Set game statistics stored in the game's Textbox control to zero
    txtWins.Text = 0
    txtLosses.Text = 0
    txtTies.Text = 0

End Sub
```

In order to initiate game play, the player must click on the Button control labeled Play. This button initiates the game's 1.5-second countdown process by setting the Value property of the ProgressBar control equal to 0 and then enabling the Timer control. This procedure also clears the display of any leftover text in the txtOutput (Textbox) control and sets the display of blank bitmap images in the game's two PictureBox controls. The code for the btnPlay_Click event Sub procedure is shown below.

```
'This procedure initiates the game's 1.5-second countdown
Private Sub btnPlay_Click(ByVal sender As System.Object, _
   ByVal e As System.EventArgs) Handles btnPlay.Click
```

```
pgbCountDown.Value = 0 'Set ProgressBar to show 0 percent progress
tmrControl.Enabled = True 'Start countdown by enabling the Timer
txtOutput.Text = "" 'Clear out any text stored in the Textbox
pcbLeft.Image = imlHands.Images.Item(6)  'Load a blank Bitmap
pcbRight.Image = imlHands.Images.Item(6) 'Load a blank Bitmap
```

End Sub

The Timer control is responsible for controlling the timing of the game. It simulates the amount of time that it typically takes for two players to manually sync up by performing a 1.5-second countdown. The Timer controls Interval property was set at design time to 500, which equates to a half-second. The value of the intCounter variable is incremented by 1 upon each tick of the Timer control.

The tmrControl_Tick procedure, shown below, uses a Select Case block to keep track of time. Once the first half-second has passed, the value of intCounter will be 1 and the ProgressBar control's Value property is set to 33, in order to provide the player with a visual indicator that a third of the countdown has elapsed. After the passage of a full second, the second Case statement is triggered and the ProgressBar control's Value property is updated to show that two-thirds of the countdown have elapsed.

```
'This procedure controls the timing of game play
Private Sub tmrControl_Tick(ByVal sender As System.Object, _
  ByVal e As System.EventArgs) Handles tmrControl.Tick

    intCounter += 1  'Increment counter

    'Determine the actions to take based on the counter's value
    Select Case intCounter
        Case 1  'At .5 seconds
            pgbCountDown.Value = 33 'Set ProgressBar to show 33%
        Case 2  'At 1 second
            pgbCountDown.Value = 66 'Set ProgressBar to show 66%
        Case 3  'At 1.5 seconds
            pgbCountDown.Value = 100 'Set ProgressBar to show 100%
            'Enable the 3 game choice buttons
            btnRock.Enabled = True
            btnPaper.Enabled = True
            btnScissors.Enabled = True
```

```
        Case 4  'At 2 seconds
            intCounter = 0  'Set counter to zero
            tmrControl.Enabled = False 'Disable the Timer Control
            'Disable the 3 game choice buttons
            btnRock.Enabled = False
            btnPaper.Enabled = False
            btnScissors.Enabled = False
            pgbCountDown.Value = 0 'Set ProgressBar to show 0%
        Case Else
    End Select

End Sub
```

At 1.5 seconds, the ProgressBar control's Value property is updated to show that the count-down is complete. At this point, the buttons representing the Rock, Paper and Scissors options are enabled, and the player has a half-second in which to make a choice of which button to click. Once the last half-second interval has elapsed, the last Case statement is triggered. As a result, the value of intCounter is reset to 0, the three option buttons are disabled, the Timer control is disabled, and the ProgressBar control is cleared by setting its Value property to 0.

The code for the Button control event representing the selection of the Rock option is shown below. It includes two Dim statements that define local variables used to store both the player's and the computer's choices. The last four statements in this procedure display a graphic representing the player's choice of Rock, sets the strPlayerPick variable equal to Rock, calls on the ComputerTurn() procedure function to retrieve the computer's choice, and then passes the player's and computer's choices to the CheckGameResults() procedure for processing (to determine the results of the game).

```
'This procedure executes when the player selects Rock
Private Sub btnRock_Click(ByVal sender As System.Object, _
  ByVal e As System.EventArgs) Handles btnRock.Click

    Dim strPlayerPick As String 'Used to store player's move
    Dim strComputerPick As String 'Used to store computer's move

    'Load Bitmap representing a Rock into the right-most PictureBox
    pcbRight.Image = imlHands.Images.Item(3)
```

```
strPlayerPick = "Rock" 'Set the player's move equal to Rock

'Run procedure that determines the computer's move
strComputerPick = ComputerTurn()

'Run procedure that determines who has won the game
CheckGameResults(strPlayerPick, strComputerPick)
```

End Sub

The Click event procedure for the Button control representing the Paper option is shown below. Its code is almost identical to that of the Button control for the Rock option, except that it reflects the player's choice of Paper as the move.

```
'This procedure executes when the player selects Paper
Private Sub btnPaper_Click(ByVal sender As System.Object, _
  ByVal e As System.EventArgs) Handles btnPaper.Click

    Dim strPlayerPick As String 'Used to store player's move
    Dim strComputerPick As String 'Used to store computer's move

    'Load Bitmap representing Paper into the right-most PictureBox
    pcbRight.Image = imlHands.Images.Item(1)

    strPlayerPick = "Paper" 'Set the player's move equal to Paper

    'Run procedure that determines the computer's move
    strComputerPick = ComputerTurn()

    'Run procedure that determines who has won the game
    CheckGameResults(strPlayerPick, strComputerPick)
```

End Sub

The code for the Button control representing the Scissors option is shown below. As you can see, it is only a slight variation of the previous two procedures.

```
'This procedure executes when the player selects Scissors
Private Sub btnScissors_Click(ByVal sender As System.Object, _
  ByVal e As System.EventArgs) Handles btnScissors.Click

    Dim strPlayerPick As String 'Used to store player's move
    Dim strComputerPick As String 'Used to store computer's move

    'Load Bitmap representing Scissors into the right-most PictureBox
    pcbRight.Image = imlHands.Images.Item(5)

    strPlayerPick = "Scissors" 'Set player's move equal to Scissors

    'Run procedure that determines the computer's move
    strComputerPick = ComputerTurn()

    'Run procedure that determines who has won the game
    CheckGameResults(strPlayerPick, strComputerPick)

End Sub
```

The ComputerTurn() procedure, shown below, is a custom-developed Function. Therefore, you will have to manually define it before you can begin coding it. It begins by defining a local variable that will be used to store the computer's selection. Then the Random class's Next method is used to generate a random number between 1 and 3.

```
'This procedure determines the computer's move
Function ComputerTurn() As String

    'Declare a variable to hold a randomly generated number
    Dim intRandomNumber As Integer

    Dim r As New Random 'Instantiate a Random object

    'Use the Random class's Next method to get a number between 1 - 3
    intRandomNumber = r.Next(1, 3)
```

```
    If intRandomNumber = 3 Then   'Assign Rock as the computer's turn
        'Load Bitmap of Rock into left-most PictureBox
        pcbLeft.Image = imlHands.Images.Item(2)
        Return "Rock"
    End If

    If intRandomNumber = 2 Then 'Assign Scissors as the computer's turn
        'Load Bitmap of Scissors into left-most PictureBox
        pcbLeft.Image = imlHands.Images.Item(4)
        Return "Scissors"
    End If

    If intRandomNumber = 1 Then 'Assign Paper as the computer's turn
        'Load Bitmap of Paper into left-most PictureBox
        pcbLeft.Image = imlHands.Images.Item(1)
        Return "Paper"
    End If


End Function
```

The rest of the ComputerTurn() procedure processes the randomly generated number using three If…Then statements. If the random number is equal to 3, the computer's choice is set equal to Rock and the appropriate graphic is loaded into the first PictureBox control. The second and third If…Then blocks are used to process the computer choice for Paper and Scissors.

The CheckGameResults() Sub procedure, shown below, processes two arguments. The arguments passed to it are the player's and the computer's choices. This procedure is made up of a Select Case block that compares the player's choice against each of the three possible options (Rock, Paper and Scissors). Based on which of the three options match the player's choice, three embedded If…Then statements are executed in order to determine what choice the computer was assigned by the game. Once the player's and the computer's choices have been identified, the appropriate output string is posted in the txtOutput (TextBox) control, and the value stored in the TextBox controls that represent the number of games won, lost, and tied is incremented as appropriate.

```
'This procedure compares the player's move to the computer's move
Sub CheckGameResults(ByVal strPlayerPick As String, _
  ByVal strComputerPick As String)
```

```
pgbCountDown.Value = 0 'Set the ProgressBar to show 0%

Select Case strPlayerPick  'Process the player's move

    Case "Rock" 'Determine results if the player picks Rock
        If strComputerPick = "Rock" Then
            txtOutput.Text = "Rock versus Rock is a Tie!"
            'Add 1 to the TextBox that displays the # of ties
            txtTies.Text += 1
        End If
        If strComputerPick = "Scissors" Then
            txtOutput.Text = "Rock crushes Scissors. You Win!"
            'Add 1 to the TextBox that displays the # of wins
            txtWins.Text += 1
        End If
        If strComputerPick = "Paper" Then
            txtOutput.Text = "Paper covers Rock. You Lose!"
            'Add 1 to the TextBox that displays the # of losses
            txtLosses.Text += 1
        End If

    Case "Scissors" 'Determine results if the player picks Scissors
        If strComputerPick = "Rock" Then
            txtOutput.Text = "Rock breaks scissors. You Lose!"
            'Add 1 to the TextBox that displays the # of losses
            txtLosses.Text += 1
        End If
        If strComputerPick = "Scissors" Then
            txtOutput.Text = "Scissors versus Scissors is a Tie"
            'Add 1 to the TextBox that displays the # of ties
            txtTies.Text += 1
        End If
        If strComputerPick = "Paper" Then
            txtOutput.Text = "Scissors cut Paper. You Win!"
            'Add 1 to the TextBox that displays the # of wins
            txtWins.Text += 1
        End If
```

```
                Case "Paper" 'Determine results if the player picks Paper
                     If strComputerPick = "Rock" Then
                          txtOutput.Text = "Paper covers Rock. You Win!"
                          'Add 1 to the TextBox that displays the # of wins
                          txtWins.Text += 1
                     End If
                     If strComputerPick = "Scissors" Then
                          txtOutput.Text = "Scissors cut Paper. You Lose!"
                          'Add 1 to the TextBox that displays the # of losses
                          txtLosses.Text += 1
                     End If
                     If strComputerPick = "Paper" Then
                          txtOutput.Text = "Paper versus paper is a Tie!"
                          'Add 1 to the TextBox that displays the # of ties
                          txtTies.Text += 1
                     End If
          End Select

End Sub
```

Step 5: Testing the Execution of the Rock, Paper and Scissors Game

OK. That's it. The Rock, Paper and Scissors game is now ready to run. Go ahead and run the game by pressing F5 and make sure that everything works like it is supposed to. If you run into any problems, go back and double-check your typing. Once things are in order, pass it around to a few of your friends and ask them what they think.

SUMMARY

In this chapter, you learned about Visual Basic classes and namespaces. You learned how to create your own custom classes. You then learned how to instantiate new objects using your custom classes. The custom objects that you created included their own properties and methods. You also learned how to overload object methods and how to provide controlled access to data stored within your objects. On top of all this, you created the Rock, Paper and Scissors game.

Now, before you move on to Chapter 10, "Graphics, Audio, and Animation," spend a few additional minutes improving the Rock, Paper and Scissors game by implementing the following challenges.

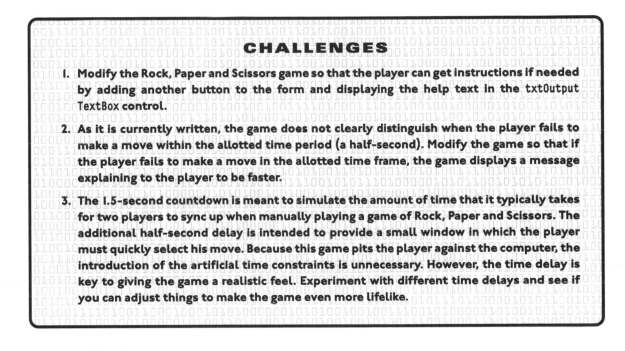

CHALLENGES

1. Modify the Rock, Paper and Scissors game so that the player can get instructions if needed by adding another button to the form and displaying the help text in the txtOutput TextBox control.

2. As it is currently written, the game does not clearly distinguish when the player fails to make a move within the allotted time period (a half-second). Modify the game so that if the player fails to make a move in the allotted time frame, the game displays a message explaining to the player to be faster.

3. The 1.5-second countdown is meant to simulate the amount of time that it typically takes for two players to sync up when manually playing a game of Rock, Paper and Scissors. The additional half-second delay is intended to provide a small window in which the player must quickly select his move. Because this game pits the player against the computer, the introduction of the artificial time constraints is unnecessary. However, the time delay is key to giving the game a realistic feel. Experiment with different time delays and see if you can adjust things to make the game even more lifelike.

INTEGRATING GRAPHICS AND AUDIO

This chapter will introduce you to various graphic and audio capabilities provided by Visual Basic 2005 Express. You will learn how to work with a number of new classes associated with the System.Drawing.Graphics namespace. Using objects created from classes stored in this namespace, you will learn how to draw custom graphics in your applications. You will also learn how to use the SoundPlayer control to enable playing sounds in your applications. In addition, you will learn how to work with the classes stored in the My namespace in order to create a small application called the Audio Jukebox. On top of all this, you will learn how to create this chapter's game project, the VB Doodle game.

Specifically, you will learn how to:

- Work with the Graphics, Pen, Pens, Brush, and Brushes classes
- Draw both graphics and text
- Work with the SoundPlayer class in order to add sounds to your applications
- Use classes in the My namespace to display a list of files and to play wave files

PROJECT PREVIEW: THE VB DOODLE GAME

In this chapter, you will demonstrate your knowledge and understanding of Visual Basic graphics capabilities by developing the VB Doodle game. VB Doodle is a drawing program that will provide players with the ability to draw freehand images as well as assistance in drawing a number of predefined shapes, such as lines and rectangles.

Figures 10.1 to 10.4 show examples from the VB Doodle game, demonstrating its functionality and overall execution flow.

FIGURE 10.1

The user interface for the VB Doodle game consists of a control panel and a drawing area.

FIGURE 10.2

VB Doodle provides the player with a range of colors to choose from.

FIGURE 10.3

The game assists the player in drawing an assortment of predefined shapes.

FIGURE 10.4

The player also has the option of making a freehand drawing using any combination of colors.

By the time you have finished the creation of the VB Doodle game, you will have demonstrated your understanding of the fundamentals of working with Visual Basic's built-in graphic drawing capabilities. You will be well prepared to move on and tackle more advanced graphics topics.

INTEGRATING GRAPHICS INTO YOUR VISUAL BASIC APPLICATIONS

Visual Basic 2005 Express provides graphic support based on GDI+ (*Graphics Device Interface*), which it implements in the form of properties and methods made available by classes organized in the System.Drawing namespace. GDI+ provides support for managing and displaying graphic images, drawing vector graphics, and drawing text.

DEFINITION

GDI+ (Graphics Device Interface) is a graphics system that provides applications with the ability to create graphics and draw text for video and print output.

GDI+ draws graphics using a coordinate system. Coordinates are measured using pixels. A graphic is rendered by specifying its starting position relative to coordinates (0,0) and other required coordinates to render a particular shape based on their distance from (0,0) on the X and Y axis, as depicted in Figure 10.5.

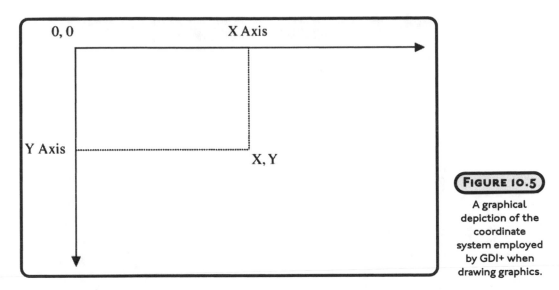

0, 0   X Axis

Y Axis

                              X, Y

FIGURE 10.5

A graphical
depiction of the
coordinate
system employed
by GDI+ when
drawing graphics.

Working with Graphic Images

As you have seen in earlier chapters, Visual Basic makes it relatively easy to add the display of graphic images to applications using the `PictureBox` control. Other controls, such as the `Button` control, also provide the ability to display bitmaps. Visual Basic provides built-in support for numerous types of graphic files, including .bmp, .jpeg, and .gif.

DEFINITION

A pixel (picture element) is a unit of measure. The computer's display is measured in terms of the number of pixels that it displays (for example, 800 x 600, 1024 x 786, and so on).

As you have already seen, you can configure the `PictureBox` control's `Image` property to display a graphic image. You also learned through the creation of the Dice Poker game, shown in Figure 10.6, that you can preload graphic images into an `ImageList` control and then display these images in any control capable of displaying them.

GDI+ support for images also includes the ability to manipulate them in many different ways, including stretching, centering, and zooming.

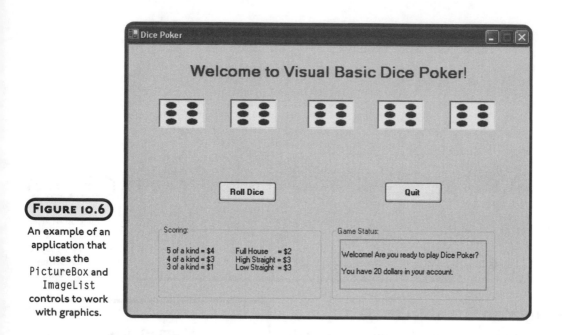

FIGURE 10.6

An example of an application that uses the PictureBox and ImageList controls to work with graphics.

Drawing Vector Graphics

Instead of simply rendering a copy of an already existing graphic image, GDI+ provides Visual Basic with the ability to draw (from scratch) images using coordinates passed to various methods. Visual Basic allows you to draw on various surfaces, including Button and Form backgrounds. You can execute methods that can draw lines, ellipses, rectangles, polygons, pie shapes, arcs, curved shapes, and so on. For example, to draw a rectangle, you only have to call on the appropriate method and pass it the coordinates of the starting and end points for the figure.

Working with the Graphics Class

In order to draw a graphic, you need a surface to draw it on, such as a Form or Button control. Before you can start drawing, you must create a Graphics object for the drawing surface you intend on using. The first step in completing this task is to set up an instance of the Graphics class within your application, as demonstrated below.

```
Dim MyGraphics As System.Drawing.Graphics
```

Once this has been done, you call on the CreateObjects() function in order to establish a pointer to the control or form to be used as the drawing surface, as demonstrated below.

```
Private Sub frmMain_Load(ByVal sender As System.Object, _
  ByVal e As System.EventArgs) Handles MyBase.Load

    FormGraphic = Me.CreateGraphics()

End Sub
```

In this example, the object variable FormGraphic has been set to use the frmMain form (Me) as a drawing surface. Once the Graphics class reference has been defined and the drawing surface established, you can begin drawing graphics within your application by calling on any of the Graphics class's methods, as listed in Table 10.1.

TABLE 10.1: DRAWING METHODS ASSOCIATED WITH THE SYSTEM.DRAWING.GRAPHICS CLASS

Method	Description
Clear	Clears the drawing surface
DrawArc	Draws an arc
DrawBezier	Draws a bezier curve
DrawBeziers	Draws a collection of bezier curves
DrawClosedCurve	Draws a closed curve
DrawCurve	Draws a curve
DrawEllipse	Draws an ellipse
DrawIcon	Draws an icon
DrawIconUnstretched	Draws the image without scaling its image
DrawImage	Draws an image
DrawImageUnscaled	Draws an image without scaling its size
DrawLine	Draws a line
DrawLines	Draws a collection of line segments
DrawPath	Draws a graphics path
DrawPie	Draws a pie shape
DrawPolygon	Draws a polygon
DrawRectangle	Draws a rectangle

continued

TABLE 10.1: DRAWING METHODS ASSOCIATED WITH THE SYSTEM.DRAWING.GRAPHICS CLASS	
DrawRectangles	Draws a collection of rectangles
DrawString	Draws a text string
FillClosedCurve	Draws a filled curve
FillEllipse	Draws a filled ellipse
FillPath	Draws a filled path
FillPie	Draws a filled pie
FillPolygon	Draws a filled polygon
FillRectangle	Draws a filled rectangle
FillRectangles	Draws a collection of filled rectangles
FillRegion	Draws a filled region

Working with the Pen Class

One way in which to draw a graphic using the Graphics class is with the Pen class. This is done as demonstrated below.

```
FormGraphic.DrawLine(pen, Coordinates)
```

In this example, Pen represents a Pen object and *Coordinates* represents the start and ending point for a line. The Pen class is located in the System.Drawing namespace. It allows you to specify how you want a given image to be drawn. One Pen property is Color, which allows you to specify the color of the line to be drawn. Another Pen property is Brush, which is used to retrieve or set a Brush object for the Pen. Using methods associated with the Brush class, you can draw filled-in shapes.

In order to specify a color when drawing shapes with the Pen class or filling in shapes with the Brush class, you can specify any of a large collection of predefined colors that are provided by these classes. Table 10.2 provides a complete list of the colors provided by these two classes.

The following example demonstrates the syntax involved in drawing a green line using the Pen class.

```
FormGraphic.DrawLine(Pen.Green, coordinates)
```

Similarly, the following syntax demonstrates how to formulate a statement that fills in a red rectangle shape using the Brush class.

```
FormGraphic.FillRectangle(Brush.Red, coordinates)
```

TABLE 10.2: PREDEFINED COLORS PROVIDED BY THE PENS AND BRUSHES CLASSES

AliceBlue	DarkTurquoise	LightSkyBlue	Peru
AntiqueWhite	DarkViolet	LightSlateGray	Pink
Aqua	DeepPink	LightSteelBlue	Plum
Aquamarine	DeepSkyBlue	LightYellow	PowderBlue
Azure	DimGray	Lime	Purple
Beige	DodgerBlue	LimeGreen	Red
Bisque	Firebrick	Linen	RosyBrown
Black	FloralWhite	Magenta	RoyalBlue
BlanchedAlmond	ForestGreen	Maroon	SaddleBrown
Blue	Fuchsia	MediumAquamarine	Salmon
BlueViolet	Gainsboro	MediumOrchid	SandyBrown
Brown	GhostWhite	MediumPurple	SeaGreen
BurlyWood	Gold	MediumSeaGreen	SeaShell
CadetBlue	Goldenrod	MediumSeaGreen	Sienna
Chartreuse	Gray	MediumSlateBlue	Silver
Chocolate	Green	MediumSpringGreen	SkyBlue
Coral	GreenYellow	MediumTurquoise	SlateBlue
CornflowerBlue	Honeydew	MediumVioletRed	SlateGray
Cornsilk	HotPink	MidnightBlue	Snow
Crimson	IndianRed	MintCream	SpringGreen
Cyan	Indigo	MistyRose	SteelBlue
DarkBlue	Ivory	Moccasin	Tan
DarkCyan	Khaki	NavajoWhite	Teal
DarkGoldenrod	Lavender	Navy	Thistle
DarkGray	LavenderBlush	OldLace	Tomato

TABLE 10.2: PREDEFINED COLORS PROVIDED BY THE PENS AND BRUSHES CLASSES			
DarkGreen	LawnGreen	Olive	Transparent
DarkKhaki	LemonChiffon	OliveDrab	Turquoise
DarkMagenta	LightBlue	Orange	Violet
DarkOliveGreen	LightCoral	OrangeRed	Wheat
DarkOrange	LightCyan	Orchid	White
DarkOrchid	LightGoldenrodYellow	PaleGoldenrod	WhiteSmoke
DarkRed	LightGray	PaleGreen	Yellow
DarkSalmon	LightGreen	PaleTurquoise	YellowGreen
DarkSeaGreen	LightPink	PaleVioletRed	
DarkSlateBlue	LightSalmon	PapayaWhip	
DarkSlateGray	LightSeaGreen	PeachPuff	

Drawing Basic Shapes

The best way to learn how to work with the Graphics class is to experiment with it. Let's begin with a couple of quick examples. The first example, shown below, demonstrates how to draw a green square.

```
Public Class frmMain

    Private Sub btnDraw_Click(ByVal sender As System.Object, _
      ByVal e As System.EventArgs) Handles btnDraw.Click

        'Declare an object based on the Graphics class
        Dim FormGraphic As System.Drawing.Graphics

        'Declare and instantiate an object based on the Pen class and
        'set its color and width
        Dim MyPen As New Pen(Color.Green, 3)

        'Declare and instantiate an object based on the Rectangle class
        'and set its coordinates
        Dim MyRectangle As New Rectangle(20, 20, 250, 250)
```

```
'Set the form's background as the drawing surface
FormGraphic = Me.CreateGraphics()

'Draw the shape
FormGraphic.DrawRectangle(MyPen, MyRectangle)

    End Sub

End Class
```

In this example, the program statements that draw the square shape are executed after the user clicks on the Button control labeled Draw. As you can see, it does not take many lines of code to create this simple drawing. The first statement defines an object variable named FormGraphic based on the System.Drawing.Graphics class. The second statement defines an object variable named MyPen as a Pen object, setting the object's Color property equal to green and its line width to 3 pixels (the default width is 1 pixel). The third statement defines an object variable named MyRectangle as a Rectangle object, passing the object the coordinates of the drawing's starting location (20, 20) and its length position (250, 250) relative to the upper left-hand corner of the drawing surface (frmMain). Take note of the use of the New keyword in the second and third statements. By adding this keyword, you are able to declare and instantiate an object in the same statement. The fourth statement sets the form's background as the drawing surface. The last statement executes the Graphics class's DrawRectangle method, passing it the object variables representing the Pen object and Rectangle object.

 TRICK Even though this example draws a square shape, I had to use the Rectangle class and the DrawRectangle method because there is no Square object or DrawSquare method.

Figure 10.7 shows the drawing that is produced when this example is executed.

The next example demonstrates how to draw a filled-in circle. As you can see, it is very similar to the previous example.

FIGURE 10.7

Using the
Graphics class's
DrawRectangle
method to draw a
square.

```vbnet
Public Class frmMain

    Private Sub btnDraw_Click(ByVal sender As System.Object, _
      ByVal e As System.EventArgs) Handles btnDraw.Click

        'Declare an object based on the Graphics class
        Dim FormGraphic As System.Drawing.Graphics
        'Declare and instantiate a SolidBrush and set its color
        Dim MyBrush As New SolidBrush(Color.Blue)
        'Declare and instantiate a Rectangle and set its coordinates
        Dim MyRectangle As New Rectangle(20, 20, 250, 250)

        'Set the form's background as the drawing surface
        FormGraphic = Me.CreateGraphics()

        'Draw the shape
        FormGraphic.FillEllipse(MyBrush, MyRectangle)

    End Sub

End Class
```

Like the previous example, this example draws a filled-in circle only after the user has clicked on the `Button` control labeled `Draw`. The first statement defines an object variable named `FormGraphic` based on the `System.Drawing.Graphics` class. The second statement defines an object variable named `MyBrush` based on the `SolidBrush` class, setting the object's `Color` property equal to `Blue`. The third statement defines an object variable named `MyRectangle` based on the `Rectangle` class, passing the object the coordinates of the drawing's starting location (20, 20) and its length position (250, 250). I had to use the `Rectangle` class to outline the starting location and dimensions of the drawing because the .NET Framework does not provide an `Ellipse` class. Fortunately, an ellipse is drawn using the same set of coordinates as those required to draw a rectangle shape. The last statement executes the `Graphics` class's `DrawEllipse` method, passing it the object variables representing the `SolidBrush` object and `Rectangle` object.

 TRICK Even though this example draws a circle shape, I had to use the `Ellipse` class and the `Graphics` class's `FillEllipse` method because there is no `Circle` class of `FillCircle` method.

Figure 10.8 shows the drawing that is produced when this example is executed.

FIGURE 10.8

Drawing a filled-in circle using the Graphics object's FillEllipse method.

Drawing Text

In addition to displaying and drawing graphics images, Visual Basic's GDI+ implementation provides you with the ability to draw text as a graphic image using the `Graphics` class's `DrawString` method. For example, one way to call on this method is shown below.

```
Dim objName As System.Drawing.Graphics
objName(TextString, FontType, BrushColor, Coordinates)
```

ObjName is the name that you chose to assign to the new instance of the Graphics class. TextString represents the string to be written as a graphic. FontType identifies the type of font to be used (Arial, Courier, and so on). BrushColor specifies the color to be used and Coordinates represents the X and Y coordinates for the upper left-hand side of the starting position of the text image.

The following statement provides an example of how to create a text graphic drawing.

```
Public Class frmMain

    Private Sub frmMain_Paint(ByVal sender As Object, _
       ByVal e As System.Windows.Forms.PaintEventArgs) Handles Me.Paint

        'Declare and instantiate a Font and specify property settings
        Dim MyFont = New Font("Arial", 32, FontStyle.Bold)

        'Draw the specified text and set its color and coordinates
        e.Graphics.DrawString(DateTime.Now(), MyFont, Brushes.Red, 10, 50)

    End Sub

End Class
```

In this example, the statements that draw the text image have been placed inside the frmMain_Paint procedure. This event procedure automatically executes anytime a form needs to be repainted, including when the form is first displayed. In this example's first statement, a Font object variable named MyFont is instantiated and passed arguments that set its font type, font size, and font style. The second statement draws a text string using the Graphics class's DrawString method. Notice that the Graphics class is referenced as e.Graphics in this example. I was able to set up the reference to the Graphics class this way because the Paint event procedure automatically generates a reference to the System.Drawing class in the form of a variable named e.

The graphic text to be written is supplied by the DateTime class's Now() method. Font information is supplied by passing the DrawString method the MyFont object. Finally, the Brushes.Red argument is used to specify the color of the text, and the coordinates (10, 50) are passed in order to specify the location where the graphic text should start being written.

Figure 10.9 shows the output generated when this example is run.

FIGURE 10.9

Visual Basic allows you to draw text as a graphic.

ADDING SOUNDS TO YOUR APPLICATIONS

Many Windows applications use sound to communicate with users. Some applications play a sound to indicate when a specific event occurs, such as when the application has finished loading or has run into a problem. Visual Basic 2005 Express provides support for playing sounds in the form of wave files.

DEFINITION

A wave file is a digital audio file with a .wav file extension that was originally developed by Microsoft. Wave files store uncompressed raw audio data and are supported by all Windows operating systems as well as by non-Windows platforms such as the Macintosh.

There are plenty of different sources of wave files at your disposal. For example, you can download an untold number of wave files from the Internet. You will also find an assortment of wave files on your computer. Windows XP, for example, stores a number of wave files in the C:\Windows\Media folder.

TRICK

If you cannot find a wave file that provides the sound you want played by your application, you can always make your own custom wave file using the Sound Recorder utility provided with Windows. To access the Sound Recorder, click on Start, All Programs, Accessories, Entertainment, and then Sound Recorder. The Sound Recorder utility will appear as shown in Figure 10.10.

FIGURE 10.10

Using the Windows Sound Recorder utility to create a custom wave file.

Working with the SoundPlayer Class

You can play a wave file within your applications using the SoundPlayer class. You can programmatically create a new SoundPlayer object, as demonstrated below.

```
Dim MySound As New SoundPlayer
```

Once instantiated, you can use the MySound variable to access properties and methods belonging to the SoundPlayer class, including those listed below.

- **SoundLocation.** A SoundPlayer property that is used to specify the location of the wave file to be played
- **Play().** A SoundPlayer method that plays the wave file specified by the SoundPlayer class's SoundLocation property
- **PlayLooping().** A SoundPlayer method that repeatedly plays the wave file specified by the SoundPlayer class's SoundLocation property
- **Stop().** A SoundPlayer method that stops playing any currently executing sound

The following example provides a demonstration of how to instantiate an object based on the SoundPlayer class and then use it to repeatedly play a wave file when the application loads.

```
'Import the System.Media namespaces
Imports System.Media

Public Class frmMain

    'Declare and instantiate the SoundPlayer
    Private MySound As New SoundPlayer

    Private Sub frmMain_Load(ByVal sender As System.Object, _
      ByVal e As System.EventArgs) Handles MyBase.Load

        'Specify the location of the wave file
        MySound.SoundLocation = "C:\Windows\Media\chimes.wav"
        MySound.PlayLooping()  'Repeatedly play the sound file

    End Sub

End Class
```

Note the inclusion of the `Imports System.Media` statement at the beginning of this example. This statement tells Visual Basic to include a reference to the `System.Media` namespace, which is required in order to get access to the `SoundPlayer` **Class.**

RAD Development with the My Namespace

One of the few real differences between Visual Basic 2003 and Visual Basic 2005 is the expansion of the .NET Framework's class library, which includes a number of new classes. One collection of classes in particular that is of special interest is the collection that makes up the new `My` namespace. The `My` namespace provides access to a number of classes that can be used to instantiate objects that greatly facilitate rapid application development. These classes include:

- **`My.Application`.** Gets information about the currently running application, such as its name and version
- **`My.Computer`.** Gets information about the local computer, including its hardware
- **`My.User`.** Gets information about the current user, including username and domain name
- **`My.Forms`.** Gets information regarding any currently open application forms

You can use properties and methods belonging to the `My.Computer` class to quickly and easily add the ability to play wave audio files in your Visual Basic applications. To demonstrate this, let's develop a new application called the Audio Jukebox. This application will use properties and methods belonging to the `My.Computer` class to play `.wav` files. Specifically, it will use the `Play` method belonging to the `Audio` class, which is a subclass of the `My.Computer` class, to play a wave file. It will also use the `FileSystem` subclass's `GetFiles` method to generate a list of wave files and the `FileSystem` class's `CurrentDirectory` property to specify the location of these wave files. Figure 10.11 shows what the application will look like when you have finished building it.

The application's user interface is made up of a form with a `ListBox` and `Button` control. Assign a name of `lbxWaveFiles` to the `ListBox` control and a name of `btnPlay` to the `Button` control. Then add the following code to the application as shown below.

DEFINITION

A ListBox control is used to display a list of items from which a selection can be made.

FIGURE 10.11

The Audio
Jukebox
application
demonstrates
how to control
the play of
various wave
files.

One way to populate a ListBox control with a list of items is to use the ListBox class's DataSource property. Once populated, you can use the ListBox class's SelectedItem property to determine which item is selected by the user. The audio Jukebox application demonstrates how to use the DataSource property to display a list of wave files and the SelectedItem property to determine which wave file is selected for play.

```
Public Class frmMain

    Private Sub frmMain_Load(ByVal sender As System.Object, _
      ByVal e As System.EventArgs) Handles MyBase.Load

        'Specify the location of the wave files to be displayed by the
        'application
        My.Computer.FileSystem.CurrentDirectory = "C:\Windows\Media"

        'Load a list of wave files into the ListBox control

        lbxWaveFiles.DataSource = My.Computer.FileSystem.GetFiles( _
          My.Computer.FileSystem.CurrentDirectory, _
          FileIO.SearchOption.SearchTopLevelOnly, "*.wav")

    End Sub

    Private Sub btnPlay_Click(ByVal sender As System.Object, _
      ByVal e As System.EventArgs) Handles btnPlay.Click
```

```
        'Play the selected wave file
        My.Computer.Audio.Play(lbxWaveFiles.SelectedItem.ToString)

    End Sub

End Class
```

The first statement requires a little explanation. It begins with the My class. This class provides access to the Computer class. The Computer class has a property named FileSystem, which provides access to the FileSystem class, which in turn has a property named CurrentDirectory, which is set equal to "C:\Windows\Media".

The second statement populates the ListBox control with a list of wave files located in the "C:\Windows\Media" folder. This statement also requires some additional explanation. This statement works by executing the My.Computer.FileSystem.GetFiles method, which is passed three arguments in the following order: target folder, a value specifying whether subfolders should be recursively displayed (FileIO.SearchOption.Search-TopLevelOnly), and a string specifying the files to be retrieved. In the case of this example, all files with a .wav file extension are displayed.

In order to use the application, the user must select one of the wave files displayed in the ListBox control and then click on the Button control labeled Play, which then uses the Audio class's Play method to play the selected wave file.

As you can see, the My namespace and the objects that can be generated from its classes provide you with the ability to perform complex tasks with very little coding and offer yet another alternative for adding sound to your Visual Basic applications.

BACK TO THE VB DOODLE GAME

It is time to turn your attention back to the development of this chapter's game project, the VB Doodle game. The VB Doodle game is a drawing program. You will create it by following the five basic development steps that have been used in the creation of all the previous chapter game projects.

Designing the Game

The VB Doodle game is executed using a single window and is made up of one form and the 11 controls listed in Table 10.3.

TABLE 10.3: FORM CONTROLS FOR THE VB DOODLE GAME

Control Type	Control Name	Description
Panel1	pnlControl	Panel control located on the left-hand side of the user interface where game controls are displayed
Label1	lblControls	Identifies the location of the controls for the VB Doodle application
Label2	lblColor	Identifies the ComboBox control where the player makes color selections
Button1	btnRectangle	Initiates the process of drawing a rectangle
Button2	btnLine	Initiates the process of drawing a line
Button3	btnCircle	Initiates the process of drawing an ellipse
Button4	btnFillRectangle	Initiates the process of drawing a filled-in rectangle
Button5	btnFillCircle	Initiates the process of drawing a filled-in ellipse
Button6	btnDraw	Initiates the process of making a freehand drawing
Button7	btnClear	Initiates the clearing of the drawing area
ComboBox1	cbxColor	Lists the available color choices provided by the application

Step 1: Creating a New Visual Basic Project

The first step in creating the VB Doodle game is to open up Visual Basic and create a new project as outlined below.

1. If you have not already done so, start up Visual Basic 2005 Express and then click on File and select New Project. The New Project dialog will appear.

2. Select the Windows Application template.

3. Type VB Doodle as the name of your new application in the Name field located at the bottom of the New Project window.

4. Click on OK to close the New Project dialog.

Visual Basic will now create a new project for you and display a new form upon which you will design the game's user interface.

Step 2: Creating the User Interface

The first step in designing the game's user interface is to add the appropriate controls to the form and then move and resize them to the right locations. Use Figure 10.12 as a reference as you go through each of the following steps to make sure that you know where each control should be placed and their approximate sizes.

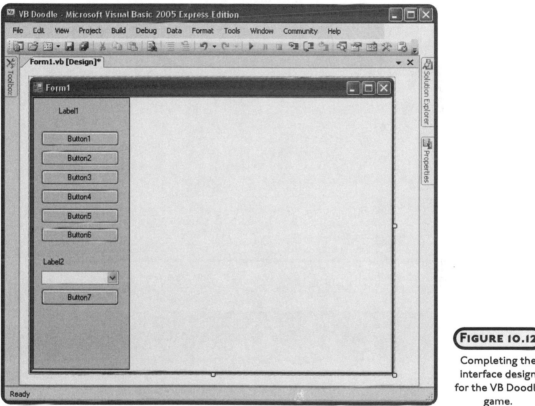

FIGURE 10.12

Completing the interface design for the VB Doodle game.

1. Resize Form1 by setting its Size property to 586, 458.
2. Add a Panel control to the left-hand side of the form and resize it until it takes up approximately 25 percent of the available form space.
3. Add and center a Label control on the top of the Panel control.
4. Add six Button controls under the Label control.
5. Add a second Label control beneath the last button that you added to the Panel control.
6. Add a ComboBox control just under the second Label control.
7. Finally, add one more Button control on the Panel control.

The overall layout of the VB Doodle game's user interface is complete. You are now ready to start customizing form and control properties.

Step 3: Customizing Form and Control Properties

Now let's start customizing the properties associated with the form and its controls. Start by changing the form properties listed in Table 10.4.

TABLE 10.4: PROPERTY CHANGES FOR FORM1

Property	Value
Name	frmMain
BackColor	White
FormBorderStyle	Fixed3D
Size	586, 458
StartPosition	CenterScreen
Text	VB Doodle

Next, modify the properties listed in Table 10.5 for the Panel control.

TABLE 10.5: PROPERTY CHANGES FOR PANEL CONTROL

Property	Value
Name	pnlControl
Anchor	Top, Bottom, Left
BackColor	LightGray
BorderStyle	FixedSingle

TRICK Take special note of the Anchor property setting. It has been set so that the panel control will automatically resize itself if the form is resized. This provides the player with the flexibility to change the size of the drawing area by maximizing the form without affecting the size and appearance of the Panel control.

Next, modify the properties listed in Table 10.6 for the two Label controls.

TABLE 10.6: PROPERTY CHANGES FOR LABEL CONTROLS

Control	Property	Value
Label1	Name	lblControls
	Font.Bold	True
	Text	Controls
Label2	Name	lblColor
	Font.Bold	True
	Text	Select Color:

Now modify the properties listed in Table 10.7 for the seven Button controls.

TABLE 10.7: PROPERTY CHANGES FOR BUTTON CONTROLS

Control	Property	Value
Button1	Name	btnRectangle
	Text	Rectangle
Button2	Name	btnLine
	Text	Line
Button3	Name	btnCircle
	Text	Circle
Button4	Name	btnFillRectangle
	Text	Fill Rectangle
Button5	Name	btnFillCircle
	Text	Fill Circle
Button6	Name	btnDraw
	Text	Draw
Button7	Name	btnClear
	Text	Clear

Now modify the properties listed in Table 10.8 for the ComboBox control.

TABLE 10.8: PROPERTY CHANGES FOR COMBOBOX CONTROL

Property	Value
Name	cbxColor
Items	Red
	Green
	Blue
	Black
	Yellow
	Purple
Text	**Red**

That is it. You have finished making all the design-time property changes to the VB Doodle application's form and control properties.

Step 4: Adding a Little Programming Logic

The first step in writing the code for the VB Doodle game is to define class-level variables that the application will need in order to run, as shown below.

```
Public Class frmMain

    'Declare a variable representing the System.Drawing.Graphics class
    Private FormGraphic As Graphics

    'Declare variables representing the Point class
    Private StartPoint As Point
    Private EndPoint As Point

    'Declare a variable that will be used to store and track the drawing
    'option selected by the player
    Private strCurrentAction As String = "Line"
```

```
'Declare a variable to be used as a counter
Private intCounter As Integer = 0

'Declare an array
Private apntArray() As Point
```

End Class

The first declaration statement defines an object variable that will be used to represent the Graphics class. The second and third statements define object variables that will be used to represent the Point class. The third statement defines a string variable name, strCurrentAction, that will be used by the application to keep track of the currently selected drawing option. The last two statements are used to define a variable that will be used to keep track of the number of elements stored in an array named apntArray.

One of the procedures within the application allows the player to make a freehand drawing. This is accomplished by storing coordinates representing the location of the pointer in the apntArray as the player moves the mouse around when drawing freehand and then passing these coordinates to the DrawLines method.

DEFINITION

A *Point* class is a member of the System.Drawing namespace. The Point class can be used as a mechanism for storing sets of coordinates.

The next thing to do is to set up the application so that it associates the FormGraphic object variable with its drawing surface (the form), which you can do by modifying the frmMain_Load procedure as shown below.

```
'This procedure executes when the VB Doodle game loads
Private Sub frmMain_Load(ByVal sender As System.Object, _
  ByVal e As System.EventArgs) Handles MyBase.Load

    'Create an instance of the Graphics class
    objFormGraphic = Me.CreateGraphics

End Sub
```

Regardless of which type of drawing operation the player wishes to make, such as drawing a line, a rectangle, or a freehand image, everything begins when the player clicks on the mouse button in order to set the starting point for whatever shape is being drawn. Therefore, you will need to modify the frmMain_MouseDown procedure as shown below in order to capture this initial set of coordinates and assign it to the StartPoint variable.

```
'This procedure captures the coordinates used to draw shapes
Private Sub frmMain_MouseDown(ByVal sender As Object, _
   ByVal e As System.Windows.Forms.MouseEventArgs) Handles Me.MouseDown

     'Create an instance of the point class and assign coordinates
     StartPoint = New Point(e.X, e.Y)


End Sub
```

The next procedure to set up is the frmMain_MouseMove Sub procedure, shown below.

```
'This procedure captures coordinates for freehand drawings
Private Sub frmMain_MouseMove(ByVal sender As Object, _
   ByVal e As System.Windows.Forms.MouseEventArgs) Handles Me.MouseMove

     'The button labeled Draw was clicked
     If strCurrentAction = "Draw" Then

         'The player must press and hold down the left mouse button
         If e.Button = Windows.Forms.MouseButtons.Left Then
             'Create an instance of the Point class and assign a set
             'of coordinates
             Dim DrawPoint As New Point(e.X, e.Y)

             'Resize the array and keep all existing data
             ReDim Preserve apntArray(intCounter)

             'Add the most recently collected set of coordinates
             apntArray(intCounter) = objPoint
             intCounter += 1  'Increment the counter
```

```
        'A minimum of 2 sets of coordinates is required to draw
        If intCounter >= 2 Then
            'Call procedure that does the actual drawing
            SelectAndDraw("Draw", apntArray)
        End If

    End If

  End If

End Sub
```

This procedure is responsible for collecting the coordinates of the mouse as the player moves it around the form when creating a freehand image (when the value of strCurrentAction is equal to "Draw"). However, coordinates are only recorded if the player is holding down the left mouse button when the mouse is being moved (if e.Button = Windows.Forms.MouseButtons.Left Then). Individual coordinates are stored as object variables named DrawPoint and then assigned to the apntArray. The intCounter variable, which is incremented by one with the addition of every new set of coordinates, it used to assign the index number of each new array entry.

The coordinates stored in the apntArray are then passed on to the SelectAndDraw procedure, where the Graphics class's DrawLines method will be used to draw the image on the form. The DrawLines method requires a minimum of two sets of coordinates in order to execute. Therefore, the SelectAndDraw procedure is only called if the value of intCounter is greater than or equal to 2.

The player can release the left mouse button at any time when making a freehand drawing in order to change colors or to reposition the pointer to a new location to add another freehand drawing to the form. Therefore, whenever the player releases the mouse button, the application will need to reset the intCounter variable to 0 and reinitialize the apntArray array. In addition, the application will need to capture the location of the last set of coordinates for the freehand image. You can set all this up by modifying the frmMain_MouseUp procedures as shown below.

```
'This procedure runs when the player releases the left mouse button
Private Sub frmMain_MouseUp(ByVal sender As Object, _
  ByVal e As System.Windows.Forms.MouseEventArgs) Handles Me.MouseUp
```

```
        intCounter = 0   'Reset the counter to zero
        ReDim apntArray(intCounter)   'Reset the array

        EndPoint = New Point(e.X, e.Y)   'Capture last set of coordinates
        DrawGraphic()   'Call procedure that draws the shape

End Sub
```

As you can see, the apntArray is reset using the ReDim keyword (without using the Preserve keyword). Once the coordinates of the pointer's last location (when the left mouse button was released) have been captured, a procedure named DrawGraphic is called.

The DrawGraphic procedure, shown below, is responsible for laying out the required coordinates for a drawing based on the value assigned to the strCurrentAction variable.

```
'This procedure assembles the coordinates required to draw shapes
Private Sub DrawGraphic()

        'Assemble coordinates for a rectangle drawing
        If strCurrentAction = "Rectangle" Then
            'Declare variable representing a rectangle
            Dim ShapeCoordinates As Rectangle
            'Instantiate a rectangle object and assign its coordinates
            ShapeCoordinates = _
              New Rectangle(Math.Min(EndPoint.X, StartPoint.X), _
                  Math.Min(EndPoint.Y, StartPoint.Y), _
                  Math.Abs(EndPoint.X - StartPoint.X), _
                  Math.Abs(EndPoint.Y - StartPoint.Y))
            'Call procedure to draw shape
            SelectAndDraw("Rectangle", ShapeCoordinates)
        End If

        'Call procedure to draw a line
        If strCurrentAction = "Line" Then
            SelectAndDraw("Line")
        End If

        'Assemble coordinates for a circle drawing
        If strCurrentAction = "Circle" Then
            'Declare variable representing a rectangle
```

```
        Dim ShapeCoordinates As Rectangle
        'Instantiate a rectangle object and assign its coordinates
        ShapeCoordinates = _
        New Rectangle(Math.Min(EndPoint.X, StartPoint.X), _
          Math.Min(EndPoint.Y, StartPoint.Y), _
          Math.Abs(EndPoint.X - StartPoint.X), _
          Math.Abs(EndPoint.Y - StartPoint.Y))
        'Call procedure to draw shape
        SelectAndDraw("Ellipse", ShapeCoordinates)
End If


'Assemble coordinates for a filled rectangle drawing
If strCurrentAction = "FillRectangle" Then
        'Declare variable representing a rectangle
        Dim ShapeCoordinates As Rectangle
        'Instantiate a rectangle object and assign its coordinates
        ShapeCoordinates = _
          New Rectangle(Math.Min(EndPoint.X, StartPoint.X), _
          Math.Min(EndPoint.Y, StartPoint.Y), _
          Math.Abs(EndPoint.X - StartPoint.X), _
          Math.Abs(EndPoint.Y - StartPoint.Y))
        'Call procedure to draw shape
        SelectAndDraw("FillRectangle", ShapeCoordinates)
End If


'Assemble coordinates for a filled circle drawing
If strCurrentAction = "FillCircle" Then
        'Declare variable representing a rectangle
        Dim ShapeCoordinates As Rectangle
        'Instantiate a rectangle object and assign its coordinates
        ShapeCoordinates = _
          New Rectangle(Math.Min(EndPoint.X, StartPoint.X), _
          Math.Min(EndPoint.Y, StartPoint.Y), _
          Math.Abs(EndPoint.X - StartPoint.X), _
          Math.Abs(EndPoint.Y - StartPoint.Y))
```

```
          'Call procedure to draw shape
          SelectAndDraw("FillCircle", ShapeCoordinates)
     End If

End Sub
```

For example, if strCurrentAction is equal to Rectangle, an object variable named ShapeCoordinates is declared representing the Rectangle class. The coordinates for the drawing are then laid out and the SelectAndDraw procedure is called and passed a string representing the shape to be drawn and the coordinates required to draw it.

 TRICK

The way that the coordinates are assembled for a rectangle shape requires a little extra examination. As you can see, both the Math class's Min and Abs methods are used. To understand what is going on here, you must first remember that the rectangle will be drawn from left to right, and that the point in its upper-left corner is determined based on its relationship to the (0,0) coordinates. This is true even if the player decides to draw the rectangle right to left.

The first use of Math.Min determines whether the EndPoint.X or StartPoint.X coordinates is the leftmost coordinate by returning a value representing the lower of the two coordinates. Likewise, the second use of Math.Min determines whether the EndPoint.Y or the StartPoint.Y coordinates is the topmost coordinate. Once the coordinate of the top left corner is identified, the first Math.Abs method is used to retrieve an absolute number representing the length of the rectangle along the X axis by subtracting the difference between EndPoint.X and StartPoint.X. Likewise, the length of the rectangle's Y axis is determined by returning the absolute value of EndPoint.Y minus StartPoint.Y.

DEFINITION

An absolute number is a non-negative number. For example, the absolute value of -9 is 9. By the same token, the absolute value of 9 is also 9.

Now it is time to begin adding code to the Click event for each of the game's Button controls. The code for the btnRectangle_Click procedure is shown below. When selected, it sets the value of strCurrentAction equal to "Rectangle" in order to allow the player to indicate what type of drawing to make.

```
'This procedure runs when the button labeled Rectangle is clicked
Private Sub btnRectangle_Click(ByVal sender As System.Object, _
  ByVal e As System.EventArgs) Handles btnRectangle.Click

    strCurrentAction = "Rectangle"

End Sub
```

The code for the `btnLine_Click` procedure is shown below.

```
'This procedure runs when the button labeled Line is clicked
Private Sub btnLine_Click(ByVal sender As System.Object, _
  ByVal e As System.EventArgs) Handles btnLine.Click

    strCurrentAction = "Line"

End Sub
```

The code for the `btnCircle_Click` procedure is shown below.

```
'This procedure runs when the button labeled Circle is clicked
Private Sub btnCircle_Click(ByVal sender As System.Object, _
  ByVal e As System.EventArgs) Handles btnCircle.Click

    strCurrentAction = "Circle"

End Sub
```

The code for the `btnFillRectangle_Click` procedure is shown below.

```
'This procedure runs when the button labeled Fill Rectangle is clicked
Private Sub btnFillRectangle_Click(ByVal sender As System.Object, _
  ByVal e As System.EventArgs) Handles btnFillRectangle.Click

    strCurrentAction = "FillRectangle"

End Sub
```

The code for the `btnFillCircle_Click` procedure is shown below.

```
'This procedure runs when the button labeled Fill Circle is clicked
Private Sub btnFillCircle_Click(ByVal sender As System.Object, _
  ByVal e As System.EventArgs) Handles btnFillCircle.Click

    strCurrentAction = "FillCircle"

End Sub
```

The code for the btnDraw_Click procedure is shown below.

```
'This procedure runs when the button labeled Draw is clicked
Private Sub btnDraw_Click(ByVal sender As System.Object, _
  ByVal e As System.EventArgs) Handles btnDraw.Click

    strCurrentAction = "Draw"

End Sub
```

The code for the btnClear_Click procedure is shown below. Instead of setting a variable as was done in the other Button object Click event procedures, this procedure executes the Graphics object's Clear method, passing it Me.BackColor in order to clear out the drawing area (the form's background).

```
'This procedure runs when the button labeled Clear is clicked
Private Sub btnClear_Click(ByVal sender As System.Object, _
  ByVal e As System.EventArgs) Handles btnClear.Click

    FormGraphic.Clear(Me.BackColor)

End Sub
```

The last procedure that you'll need to set up for the VB Doodle game is the SelectAndDraw Sub procedure, which is shown below. This procedure uses a Select Case block to process the strShape argument that is passed to it. Then, based on the appropriate match, a call is made to the appropriate Graphics object method.

```
'This procedure draws the selected shape
Private Sub SelectAndDraw(ByVal strShape As String, _
  Optional ByVal Coordinates As Object = "")
```

```
 'Declare and instantiate a Pen object and assign its color
Dim Pen1 As New Pen(Color.FromName(cbxColor.Text))

 'Declare and instantiate a SolidBrush object and assign its color
Dim Brush1 As New SolidBrush(Color.FromName(cbxColor.Text))

 'Process the procedure arguments and draw
Select Case strShape
Case "Line"
     FormGraphic.DrawLine(Pen1, StartPoint, EndPoint)
         Case "Rectangle"
     FormGraphic.DrawRectangle(Pen1, Coordinates)
         Case "Ellipse"
     FormGraphic.DrawEllipse(Pen1, Coordinates)
         Case "FillRectangle"
     FormGraphic.FillRectangle(Brush1, Coordinates)
         Case "FillCircle"
     FormGraphic.FillEllipse(Brush1, Coordinates)
         Case "Draw"
     FormGraphic.DrawLines(Pen1, Coordinates)
End Select

End Sub
```

Step 5: Testing the Execution of the VB Doodle Game

OK. That's it. The VB Doodle game is now ready to run. Go ahead and run the game by pressing F5, and make sure that everything works like it is supposed to. If you run into any problems, go back and double-check your typing.

SUMMARY

In this chapter, you learned how to work with various classes and objects that provide the ability to work with graphics and audio. This included learning how to work with the `System.Drawing.Graphics` namespace. You learned how to instantiate the `Graphics` object as well as the `Pens` and `Brushes` objects and to use their properties and methods to create various drawing applications. You also learned how to add sound to your Visual Basic applications using the `SoundPlayer` control and class. In addition, you learned a little about the `My` namespace and how to use properties and methods belonging to the `My.Computer` class as an alternative means for playing wave files. On top of all this, you learned how to create the VB Doodle game.

Now, before you move on to Chapter 11, "Debugging Visual Basic Applications," and start learning various tools and techniques for debugging your Visual Basic applications, take a few extra minutes to improve the VB Doodle game by completing the following challenges.

CHALLENGES

1. As the game is currently written, it is not always clear what type of shape the player is working with. To make the application easier to use, add a status bar control and use it to display a string identifying the currently selected shape.

2. The `Graphics` class provides the ability to create numerous other shapes besides rectangles, ellipses, and lines. Enhance the VB Doodle game to support other shapes, such as the pie, arc, and polygon. You can get information on the arguments that need to be supplied to create each of the shapes using Visual Basic's Help system.

3. The Visual Basic `Pens` and `Brushes` classes provide access to many dozens of predefined colors. Expand the VB Doodle game's list of supported colors to give the player additional choices.

4. Use the `MessageBox.Show` method to require that the player confirm the desire to clear the drawing area before allowing the `btnClear_Click` event procedure to execute.

5. Make the VB Doodle game a little more exciting by adding some sound effects. For example, consider playing the `C:\Windows\Media\Tada.wav` file when the application first loads. Also, find a different sound to play when the player switches colors and when the player clicks on the button that clears the drawing surface.

DEBUGGING VISUAL
BASIC APPLICATIONS

Welcome to the final chapter in this book. In this chapter, you will learn how to deal with syntax, logic, and run-time errors. This will include learning how to set up breakpoints in order to track variable status and program flow. You will learn how to work with a number of debugging windows. You also will learn how to develop custom exception handling routines. In addition, you will get the chance to apply what you learn through the development of the chapter's game project, the Tic-Tac-Toe game.

Specifically, you will learn:

- About the different types of errors that can occur
- How to set breakpoints and to step through code execution
- How to use various debugging windows
- How to create exception-handling routines

PROJECT PREVIEW: THE TIC-TAC-TOE GAME

As this chapter's game project, you will develop a two-player Visual Basic version of the Tic-Tac-Toe game. You will track and validate player moves and determine when a game is won, lost, or tied. Figures 11.1 to 11.3 show examples from the Tic-Tac-Toe game, demonstrating its functionality and overall execution flow.

FIGURE 11.1

The Tic-Tac-Toe game begins by displaying a blank game board.

FIGURE 11.2

The game keeps track of each player's turn.

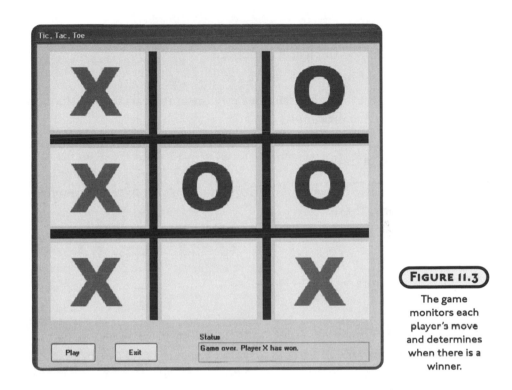

FIGURE 11.3

The game monitors each player's move and determines when there is a winner.

By the time you have created and run this game, you will have completed the last game project in this book and will be well on your way to becoming a Visual Basic programmer. By completing this game and the other games in this book, you will have established a solid collection of code, which you can expand and build upon to create even more intricate and powerful Visual Basic applications.

DEALING WITH ERRORS

As your Visual Basic programs grow larger and more complex, errors are going to happen. That is just the way things work. Even the most experienced programmers run into errors all the time. Visual Basic applications are subject to many different types of errors. The occurrence of an error causes an application to behave inappropriately and is often referred to as a bug. Your job as a programmer is to seek out and remove (or handle) these bugs.

There are many things that you can do to minimize the number of errors in your applications. For starters, you can sit down and plan out the overall design of your applications before you start writing them. Once created, you should test your applications extensively to look for bugs. Other good programming practices that you should consider include:

- Creating a simple and easy-to-use interface
- Providing users with clear instructions
- Validating user input data before accepting it
- Using consistent naming schemes for constants, variables, objects, arrays, and Function and Sub procedures
- Anticipating specific situations where errors might occur and trying to deal with them programmatically

There are three basic categories of errors that you will experience when developing Visual Basic applications. These are:

- Syntax errors
- Logical errors
- Run-time errors

Syntax Errors

The most common type of error is a syntax error. A syntax error occurs when you key in a statement that does not conform to Visual Basic's rules. Syntax errors are often the result of typos, such as when you accidentally mistype a keyword or leave out a required parameter.

DEFINITION

A syntax error is an error that occurs when you do not write a code statement according to the rules of the programming language.

Visual Basic identifies syntax errors in your programming statements as you finish typing them by underlining the errors, as demonstrated in Figure 11.4. If you move the pointer over a syntax error, a ToolTip will display a brief error message.

Because syntax errors are identified for you as you key in your Visual Basic program statements, they are easy to locate and correct. You can also view syntax errors from the Error List window, as shown at the bottom of Figure 11.4. This window will automatically open during application development if you attempt to run a Visual Basic application that has a syntax error in it. The window shows each error, provides a brief description of the error, and identifies the line number of the statement that contains the error. If you want, you can double-click on an error listed in the Error List window and Visual Basic will respond by locating the statement that contains it in the code editor.

FIGURE 11.4

The compiler flags Visual Basic syntax errors by underlining them with a jagged blue line.

TRICK

Sometimes you might miss when Visual Basic flags a syntax error in your code. To help prevent this from happening, you might want to keep the Error List window open while you are writing code. You can do this by clicking on the View menu and then selecting the Error List menu item.

Logical Errors

Logical errors are errors caused by a mistake on the programmer's part. For example, you might accidentally add together two numbers that should have been subtracted. The end result is that everything runs fine but the output is not what you expect. Another example of a logical error is when you accidentally set up an endless loop.

Visual Basic won't be able to flag or report your logical errors. The best way to deal with logical errors is to try and prevent them in the first place by taking extra care in the formulation of your programming logic. Organize your Visual Basic applications into procedures by assigning each procedure one specific task to perform. Then do your best to test out each procedure as you go. However, even the best laid plans often go awry, and when this occurs, there is no substitute for careful testing as a means of identifying logical errors.

DEFINITION

A logical error is created when the programmer makes a mistake in laying out the logic used to perform a given task.

Run-Time Errors

A third category of errors is the run-time error, which occurs whenever a statement attempts to do something that is not possible. For example, a run-time error will occur if an application attempts to access a disk drive that does not exist or if a broken network connection prevents the access of a network file.

DEFINITION

A run-time error occurs when an application attempts to perform an illegal action.

Unlike syntax errors, the compiler won't flag run-time errors for you. In fact, if a seldom-used procedure contains code that might produce a run-time error and you don't carefully test the functionality provided by that procedure, you may not catch the run-time error at all, in which case, the user will be left to discover it.

If you come across a run-time error when running your Visual Basic application in debug mode, you'll receive an error message like the one shown in Figure 11.5. However, if you don't catch the run-time error during testing and development, your application may or may not display an error message when its release version is being executed. Worse still, your application may simply lock up and stop responding.

FIGURE 11.5

An example of a Visual Basic run-time error displayed when an application is being executed in design mode.

A run-time error can also occur if the user passes your application some unanticipated input. Therefore, it is important that you add logic to your applications to validate, as much as possible, all user input. It is also critical to test all of the functionality provided by your Visual Basic applications as thoroughly as possible in order to minimize the possible of running into unexpected run-time errors. However, try as you may, there is no way to completely avoid run-time errors. For example, sometimes hardware just fails or the network goes down. If your application requires these resources to execute, then run-time errors will eventually occur. However, as you'll learn later in this chapter, Visual Basic provides you with the ability to develop exception handlers so that you can recover from or at least gracefully respond to unavoidable run-time errors.

ESTABLISHING BREAKPOINTS

Visual Basic 2005 Express provides you with a number of tools for tracking down and dealing with errors. Using these tools, you can track down errors by monitoring your program code statements as they execute in order to examine variable and property values and to observe the execution flow of your application as it moves from statement to statement.

Up to this point in the book, you have executed your Visual Basic applications mostly in design mode by pressing the F5 key within the Visual Basic IDE. However, you also learned how to create standalone executable versions of your Visual Basic applications, known as run-time mode. Now it's time to learn about a third mode of application execution, break mode.

In break mode, you are able to pause the execution of your application and examine its status before resuming execution. This can be a very effective tool for tracking down and locating statements that may be incorrectly setting variable and property values. Break mode allows you to step through each line of your program code, to see what procedures have been called, and to examine variable and property values.

Setting Up Breakpoints

To set up a breakpoint within your application, click on the left-hand margin of the code editor on the line where you wish to place the breakpoint. Once the breakpoint has been set, a circular marker is displayed in the margin, and the line of code where the breakpoint is set is highlighted, as demonstrated in Figure 11.6.

FIGURE 11.6

Using a breakpoint to pause an application's execution.

Place your breakpoints at locations within your applications where you suspect a problem may be occurring. You can set as many breakpoints as you wish. When you press F5 to run your application and a breakpoint is reached, program execution pauses and the circular marker for the current breakpoint changes to display an arrow, as demonstrated in Figure 11.7.

FIGURE 11.7

The Visual Basic IDE changes the highlight of the currently active breakpoint.

TRICK Once you have resolved any errors that you may have and no longer need any breakpoints, you can remove them by clicking on the circular markers located in the left-hand margin.

You can learn a lot about what is going on in your application by setting a breakpoint and then examining the value of properties and variables to see what they have been set to. For example, at the bottom of Figure 11.7, you can see that the Locals window and the Immediate Window have been opened. The Locals window displays information about variables within the current context, including their current value and type. If you want, you can even change the value assigned to a variable displayed in the Locals window.

You can also use the Immediate Window to query the value of a variable or property. For example, if you look at the Immediate Window in Figure 11.7, you will see where I checked on the value assigned to the intUpperLimit variable by typing in a question mark followed by the name of the variable.

By using breakpoints and the windows mentioned above, you can track down many errors by locating the statements in your applications that inappropriately modify variable or property values.

Stepping through Code Execution

Another important feature provided by Visual Basic when executing an application in break mode is the ability to step through program statements. This allows you to identify a section of code where you think an error may be located (by setting a breakpoint) and then to step through and execute each subsequent statement a line at a time. This lets you follow the execution flow of an entire process, pausing at any point along the way to check on the value of related variables and properties.

Visual Basic provides you with three different ways to step through your program statements, as listed below:

- **Step Into.** Executes the breakpoint statement and then pauses before the execution of statements that follow
- **Step Over.** Executes entire procedures, pausing before the execution of the next procedure
- **Step Out.** Used inside a procedure in order to return to the calling procedure where program flow is then paused

You can selectively choose which of these step options you wish to use at any moment by clicking on their icons, which are located in the Visual Basic standard toolbar, as shown in Figure 11.8.

Continue

Break All

Stop Debugging

Step Into

Step Over

Step Out

FIGURE 11.8

Using the Debug icons on the standard toolbar to step through program statements.

DEVELOPING EXCEPTION HANDLERS

Run-time errors, also referred to as *exceptions*, can occur for many different reasons. Examples include collecting and processing user input that may not be valid and attempting to access local computer and network resources that may not be available. Obviously, it would be best if your applications were written in such a way that they could handle these unexpected exceptions without blowing up or confusing your users with cryptic error messages.

In order for your applications to be able to handle exceptions, you need to anticipate the locations within your applications where errors are most likely to occur and then develop code that handles the problem. For example, if an error could occur due to incorrect user input, then you should incorporate input validation checks into your applications. If your application needs to access local network hardware resources, you should add logic that notifies the user if the required resources are unavailable. There are numerous other ways of dealing with exceptions. For example, you might:

- Reword cryptic error messages
- Provide the user with additional instruction
- Apologize for the error and close down the application
- Request that the user report the error

Visual Basic 2005 Express Edition provides two programmatic tools that allow you to establish exception handling routines, unstructured and structured. By adding exception-handling logic into your Visual Basic applications, you can attempt to prevent exceptions from creating havoc with your applications, potentially causing them to crash.

A Run-time Exception Demonstration

To see firsthand just how Visual Basic handles exceptions, create a new Visual Basic application and modify its Load event procedure as shown below.

```
Public Class Form1

    Dim intX As Integer = 0
    Dim intY As Integer = 10
    Dim intZ As Integer

    Private Sub Form1_Load(ByVal sender As System.Object, _
      ByVal e As System.EventArgs) Handles MyBase.Load

        intZ = intY / intX

    End Sub


End Class
```

This application has been designed with a flaw in it that will produce an overflow error when it attempts to divide intY (10) by intX (0), because within Visual Basic, division by zero is impossible. Once you have everything keyed in, press F5 to test your application. Your application immediately runs into trouble and stops executing. Figure 11.9 shows the error message that is displayed.

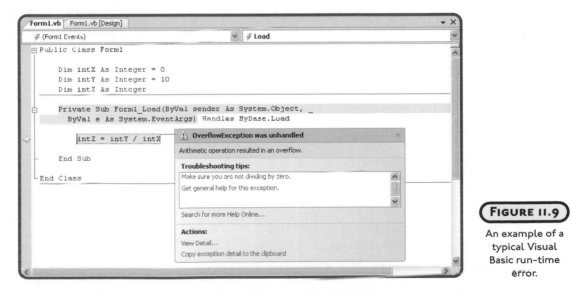

FIGURE 11.9

An example of a typical Visual Basic run-time error.

Create an executable version of your application by saving your application, clicking on the Build menu, and selecting the Build menu item. Locate and run the executable (Release) version of your new program. When you do, the error shown in Figure 11.10 will appear. Click on Quit to dismiss the error message and stop the execution of your application.

FIGURE 11.10

Examining the error message generated when your application runs into an unhandled exception at run-time.

Clearly, you don't want the users of your Visual Basic applications to see error messages like these. To avoid this, you will need to test your applications extensively to make them as bug-free as possible. In situations where you cannot eliminate the possibility of an error, you will need to develop effective exception handlers.

Unstructured Exception Handlers

The first option for creating an exception handling routine is the unstructured approach, which uses the On Error GoTo statement and causes the application to redirect program flow to a specified procedure in the event an error occurs. To see how the On Error GoTo statement works, modify your application as shown below.

```
Public Class Form1

    Dim intX As Integer = 0
    Dim intY As Integer = 10
    Dim intZ As Integer

    Private Sub Form1_Load(ByVal sender As System.Object, _
       ByVal e As System.EventArgs) Handles MyBase.Load

        On Error GoTo GenericExceptionHandler
```

```
        intZ = intY / intX

        Exit Sub

    GenericExceptionHandler:

        MessageBox.Show("Error: " & Err.Description & _
            ControlChars.CrLf & ControlChars.CrLf & _
            "Please inform the developer of this error.")

    End Sub

End Class
```

By adding the `On Error GoTo` statement at the beginning of the `Load` event procedure, you have instructed Visual Basic to transfer the program flow to the `GenericException-Handler:` statement in the event that an error occurs. The `intZ = intY / intX` statement will generate an overflow error. As a result, the next statement is skipped (`Exit Sub`) and the first statement located after the `GenericExceptionHandler:` statement (which is just a callable label embedded within the code) executes.

Whenever an error occurs, Visual Basic automatically exposes information about the error in the form of an object named `Err`. Using properties belonging to the `Err` object, such as the `Description` property, you can determine what type of error has occurred and try to handle it in some manner. In the previous example, the end result of adding the unstructured exception handler to the application is that the error message shown in Figure 11.11 is displayed when your application is executed.

FIGURE 11.11

Using an exception handler to generate a more user-friendly error message.

Using the unstructured approach to set up event handlers is considered to be old school, and I don't recommend that you use it. I have provided you with an example of how the `On Error GoTo` statement works here just to give you a feel of what it looks like and how it works. Chances are that as you start working with other people's code, you will come across its use somewhere along the line.

Structured Exception Handlers

Microsoft's recommended approach to developing exception handlers is the structured option, which uses the Try…Catch…Finally statement. Using the Try…Catch…Finally statement, you can block off program statements where errors are likely to occur and then attempt to handle them.

To use the Try…Catch…Finally statement, place the statements where exceptions may occur within the Try block and then place statements designed to handle the exception in the Catch block. If different exceptions are possible, you can insert additional Catch blocks, each designed to handle a different type of exception. Lastly, you can include an optional Finally block, which will always execute, regardless of whether an execution occurred at all or which Catch block executed. When included, the Finally block is always executed last and provides a place to store any program statements that will always have to be executed.

The following example demonstrates how to apply the Try…Catch…Finally statement to develop an exception handler for the previous example.

```
Public Class Form1

    Dim intX As Integer = 0
    Dim intY As Integer = 10
    Dim intZ As Integer

    Private Sub Form1_Load(ByVal sender As System.Object, _
        ByVal e As System.EventArgs) Handles MyBase.Load

        Try
            intZ = intY / intX

        Catch ex As OverflowException
            MessageBox.Show("Error: The application has attempted " & _
                "to divide a number by 0.")

        Catch ex As Exception
            MessageBox.Show("Error: " & ex.Message)

        Finally
```

```
        MessageBox.Show("Please inform the developer if any " & _
            "errors occurred.")

      End Try

    End Sub

End Class
```

TRICK The order in which Catch blocks occur is important. Visual Basic will execute the first Catch block that matches the specified criteria. When using multiple Catch blocks, always put the most specific Catch statements first, followed by the more general ones.

The statement that is likely to cause the error (a certainty in this example) is placed inside the Try block. Next, a Catch block is set up to handle the occurrence of an Overflow-Exception. Note that a variable named ex has been declared. This variable will be used to access an Exception object that Visual Basic automatically generates when an exception occurs. By examining properties belonging to this object, you can get information about the exception.

A second Catch block is set up to handle all other types of exceptions not handled by previous Catch blocks. A Finally block is then specified that will execute every time the form's Load event procedure executes, even if an exception doesn't occur.

TRICK You can view a list of possible exceptions by typing Catch followed by a variable name and the keyword As when working with the code editor, as demonstrated in Figure 11.12.

Although the example that I have shown you here is relatively simple, it presents you with

FIGURE 11.12

Using IntelliSense
to examine
exceptions.

a template that you can copy and apply when you come across the need to handle run-time errors in your applications.

> **TRICK** When deciding whether to create an exception handler in order to attempt to deal with a potential error in one of your applications, take a look at the likelihood of the exception occurring. If it is a pretty high possibility, then you should attempt to build a new procedure to your application that deals with the situation. However, if the possibility of an error occurring is unlikely (but still possible), then adding an exception handler may be the more appropriate option.

BACK TO THE TIC-TAC-TOE GAME

It is time to turn your attention to this book's final game project, the Tic-Tac-Toe game. You will create the Tic-Tac-Toe game by following the same five basic development steps that you have followed for all preceding game projects.

Designing the Game

The Tic-Tac-Toe game is played on a single window and is made up of one form and the 18 controls listed in Table 11.1.

TABLE 11.1: FORM CONTROLS FOR THE TIC-TAC-TOE GAME

Control Type	Control Name	Description
Panel1	pnlLeft	Used to represent the left vertical bar on the game board
Panel2	pnlRight	Used to represent the right vertical bar on the game board
Panel3	pnlTop	Used to represent the top horizontal bar on the game board
Panel4	pnlBottom	Used to represent the bottom horizontal bar on the game board
PictureBox1	pbxA1	The left PictureBox control on the first row of the game board
PictureBox2	pbxA2	The middle PictureBox control on the first row of the game board
PictureBox3	pbxA3	The right PictureBox control on the first row of the game board
PictureBox4	pbxB1	The left PictureBox control on the second row of the game board
PictureBox5	pbxB2	The middle PictureBox control on the second row of the game board
PictureBox6	pbxb3	The right PictureBox control on the second row of the game board
PictureBox7	pbxC1	The left PictureBox control on the third row of the game board
PictureBox8	pbxC2	The middle PictureBox control on the third row of the game board
PictureBox9	pbxC3	The right PictureBox control on the third row of the game board
Button1	btnPlay	Used to initiate game play
Button2	btnExit	Used to terminate the game
Label1	lblOutput	Identifies the TextBox control that is used to display status messages
TextBox1	txtOutput	Used to display status messages
ImageList1	imlSquares	Stores an indexed collection of graphics used to represent player moves

Step 1: Creating a New Visual Basic Project

The first step in creating the Tic-Tac-Toe game is to open up Visual Basic and create a new project, as outlined below.

1. If you have not already done so, start up Visual Basic 2005 Express Edition and then click on File and select New Project. The New Project dialog will appear.

2. Select the Windows Application template.

3. Type Tic-Tac-Toe as the name of your new application in the Name field located at the bottom of the New Project window.

4. Click on OK to close the New Project dialog.

Visual Basic will create a new project for you and display a form, which you will then use to design your new game's user interface.

Step 2: Creating the User Interface

The first step in laying out the user interface is to add controls to the form and to move and resize them to the appropriate locations. As you go through each step, make sure that you reference Figure 11.13 so that you'll know where each control needs to be placed and what size it needs to be.

1. Begin by setting the Size property of the form to 605, 591.

2. Next, create the grid lines that organize the game board by adding four Panel controls and resizing them as shown in Figure 11.13.

3. Add PictureBox controls inside each of the game board's nine cells and resize them until they take up almost all of the available space.

4. Add two Button controls to the bottom left hand corner.

5. Add a TextBox control to the bottum right-hand side of the game board and resize it as shown in Figure 11.13.

6. Add a Label control and place it just over the upper left-hand corner of the TextBox control.

7. Finally, add an ImageList control.

At this point, the overall layout of the Tic-Tac-Toe game's user interface is now complete. You can start making changes to the form and control properties.

FIGURE 11.13

Completing the
interface design
for the Tic-Tac-
Toe game.

Step 3: Customizing Form and Control Properties

Let's begin by making the required changes to properties belonging to the form object, as listed in Table 11.2.

TABLE 11.2: PROPERTY CHANGES FOR FORM1

Property	Value
Name	frmMain
ControlBox	False
Cursor	Hand
FormBorderStyle	Fixed3D
StartPosition	CenterScreen
Text	Tic-Tac-Toe

Make the property changes shown in Table 11.3 to the Panel controls.

TABLE 11.3: PROPERTY CHANGES FOR PANEL CONTROLS

Control	Property	Value
Panel1	Name	pnlLeft
	BackColor	Black
Panel2	Name	pnlRight
	BackColor	Black
Panel3	Name	pnlTop
	BackColor	Black
Panel4	Name	pnlBottom
	BackColor	Black

Make the property changes shown in Table 11.4 to the PictureBox controls.

TABLE 11.4: PROPERTY CHANGES FOR PICTUREBOX CONTROLS

Control	Property	Value
PictureBox1	Name	pbxA1
	Enabled	False
	Size	164, 134
	SizeMode	StretchImage
PictureBox2	Name	pbxA2
	Enabled	False
	Size	164, 134
	SizeMode	StretchImage

continued

TABLE 11.4: PROPERTY CHANGES FOR PICTUREBOX CONTROLS

PictureBox3	Name	pbxA2
	Enabled	False
	Size	164, 134
	SizeMode	StretchImage
PictureBox4	Name	pbxB1
	Enabled	False
	Size	164, 134
	SizeMode	StretchImage
PictureBox5	Name	pbxB2
	Enabled	False
	Size	164, 134
	SizeMode	StretchImage
PictureBox6	Name	pbxB3
	Enabled	False
	Size	164, 134
	SizeMode	StretchImage
PictureBox7	Name	pbxC1
	Enabled	False
	Size	164, 134
	SizeMode	StretchImage
PictureBox8	Name	pbxC2
	Enabled	False
	Size	164, 134
	SizeMode	StretchImage
PictureBox9	Name	pbxC3
	Enabled	False
	Size	164, 134
	SizeMode	StretchImage

Make the property changes shown in Table 11.5 to the Button controls.

TABLE 11.5: PROPERTY CHANGES FOR BUTTON CONTROLS

Control	Property	Value
Button1	Name	btnPlay
	Text	Play
Button2	Name	btnExit
	Text	Exit

Make the property changes shown in Table 11.6 to the Label control.

TABLE 11.6: PROPERTY CHANGES FOR LABEL CONTROL

Control	Property	Value
Label1	Name	lblOutput
	Font.Bold	True
	Text	Status

Make the property changes shown in Table 11.7 to the TextBox control.

TABLE 11.7: PROPERTY CHANGES FOR TEXTBOX CONTROL

Control	Property	Value
TextBox1	Name	txtOutput
	Font.Bold	True
	ReadOnly	True
	TabStop	False

Finally, change the name of the Name property for the ImageList control to imlSquares. Change the ImageList control's ImageSize property to 164, 134 and then add the following bitmap images to its Images property (collection) as shown in Table 11.8. You'll find copies of the Bitmap images required to complete this project, along with the source code, on this book's companion web site.

TABLE 11.8: BITMAP IMAGES TO ADD TO THE IMAGELIST CONTROLS IMAGES COLLECTION

Property	File	Index No.
Name	X.bmp	0
Name	O.bmp	1
Name	Blank.bmp	2

That's it. The user interface for this game is now complete. Let's move on to the next step and begin adding program code.

Step 4: Adding a Little Programming Logic

The first task in putting together the program code for the Tic-Tac-Toe game is to define class-level variables, as shown below. These variables represent values used by two or more procedures within the application.

```
Public Class frmMain

    Private strPlayer As String = ""    'Used to track whose turn it is

    'Declare variables representing game board cells
    Private strpbxA1 As String = "Open"
    Private strpbxA2 As String = "Open"
    Private strpbxA3 As String = "Open"
    Private strpbxB1 As String = "Open"
    Private strpbxB2 As String = "Open"
    Private strpbxB3 As String = "Open"
    Private strpbxC1 As String = "Open"
    Private strpbxC2 As String = "Open"
    Private strpbxC3 As String = "Open"

End Class
```

The first statement defines a variable named strPlayer, which is used to keep track of each player's turn. The remaining statements are used to keep track of when each of the game board cells have been selected by a player.

The form's Load event procedure, shown below, is responsible for preparing the game for initial play. This is accomplished by calling on two custom procedures.

```
'This procedure executes procedures required to set up the game
Private Sub frmMain_Load(ByVal sender As System.Object, _
   ByVal e As System.EventArgs) Handles MyBase.Load

    SetGameDefaults()  'Call procedure that sets default assignments

    ClearBoard()  'Call procedure that clears the game board

End Sub
```

The first procedure called by the form's Load event procedure is the SetGameDefaults procedure, shown below. When called, this procedure displays instructions in the TextBox control and sets Player X as the first player.

```
'This procedure sets default assignments
Private Sub SetGameDefaults()

    txtOutput.Text = "Click on Play to begin"  'Display opening message
    strPlayer = "Player X"  'Set Player X to go first

End Sub
```

The second procedure called by the form's Load event procedure is the ClearBoard procedure, shown below. This procedure is responsible for clearing off the game board by displaying blank squares in each of the game's PictureBox controls. The procedure also sets the values assigned to the variables used to track the status of each game board cell to Open.

```
'This procedure clears out the game board
Private Sub ClearBoard()

    'Load a blank image into each game board cell
    pbxA1.Image = imlSquares.Images(2)
    pbxA2.Image = imlSquares.Images(2)
    pbxA3.Image = imlSquares.Images(2)
```

```
pbxB1.Image = imlSquares.Images(2)
pbxB2.Image = imlSquares.Images(2)
pbxB3.Image = imlSquares.Images(2)
pbxC1.Image = imlSquares.Images(2)
pbxC2.Image = imlSquares.Images(2)
pbxC3.Image = imlSquares.Images(2)

'Mark each game board cell as open and available for selection
strpbxA1 = "Open"
strpbxA2 = "Open"
strpbxA3 = "Open"
strpbxB1 = "Open"
strpbxB2 = "Open"
strpbxB3 = "Open"
strpbxC1 = "Open"
strpbxC2 = "Open"
strpbxC3 = "Open"
```

End Sub

Game play cannot begin until the first player (Player X) clicks on the Button control labeled Play, at which time the btnPlay procedure, shown below, is executed. This procedure is responsible for executing two custom procedures. The first procedure that is called is the ClearBoard procedure, which we have already examined. The second procedure called is the PlayGame procedure.

```
'This procedure executes when the button labeled Play is clicked
Private Sub btnPlay_Click(ByVal sender As System.Object, _
   ByVal e As System.EventArgs) Handles btnPlay.Click

   ClearBoard()  'Call the procedure that clears out the game board

   PlayGame()   'Call the procedure that begins game play
```

End Sub

The PlayGame procedure, shown below, displays a text message in the game's TextBox control in order to identify whose turn it is. In addition, the procedure enables each of the PictureBox controls on the game board. This allows the first player to make the first move. Finally, this procedure disables the btnPlay Button control.

```
'This procedure begins game play
Private Sub PlayGame()

    'Post message that identifies whose turn it is
    txtOutput.Text = strPlayer & "'s turn."

    'Enable all game board cells
    pbxA1.Enabled = True
    pbxA2.Enabled = True
    pbxA3.Enabled = True
    pbxB1.Enabled = True
    pbxB2.Enabled = True
    pbxB3.Enabled = True
    pbxC1.Enabled = True
    pbxC2.Enabled = True
    pbxC3.Enabled = True
    btnPlay.Enabled = False 'Disable access to the button labeled Play

End Sub
```

Players can end the game at any time by clicking on the Button control labeled Exit, in which case the btnExit procedure, shown below, is executed.

```
'This procedure executes when the button labeled Exit is clicked
Private Sub btnExit_Click(ByVal sender As System.Object, _
  ByVal e As System.EventArgs) Handles btnExit.Click

    Application.Exit()

End Sub
```

Each cell on the game board is made up of a PictureBox control. The following statements make up the Click event procedure for the game's first PictureBox control.

```
'This procedure executes when a player clicks on the first cell
'in the first row
Private Sub pbxA1_Click(ByVal sender As System.Object, _
  ByVal e As System.EventArgs) Handles pbxA1.Click
```

```
    Dim strGameOver As String = ""    'Used to track game status

    'Notify the player if the cell has already been selected
    If strpbxA1 <> "Open" Then
        txtOutput.Text = "The square has already been taken." & _
            ControlChars.CrLf & strPlayer & "'s turn."
        Return    'Leave the Sub procedure
    End If

    If strPlayer = "Player X" Then
        pbxA1.Image = imlSquares.Images(0)
        strpbxA1 = "Player X"
    Else
        pbxA1.Image = imlSquares.Images(1)
        strpbxA1 = "Player 0"
    End If

    'Call the procedure that checks to see if the game has been won
    strGameOver = CheckForWinner()

    'Call the procedure that switched player turns or displays a
    'message declaring a winner
    DetermineGameStatus(strGameOver)

End Sub
```

This procedure declares a local variable named strGameOver. Next, an If…Then code block is used to check whether the cell has already been selected by examining the value assigned to the corresponding strpbxA1 variable. If the cell is available, an If…Then…Else code block displays a graphic representing the current player in the call. A call is then made to the CheckForWinner function procedure. If the game has been won, the CheckForWinner Function procedure will return a string of either Player X or Player 0, which is then passed on to the DetermineGameStatus procedure.

The code for the second PictureBox control in the first row is shown below. As you can see, except for the changes in references that reflect the second cell instead of the first cell, the code is identical to that of the pbxA1_Click procedure.

```
'This procedure executes when a player clicks on the second cell
'in the first row
Private Sub pbxA2_Click(ByVal sender As System.Object, _
  ByVal e As System.EventArgs) Handles pbxA2.Click

    Dim strGameOver As String = ""  'Used to track game status

    'Notify the player if the cell has already been selected
    If strpbxA2 <> "Open" Then
        txtOutput.Text = "The square has already been taken." & _
            ControlChars.CrLf & strPlayer & "'s turn."
        Return  'Leave the Sub procedure
    End If

    If strPlayer = "Player X" Then
        pbxA2.Image = imlSquares.Images(0)
        strpbxA2 = "Player X"
    Else
        pbxA2.Image = imlSquares.Images(1)
        strpbxA2 = "Player O"
    End If

    'Call the procedure that checks to see if the game has been won
    strGameOver = CheckForWinner()

    'Call the procedure that switched player turns or displays a
    'message declaring a winner
    DetermineGameStatus(strGameOver)

End Sub
```

The code for the third PictureBox control on the first row is shown below.

```
'This procedure executes when a player clicks on the third cell
'in the first row
Private Sub pbxA3_Click(ByVal sender As System.Object, _
  ByVal e As System.EventArgs) Handles pbxA3.Click

    Dim strGameOver As String = ""  'Used to track game status
```

```
'Notify the player if the cell has already been selected
If strpbxA3 <> "Open" Then
    txtOutput.Text = "The square has already been taken." & _
        ControlChars.CrLf & strPlayer & "'s turn."
    Return  'Leave the Sub procedure
End If


If strPlayer = "Player X" Then
    pbxA3.Image = imlSquares.Images(0)
    strpbxA3 = "Player X"
Else
    pbxA3.Image = imlSquares.Images(1)
    strpbxA3 = "Player O"
End If


'Call the procedure that checks to see if the game has been won
strGameOver = CheckForWinner()

'Call the procedure that switched player turns or displays a
'message declaring a winner
DetermineGameStatus(strGameOver)


End Sub
```

The code for the first PictureBox control on the second row is shown below.

```
'This procedure executes when a player clicks on the first cell
'in the second row
Private Sub pbxB1_Click(ByVal sender As System.Object, _
  ByVal e As System.EventArgs) Handles pbxB1.Click

    Dim strGameOver As String = ""  'Used to track game status

    'Notify the player if the cell has already been selected
    If strpbxB1 <> "Open" Then
        txtOutput.Text = "The square has already been taken." & _
            ControlChars.CrLf & strPlayer & "'s turn."
        Return  'Leave the Sub procedure
    End If
```

```
    If strPlayer = "Player X" Then
        pbxB1.Image = imlSquares.Images(0)
        strpbxB1 = "Player X"
    Else
        pbxB1.Image = imlSquares.Images(1)
        strpbxB1 = "Player O"
    End If


    'Call the procedure that checks to see if the game has been won
    strGameOver = CheckForWinner()

    'Call the procedure that switched player turns or displays a
    'message declaring a winner
    DetermineGameStatus(strGameOver)

End Sub
```

The code for the second PictureBox control on the second row is shown below.

```
'This procedure executes when a player clicks on the second cell
'in the second row
Private Sub pbxB2_Click(ByVal sender As System.Object, _
  ByVal e As System.EventArgs) Handles pbxB2.Click

    Dim strGameOver As String = ""   'Used to track game status

    'Notify the player if the cell has already been selected
    If strpbxB2 <> "Open" Then
        txtOutput.Text = "The square has already been taken." & _
            ControlChars.CrLf & strPlayer & "'s turn."
        Return   'Leave the Sub procedure
    End If

    If strPlayer = "Player X" Then
        pbxB2.Image = imlSquares.Images(0)
        strpbxB2 = "Player X"
    Else
        pbxB2.Image = imlSquares.Images(1)
        strpbxB2 = "Player O"
```

```
    End If

    'Call the procedure that checks to see if the game has been won
    strGameOver = CheckForWinner()

    'Call the procedure that switched player turns or displays a
    'message declaring a winner
    DetermineGameStatus(strGameOver)

End Sub
```

The code for the third PictureBox control on the second row is shown below.

```
'This procedure executes when a player clicks on the third cell
'in the second row
Private Sub pbxB3_Click(ByVal sender As System.Object, _
  ByVal e As System.EventArgs) Handles pbxB3.Click

    Dim strGameOver As String = ""   'Used to track game status

    'Notify the player if the cell has already been selected
    If strpbxB3 <> "Open" Then
        txtOutput.Text = "The square has already been taken." & _
          ControlChars.CrLf & strPlayer & "'s turn."
        Return   'Leave the Sub procedure
    End If

    If strPlayer = "Player X" Then
        pbxB3.Image = imlSquares.Images(0)
        strpbxB3 = "Player X"
    Else
        pbxB3.Image = imlSquares.Images(1)
        strpbxB3 = "Player O"
    End If

    'Call the procedure that checks to see if the game has been won
    strGameOver = CheckForWinner()

    'Call the procedure that switched player turns or displays a
```

```
    'message declaring a winner
    DetermineGameStatus(strGameOver)

End Sub
```

The code for the first `PictureBox` control on the third row is shown below.

```
'This procedure executes when a player clicks on the first cell
'in the third row
Private Sub pbxC1_Click(ByVal sender As System.Object, _
  ByVal e As System.EventArgs) Handles pbxC1.Click

    Dim strGameOver As String = ""    'Used to track game status

    'Notify the player if the cell has already been selected
    If strpbxC1 <> "Open" Then
        txtOutput.Text = "The square has already been taken." & _
            ControlChars.CrLf & strPlayer & "'s turn."
        Return   'Leave the Sub procedure
    End If

    If strPlayer = "Player X" Then
        pbxC1.Image = imlSquares.Images(0)
        strpbxC1 = "Player X"
    Else
        pbxC1.Image = imlSquares.Images(1)
        strpbxC1 = "Player O"
    End If

    'Call the procedure that checks to see if the game has been won
    strGameOver = CheckForWinner()

    'Call the procedure that switched player turns or displays a
    'message declaring a winner
    DetermineGameStatus(strGameOver)

End Sub
```

The code for the second PictureBox control on the third row is shown below.

```
'This procedure executes when a player clicks on the second cell
'in the third row
Private Sub pbxC2_Click(ByVal sender As System.Object, _
  ByVal e As System.EventArgs) Handles pbxC2.Click

    Dim strGameOver As String = ""  'Used to track game status

    'Notify the player if the cell has already been selected
    If strpbxC2 <> "Open" Then
        txtOutput.Text = "The square has already been taken." & _
          ControlChars.CrLf & strPlayer & "'s turn."
        Return  'Leave the Sub procedure
    End If

    If strPlayer = "Player X" Then
        pbxC2.Image = imlSquares.Images(0)
        strpbxC2 = "Player X"
    Else
        pbxC2.Image = imlSquares.Images(1)
        strpbxC2 = "Player O"
    End If

    'Call the procedure that checks to see if the game has been won
    strGameOver = CheckForWinner()

    'Call the procedure that switched player turns or displays a
    'message declaring a winner
    DetermineGameStatus(strGameOver)

End Sub
```

The code for the third PictureBox control on the third row is shown below.

```
'This procedure executes when a player clicks on the third cell
'in the third row
Private Sub pbxC3_Click(ByVal sender As System.Object, _
  ByVal e As System.EventArgs) Handles pbxC3.Click
```

```
    Dim strGameOver As String = ""    'Used to track game status

    'Notify the player if the cell has already been selected
    If strpbxC3 <> "Open" Then
        txtOutput.Text = "The square has already been taken." & _
            ControlChars.CrLf & strPlayer & "'s turn."
        Return    'Leave the Sub procedure
    End If

    If strPlayer = "Player X" Then
        pbxC3.Image = imlSquares.Images(0)
        strpbxC3 = "Player X"
    Else
        pbxC3.Image = imlSquares.Images(1)
        strpbxC3 = "Player O"
    End If

    'Call the procedure that checks to see if the game has been won
    strGameOver = CheckForWinner()

    'Call the procedure that switched player turns or displays a
    'message declaring a winner
    DetermineGameStatus(strGameOver)

End Sub
```

The CheckForWinner Function procedure, shown below, is responsible for executing a collection of If…Then statements to see if the current player has won the game. This procedure checks each row and column, as well as diagonally. In addition, the procedure checks to see if the two players have tied, which occurs when all nine cells have been selected without a winner being declared.

```
'This procedure determines whether the game has been won and by whom
  Function CheckForWinner() As String

    'Check the first row for a winner
    If strpbxA1 = strPlayer Then
        If strpbxA2 = strPlayer Then
            If strpbxA3 = strPlayer Then
```

```
                    Return strPlayer
            End If
        End If
End If


'Check the second row for a winner
If strpbxB1 = strPlayer Then
    If strpbxB2 = strPlayer Then
        If strpbxB3 = strPlayer Then
                Return strPlayer
        End If
    End If
End If


'Check the third row for a winner
If strpbxC1 = strPlayer Then
    If strpbxC2 = strPlayer Then
        If strpbxC3 = strPlayer Then
                Return strPlayer
        End If
    End If
End If


'Check the first column for a winner
If strpbxA1 = strPlayer Then
    If strpbxB1 = strPlayer Then
        If strpbxC1 = strPlayer Then
                Return strPlayer
        End If
    End If
End If


'Check the second column for a winner
If strpbxA2 = strPlayer Then
    If strpbxB2 = strPlayer Then
        If strpbxC2 = strPlayer Then
                Return strPlayer
        End If
    End If
End If
```

```vb
        'Check the third column for a winner
        If strpbxA3 = strPlayer Then
            If strpbxB3 = strPlayer Then
                If strpbxC3 = strPlayer Then
                    Return strPlayer
                End If
            End If
        End If

        'Check diagonally from top-left to bottom-right for a winner
        If strpbxA1 = strPlayer Then
            If strpbxB2 = strPlayer Then
                If strpbxC3 = strPlayer Then
                    Return strPlayer
                End If
            End If
        End If

'Check diagonally from top-right to bottom-left for a winner
        If strpbxA3 = strPlayer Then
            If strpbxB2 = strPlayer Then
                If strpbxC1 = strPlayer Then
                    Return strPlayer
                End If
            End If
        End If

        'Check to see if the game has resulted in a tie
        Select Case "Open"
            'Check each cell to see if it has been assigned to a player
            Case strpbxA1
            Case strpbxB1
            Case strpbxB1
            Case strpbxB1
            Case strpbxB2
            Case strpbxB3
            Case strpbxC1
            Case strpbxC2
```

```
            Case strpbxC3
            Case Else 'This option executes if all cells have been assigned
                    Return "Tie"
    End Select

    Return ""

End Function
```

The DetermineGameStatus procedure, shown below, processes a single argument that identifies whether the game has been won, lost, or is still in progress. If the game is still in progress, the SwitchPlayers procedure is called in order to ready the game for the next player's turn. If the game has been won, the procedure enables the Button control labeled Play, calls the DisableSquares procedure, and displays a text message in the game's TextBox control identifying the winner of the game. Finally, if the game has ended in a tie, the btnPlay control is enabled, the DisableSquares procedure is called, and a text message is displayed in the game's TextBox control indicating that a tie has occurred.

```
'This procedure determines whether or not the game is over
Private Sub DetermineGameStatus(ByVal strGameOver As String)

    If strGameOver = "" Then  'The game is not over yet
        SwitchPlayers() 'Call procedure that switches player turns
        'Post message stating that it is time for players to switch turns
        txtOutput.Text = strPlayer & "'s turn."
    Else
        If strGameOver <> "Tie" Then  'There is a winner
            btnPlay.Enabled = True  'Enable the button labeled Play
            'Call procedure that disables game board cells
            DisableSquares()
            'Display game over message
            txtOutput.Text = "Game over. " & strGameOver & " has won."
        Else  'The game has resulted in a tie
            btnPlay.Enabled = True  'Enable the button labeled Play
            'Call procedure that disables game board cells
            DisableSquares()
            'Display game over message
```

```
            txtOutput.Text = "Game over. There was no winner."
        End If
    End If

End Sub
```

The SwitchPlayers procedure, shown below, is very straightforward. When called, it changes the value assigned to the strPlayer variable to reflect the next player.

```
'This procedure is responsible for toggling between player turns
Private Sub SwitchPlayers()

    If strPlayer = "Player X" Then
        strPlayer = "Player O"
    Else
        strPlayer = "Player X"
    End If

End Sub
```

The DisableSquares procedure, shown below, is the last procedure in the application. Its job is to disable each of the game board PictureBox controls in order to keep players from trying to take another turn once the game has ended.

```
'This procedure disables all game board cells
Private Sub DisableSquares()

    pbxA1.Enabled = False
    pbxA2.Enabled = False
    pbxA3.Enabled = False
    pbxB1.Enabled = False
    pbxB2.Enabled = False
    pbxB3.Enabled = False
    pbxC1.Enabled = False
    pbxC2.Enabled = False
    pbxC3.Enabled = False

End Sub
```

Step 5: Testing the Execution of the Tic-Tac-Toe Game

OK. That's it. The Tic-Tac-Toe game is now ready to run. Go ahead and run the game by pressing F5 and make sure that everything works like it is supposed to. If you run into any problems, try using the troubleshooting tips presented in this chapter to track down any errors. Once things are in order, pass it around to a few of your friends and ask them what they think.

SUMMARY

In this chapter, you learned about syntax, logic, and run-time errors. You learned how to set breakpoints and then to step through program execution. You also learned to work with an assortment of debugging windows and to create exception-handling routines. On top of all this, you learned how to create the Tic-Tac-Toe game.

Don't look at the completion of the material in this book as the end of your Visual Basic programming education. Think of it as a launching point. Although this book has provided you with a solid foundation, there is still plenty more to learn. Before you run off and start tackling new and bigger programming projects, why not take just a little extra time and improve the Tic-Tac-Toe game by completing the following challenges.

CHALLENGES

1. Add sound effects to the game that indicate when the game has been won or tied.

2. Add logic to the game that keeps track of the number of games won, lost, and tied for each player.

3. Add logic to the game that identifies not only when a game has been won, but how it was won (diagonally, horizontally, or vertically).

4. Finally, if you think you are up to the challenge, modify the game so that one player can play against the computer.

INDEX